Core Connections

Core Connections

Cairo Belly Dance in the Revolution's Aftermath

CHRISTINE M. ŞAHIN

OXFORD
UNIVERSITY PRESS

Oxford University Press is a department of the University of Oxford. It furthers
the University's objective of excellence in research, scholarship, and education
by publishing worldwide. Oxford is a registered trade mark of Oxford University
Press in the UK and certain other countries.

Published in the United States of America by Oxford University Press
198 Madison Avenue, New York, NY 10016, United States of America.

© Oxford University Press 2024

All rights reserved. No part of this publication may be reproduced, stored in
a retrieval system, or transmitted, in any form or by any means, without the
prior permission in writing of Oxford University Press, or as expressly permitted
by law, by license, or under terms agreed with the appropriate reproduction
rights organization. Inquiries concerning reproduction outside the scope of the
above should be sent to the Rights Department, Oxford University Press, at the
address above.

You must not circulate this work in any other form
and you must impose this same condition on any acquirer.

Library of Congress Cataloging-in-Publication Data
Names: Şahin, Christine M., author.
Title: Core connections : Cairo belly dance in the revolution's aftermath /
Christine M. Şahin.
Description: New York : Oxford University Press, 2024. |
Includes bibliographical references and index.
Identifiers: LCCN 2024001944 (print) | LCCN 2024001945 (ebook) |
ISBN 9780197613627 (hardback) | ISBN 9780197613634 (paperback) |
ISBN 9780197613641 (epub)
Subjects: LCSH: Belly dance—Egypt—Cairo—History—20th century. |
Belly dance—Social aspects—Egypt—Cairo. | Belly dancers—Egypt—Cairo.
Classification: LCC GV1798.5.S24 2024 (print) | LCC GV1798.5 (ebook) |
DDC 793.3—dc23/eng/20240131
LC record available at https://lccn.loc.gov/2024001944
LC ebook record available at https://lccn.loc.gov/2024001945

DOI: 10.1093/oso/9780197613627.001.0001

The manufacturer's authorised representative in the EU for product safety is
Oxford University Press España S.A. of El Parque Empresarial San Fernando
de Henares, Avenida de Castilla, 2 – 28830 Madrid (www.oup.es/en or
product.safety@oup.com). OUP España S.A. also acts as importer into Spain
of products made by the manufacturer.

This book is dedicated to the dancers of Cairo. Listening to the rich complexity and vulnerable strength of your life experiences through your danced wisdom has been an immeasurable blessing, honor, and privilege. Thank you for sharing your stories. Thank you for courageously stepping onto those stages and sharing your dance with the incalculable strength, heart, and guts it takes to do so. May you continue to move yourself and others into deeper ways of feeling, being, knowing, and doing. Alf Shukar.

Contents

Acknowledgments   ix
A Note on Transliteration   xiii

   Introduction   1

   Taxi Transition: *Zahma* (Traffic)   36

1. Nile Cruising Boats: Cruising the Nile while Contesting Borders, Boundaries, and Bodies   41

   Taxi Transition: *3aeesh* (Life-Bread)   100

2. Five-Star Hotels: Checking in, or Checking out? Contemporary Conditions in the Revolution's Aftermath   102

   Taxi Transition: Checkpoint   136

3. Discos: Risqué Moves and the Exposure of Policing Politics   139

   Taxi Transition: Pieces of Freedom   181

4. Pyramid Street Cabarets: Negotiating Slippery Stages and Contradictory Competitions   184

   Taxi Transition: A Final Ride as Farewell Finale   214

   Circling Back and Dropping Off: Core Continuations and Connections   216

Notes   229
Bibliography   251
Index   259

Acknowledgments

Greatest thanks to God. Thank you for, and God bless, the beautiful dancing, stories, and people within these pages and throughout the vividly remarkable city of Cairo, Egypt. This book has been vibrantly interwoven with the love, support, and intellectual rigor of many I wish to thank.

Starting in Cairo, I owe my deepest gratitude to the dancers, workers, audiences, and management throughout the *raqs sharqi* industry. Additional gratitude goes to those who helped me as in-depth research collaborators in this project. Thank you to Farah Nasri, Zara Dance, Najla Ferreira, Wael, Ahmed, Karim, Ali, Khaled, Heba, Ayman, Sayyad, and Yossry for being key research partners for this ethnography. Thank you for your patience, kindness, support, profound insights, and comradeship throughout my fieldwork. Thank you also to Shahrzad, Vanessa Friedman, Sara Farouk Ahmed, Eva A., Farida Fahmy, Aicha B., Khaled, Eman, Samia, Amaria Selene, Wael, M. Bakry, and Nashwa for your generosity, assistance, and wealth of wisdom. My greatest gratitude to Sayyad H. for keeping the history of music and dance on Mohamed Ali Street alive and for your generosity in sharing your wealth of knowledge. Particular dancers and musicians I'd like to thank include Suzy, Julia, Amina, Randa, Safiya, Aziza and her husband Ahmed, Raqia H., Dina, Sahar, Amie, Bossy, Mona, Donya, Hussein M., Luna, Kawakeb, Hamada, Tamra Henna, Tito S., Soraya, Shams, Nany, Maya M., Soraia Z., and Farah Nasri's crew: Ahmed, Wael, Mahdy, and Salah. Further, I hold the sincerest gratitude to the taxi and Uber drivers (Mohamed, Ahmed, and Khaled, among many others) who made the links between my site-specific chapters so rich and insightful.

To my core dance teachers and mentors within the United States/Cairo: Sahra C. Kent, Lynda Latifa Wilkinson, Artemis Mourat, Shahrzad, Sara al-Hadithi, and Faten S., thank you not only for teaching me steps, musicality, and performance skills, but also for instilling the critical importance of culturally contextualizing dance and my performances and understandings of it. Thank you all for giving me the support and encouragement to trust in myself and love myself, and for giving me the learning toolkit to do this ethnography with integrity and sensitive nuance as a practitioner-scholar. Sahra and Latifa, you've left such an imprint on my heart and journey that I hope to honor through this book's capacity to move and empower others as you both so poignantly embody.

This ethnography began as a doctoral dissertation many years ago at the University of California, Riverside. To my committee chair, Jacqueline Shea Murphy, I send my warmest love and enduring gratitude. From our first seminar, I resonated with you and knew we would work together to make the world a better place without compromising the integrity of the dance forms and communities we worked within. It was a blessing and honor to work with you to craft a multiply moving ethnography. To Anthea Kraut, I hope I can teach and mentor with as much care, generosity, and dynamic critical vigor as you consistently offer through your pedagogy, research, and personality. To Sherine Hafez, your theoretical perspectives throughout my research, and your heartfelt advice in all areas of my life, academic and otherwise, have been a tremendous blessing to this project and my well-being.

Other professors who have significantly impacted my thinking, pedagogy, and research include Cristina Rosa, Jose Reynoso, Imani Kai Johnson, Linda Tomko, and Jeff Sacks. Notably, Cristina Rosa's Choreographies of Writing seminar was the spark that led me to make more embodied moves in my own writing. Serendipitously, years later, it was her Dance Studies Association-led writing HUB that unlocked the key to finishing my stubborn final chapter on disco-clubs. Of course, even before graduate school, there was the impactful support, advice, and ever-inspiring teaching and insights of my undergraduate anthropology professor Patricia Sloane-White. The earliest brewing of this project and my pedagogical commitment to reach those who would rather shyly hide away in classroom corners are indebted to you.

My editor at Oxford University Press, Norman Hirschy, has been enthusiastic and invested in this project since we first spoke in Malta at a Dance Studies Association conference. His kind patience, encouraging feedback, and verve for the potential of dance scholarship too often relegated to the margins have been uplifting and grounding. Peer reviewers offered astute and valuable feedback on the manuscript that has wondrously strengthened this final version. I also send deep gratitude to *raqs sharqi* scholars Anne Vermeyden, Margaret ("Megs") Morley, and Heather ("Nisaa") Ward for offering fruitful comments on the early manuscript. I am blessed to have you all as such inspiring academic colleagues, role models, and dear friends.

The community, support, buzzing intellectual curiosity, and myriad scholarly innovations found among my academic colleagues deserve special recognition. Thank you for being so inspiring: Casey Avaunt, J. Delecave, Katie Stahl-Kovell, Chuyun Oh, Ania Nikulina, Theresa Goldbach, Ali Kheradyar, Sevi Bayraktar, Ayman A., Denise Machin, Irvin Gonzalez, Lindsay Blue, Wei-Chi Wu, Rosa Rodríguez-Frazier, and Xiomara Forbez. Additionally, my students' endless enthusiasm for choreographing better worlds while I was teaching across several Southern California universities has been integral in shaping my thinking and teaching while keeping my hope for better worlds alive. I thank Lori Officer and our SC Village senior fitness community for teaching me true leadership and the value of embodied community and strength.

The final edits of this book came as I wrapped up my first quarter as Acting Assistant Professor of Dance at the University of Washington in Seattle. The connections, community, and opportunities to empower through teaching I've experienced here have healed, reinvigorated, and reinvested me in my own core connections. I'm indebted to the UW dance community and wish to thank the wonderfully vibrant dance students I've been fortunate to work with as well as departmental colleagues: Christina Sunardi, Juliet McMains, Hannah Wiley, Alana Isiguen, Jennifer Salk, and Rachael Lincoln. I also want to thank my *raqs sharqi* students, past and present from the east to west coasts, for inspiring and supporting me. Your dedication and growth keep me moving to empower. The support and inspiration of *raqs sharqi* community members Shems, Stefanie Fatooh, Amara, Zina Saeed, Khuzama, Rhia, Samira Shuruk, Alyssa, and Wafaa also deserve special recognition.

Finally, I'd like to acknowledge my family and friends for shaping who I am as a person and for the love and support offered throughout the long journey of writing this book. Much of my academic journey has taken me far from my family, without a family of my own, in an unwavering yet often heart-wrenching dedication to creating more vibrantly beautiful and humanitarian worlds. It is the love and lessons from my family have tethered my heartstrings to this commitment. My hands shake as I attempt typing a mere shimmer of the profound radiance you've all set a light into my soul. Endless thanks and love to Amy, Glenn, Renee, Kate, Laura, Sasha, Candis, and Tucker.

To my mom, Amy Canady, thank you for instilling and nurturing my sense of Faith; it's been the seeds and roots of this project and everything I've endeavored in my life—I can't imagine my life without this sense of purpose and connection to make the world more beautiful through love, compassion, and understanding. Your support and love throughout this project have been a steadfast foundation of strength, hope, and persistence. To my dad, Glenn Canady, and in loving memory of Kathleen (Kate) Hoekstra, thanks for fostering my love for travel, coffee, and knowledge—they've combined quite well in making this book come to life. Together you've taught me how fleeting and precious life is, to be here and now. Your love has immeasurably helped me let go of my fears and get to work. To my dad and Renee Canady, together, you've taught me hope prevails after the darkest trials, that heartbreaks of all kinds make us braver and more open to extraordinary beauty. You've nurtured my wings as they spread and traveled myriad journeys, but just as meaningfully, never let me lose the rooted warmth of a loving nest to call home.

To my big sister Laura, you have been endlessly helpful in being my twenty-four-hour encyclopedia. You're the epitome of all the beauty of a big sister, and I'm so grateful for our closeness, talks, and adventures. You are my compass. Knowing you've always got my back no matter where I am in the world keeps me courageously trekking in the right direction. Thank you for being a fellow wanderer of uncommon paths. Sasha Canady, I warmly remember the care package you sent when I lost everything during Covid; thanks for helping me through an immensely difficult time. Community is everything; gratitude is grounding. Candis Sanchez, you are my phoenix. Throughout my writing, I've memorably witnessed you rise and burn brighter than the ashes the ugliness of this world would limit you to. Your vitality has been a profound motivation throughout the undertones of this book. May we all rise as fiercely as you inspire. To Tucker, my rescue, your presence in my life brings a resolute peace.

Finally, two long-term friendships of sincerest love, intellectual and humanistic depth, and constant growth deserve special attention. Thank you to Roberto Mejia and Anne "Annuni" Vermeyden. In addition to relishing in the deepest depths of scholarly dance talk over many shishas, teas, and lattes, I profoundly appreciate your friendships and presence as willing co-adventurers on various aspects of my dance scholar and practitioner journeys. You both continually inspire me to be a better person, teacher, scholar, and dancer. I'm in constant awe of both of your stunning souls and sharp social-justice oriented minds. Anne, you kindly read through and prolifically edited early drafts of this book, your compassionate insight, sharp comments, and academic thoroughness as a history doctorate and writing consultant specializing in *raqs sharqi* have wonderfully strengthened this book. As well, your endless generosity of spirit has strengthened me.

A Note on Transliteration

Arabic words in this book are italicized and have been transliterated following the International Journal of Middle East Studies (IJMES) system with simplified modifications. Transliterations do not include diacritical marks above or below letters to make the writing more accessible to a wider non-academic readership. Other simplified modifications of the IJMES system are to embody the informal colloquial Egyptian Arabic in accessible ways. For example, I use the informal 3 for the letter *'ayn* and 2 for *hamza* (represented by a ' and ' in IJMES respectively). The Egyptian colloquial "g" is transliterated as opposed to the more formal IJMES *fusha* "j" and "ee" is used for the long vowel *yaa* as opposed to the IJMES "i". For help with pronunciation for non-Arabic speakers the ' (*hamza*) is a glottal stop whereas the 3 (*3yn*) letter sounds similar to a deep and tight-throated 'ah' immediately followed with the slightest hesitation, that is, *sa3idi* sounds akin to "sAH-ee-di."

I also did not follow a uniform transliteration system for proper nouns, including people's names, instead utilizing their preferred English spellings. I also use the commonly known English names for areas, such as Cairo for *al qahira*. The same follows for Arabic and dance-related terms either familiar in English or commonly known within the international dance community, such as *sheikh*, *hijab*, *raqs sharqi*, and *awalim*, which remain italicized but follow their anglicized spellings. I have also primarily added an *s* to singular Arabic words to form an anglicized plural in these more familiar cases, such as *tahiyyas* (greetings). My hope is that this simplified system will be comfortable for specialists more familiar with Arabic terms as well as general audiences that would find the diacritical marks encumbering. The transliterated Arabic included in this book is colloquial Egyptian Arabic.

Introduction

The State of Stories

This story is an embodied practice in listening. Many would claim that this story is already finished. Many scholars and everyday citizens from Cairo, the United States, and across the globe, have already closed the book on the fate of Egypt's revolution of January 25, 2011 and its larger role in the Arab Spring political uprisings. They lament it as a failed revolution that suffered a botched and quickly extinguished ending having started as a sweeping motion of political transformation for greater equity and human dignity. The revolutionaries' demands for "bread, freedom, and social justice" that reverberated from Tahrir Square in Cairo are now left unanswered in chilling silence. After all, not every story has a happy ending.

However, my gut whispers with sensed undercurrents that ground me into a knowingness that this isn't the whole story. An in-depth centering of contemporary *raqs sharqi* ("belly dance") enlivens a different socio-political curve that is nuanced by valuing embodied knowledge and dancers' core connections sinuously weaving throughout a hierarchically splintered world. Grasping such knowledge necessitates deep listening, a life-long practice that I offer to share with you with an open hand and dedicated heart.

Pulled back into the mainstream current, when desensitized from the embodiment of core connections, a conditioned credulousness instead prevails—to the benefit of state-sanctioned stories, separations, and subjugations. Reading in particular from my role as a U.S. citizen, these narratives of the alleged "failure" of Egypt's 2011 revolution and its aftermath offer a familiar fate within a series of stories already problematically titled the "Arab Spring." This labeling denotes the conception that these antigovernment protests and uprisings for human rights, social and economic justice, and dignity throughout the Middle East and North Africa (MENA) spontaneously sprung like fresh plants after a deep winter freeze and, consequently, naturally withered off and died as the season inevitably changed.

Tunisia was the first country to begin uprisings in late 2010. Egypt followed soon after, where President Hosni Mubarak was successfully ousted from his nearly thirty-year-long reign on February 11, 2011, with the Supreme Council of the Armed Forces (SCAF) militarily taking over the country soon after. Mohammed Morsi was then elected president and governed for a short time under strict Muslim Brotherhood rules before he was overthrown by a popular military coup led by then general (now President) Abdel Fattah El-Sisi. While Egyptians were hopeful during the early transition of the revolution, the military's violence and continued repression quickly demonstrated the tangled and thick roots of the regime's "deep state." Here "deep state" refers to the enduring structures and institutions, such as the military, judiciary, and security apparatus, that have held the real power in certain nation-states. In the case of Egypt (and Tunisia as well), as historian James Gelvin explains, the 2010–2011 uprisings were unique in the MENA because other countries' deep states remained intact and in charge of the course of events, including the suppression of the revolutionary changes sought by many of the revolutionaries.[1]

This story of the revolution's death is not only familiar but validates several other stories the United States is keen to sell, such as the necessity of continued economic, political, and military intervention in the Middle East and North Africa. American audiences are left speculating, yet satiated, by such conclusions; perhaps democracy cannot take root in certain lands? At the same time, such conclusions about the Arab Spring coax us to see ourselves, the U.S. nation-state, as a type of omnipotent gardener, necessary to tend to the Middle East and North Africa as the seasons change. We grant ourselves agency and paternalistic authority over the region's growth. Though on the surface, this narrative may imply nurture and protection for the seeding and sustenance of democracy, its crux is actualized as a political minefield of power plays and ploys with an iron-fisted demarcation over humanity. In other words, the central result of this paternalistic interference is violent imperialism, oppression, division, and global inequity.

In Egypt, like many countries in the Middle East and North Africa, parallel narratives are also spun, which serve to validate dominant state-sanctioned tales by those in power who have historically wielded weaponized storytelling. In Egypt, the president, backed by the deeply rooted state military regime, prefers the role of father, just as his ousted predecessor Hosni Mubarak did. The state system perpetuates the belief that danger and disorder will devour a country run without a strictly disciplining and watchful patriarch.

INTRODUCTION 3

However, these parental safeguards have materialized as an arguably more autocratic regime than the one that sparked the 2011 revolution.

The constitution continues to be amended, and the state of emergency perpetually prolonged, to further extend and solidify President Abdel Fattah el-Sisi's rule and powers. Meanwhile, increasing numbers of peaceful dissenters and marginalized communities find their political voices, participation, and bodies austerely policed and punished.[2] While expanded gender roles and a diverse array of women-led grassroots coalitions, movements, and protesting bodies flourished throughout the revolution and its immediate wake, the same tightly controlled strategy for gender issues used pre-revolution, state feminism (critiqued for its monolithic top-down approach to further regime needs), has been reinstated.[3] Sisi has continued the legacy of neoliberalism that was implemented in President Sadat's era (1971–1981) and continued throughout Mubarak's. (This legacy is entwined with the U.S.-brokered normalization peace ties between Egypt and Israel.) Over thirty percent of industry is run by the military, which contradicts Sisi's claims to help boost the private sector. Sisi has also accepted a long-delayed 12 billion-dollar IMF loan which resulted in the flotation of the Egyptian pound, slashing subsidies, and increased reliance on Arabian Gulf aid.

Compared with Mubarak's pre-revolution era, there is higher unemployment, less capital, and continued dependence on foreign aid; the pound has drastically lost its value on the market, and there continues to be food scarcity and sky-rocketing inflation. As a result, the wide gap between the rich and the poor continues to be a source of contention. Twelve years after the revolutionary cries echoed throughout Tahrir Square in Cairo, the situation remains similar, if not worse. Egyptian politics remains increasingly autocratic, gender dynamics remain volatile, and the economy remains in critical condition.[4]

In these state-sanctioned stories, the titles may change, but the texts are merely copied and pasted, as narratives of nations operate to maintain their own power grids and citizen complacency. "This is what happened"—with neat and precisely organized benchmarks from start to finish, and now time will continue marching forward. Reading all the above as failure or death is practical, if our grasping of stories, books, and grand political-historical events is tangibly fixed, singular, and linear. However, those undercurrents return to gently nudge me. These narratives and understandings don't sit right. Knowing the world as a dancer, particularly from a dance more likely to swerve, circle, or roll rather than march stiffly in linear trajectories, I follow my gut feeling to stir up this discourse. After all, there are more steps to be considered and more moving stories to be shared.

Steps to Consider: *Raqs Sharqi* ("Belly Dance")

Lean in and listen closely, as some tales wield their power circulating subtly amidst the periphery. A youthful dancer with sparkling eyes and a well-endowed hourglass figure steps her platform stilettos onto a bar in a new Cairo disco-club. This bar will serve alcohol and act as her stage. The staccato clicks of her spiked heels are barely audible above the blasting DJ music and cheering crowd of elite younger Egyptian men and women. She struts toward the front of the bar as she suddenly folds her upper body over, hinging forward from her hips but sharply halting at a ninety-degree angle, leaving her breasts to dangle daringly in her jewel-encrusted bra and mini-skirt dance costume. She erupts into a robust chest shimmy, all the more enhanced by her bent-over position. Her full décolletage jiggles intensely, the flesh threatening to burst out from the top of her costume bra as she makes direct eye contact with the patrons standing inches in front of her quivering flesh. This provocative movement doesn't fit romanticized traditional expectations of what a "belly dance" show is. The illusory constructed nostalgia for flowing floor-length chiffon skirts and heavily beaded hip belts and bras with far less sexy cutouts is more likely to come to mind, alongside perhaps a dainty shoulder shimmy with just a hint of coy breast reverberation.

Instead, reality, like the dancer's laboring flesh, proves jarring to many. She winks, then with the next heavy drum accent flips her hair down to caress the bar then flips it back up while she returns to a standing position. The drum beats heavily, *dum dum dum*, and the dancer forcefully embodies these pounding accents with assertively articulated chest pops. Again, with each explosive upward "pop" of the dancer's chest, illusory nostalgic desire for a sensual albeit refined belly dancer shatters. Nearby, a patron records this thirty-second clip on his phone and posts it to Instagram, and so this story spreads. Multiple assessments are swiftly typed out in the "comments" section under the video and shared dozens of times across multiple national borders. The viral dissemination of this newer form of storytelling could result in diverse narratives. Yet, to a significant audience in Egypt, as well as the colossal community of belly dancers around the globe, there peculiarly exist shared and interwoven themes. Let's sit with the over-arching synopses.

"This is what became of the art of belly dance in its home country of Egypt? Thank God for the rest of us that are keeping it alive!" comments one white U.S. dancer. Other dancers from around the globe, including those from the older generation of Egyptian dancers, concur. "Belly dancing is dying, if not already dead, in the mother country." While in Egypt, a middle-aged gentleman shared, "The vulgar decay of society." Finally, another white Western dancer chimed in, in what possibly started as piqued curiosity, but immediately shut down into condemnation, "Don't they get arrested for that in those countries? She needs to be arrested!"

In this context, the rhythmic clicks of the dancer's heels are fully drowned out, not by the blasting DJ music or slightly tipsy enthusiasm of the crowd. Whatever work her dancing is doing is not being listened to as discourse, yet she keeps moving, her abdomen now glistening in sweat as she makes her next move. This too will be misread. Too aggressive, low-class, vulgar; or perhaps, simply not "belly dance."

Belly dance, correctly known as *raqs sharqi* in Arabic, is primarily a solo improvisational staged dance featuring sinuous and percussive articulation of the torso and hips that centralizes musical embodiment and the transmitted and reciprocally shared feeling of Middle Eastern, North African, Hellenic, and Turkish (MENAHT) music. *Raqs sharqi* emerged as an innovative staged dance genre at the turn of the nineteenth and twentieth centuries in the Egyptian entertainment establishments of Cairo and Alexandria; it developed from earlier traditional MENAHT dances and urban *baladi* (social dance) while also adopting influences from various international concert dances. *Raqs sharqi* as a distinct genre developed and was popularized alongside a significant shift in the sites where it was performed. It was during this time, particularly crystalizing in the period of liberal democracy, that innovative performance venues sprang up in Cairo to situate and contextualize *raqs sharqi*. The area of Ezbakiya, bordering old and new Cairo, was highlighted in the late nineteenth century by restaurants, boutiques, coffee shops, and new entertainment venues to suit the tastes of Egyptians as well as Arab and international tourists. Ezbakiya served an incredibly cosmopolitan Cairo population with entertainment serving all class levels. Adjacent to this area was Mohamed Ali Street, which became famous as the professional entertainment street where *awalim*, musicians, and singers resided and could be found to negotiate business throughout the first half of the twentieth century. New performance venues housed variety entertainment shows of local dance, largely known as *raqs sharqi* at this time, as well as international dance, singing, and other entertainment. Known by a number of terms (including music halls, *salas*, *cafés chantant*, nightclubs, and/or cabarets) these new venues provided local and global entertainment for an equally local and global spectatorship. It was during the early part of this century that *raqs sharqi* developed into what practitioners are familiar with today in terms of style, technique, musicality, and costuming.

Further, it is important to point out how the term "staged dance form" is used differently here to what the more dominant proscenium-concert or staged dance terms may typically signify from a Western perspective. In *raqs sharqi*, stages are often closer to the audience, smaller, and more circular than what audiences accustomed to Western concert dance might think of. Often the stage is just a designated area on the floor, unraised, or just cleared of seating/tables, though it may also be raised. Further, *raqs sharqi* has no "fourth wall" between the audience and performer; the interaction and charisma between dancer and audience remains of central importance to the aesthetics, meanings, and shared feeling of *raqs sharqi* in Cairo contexts.

As *raqs sharqi* developed within these newly established sites, it was thus intertwined with Egypt's larger nationalist and modernization schemes, negotiating local and global tastes, performances, and spectatorships.[5] Here, I use the term global to refer not only to European or Western cultural flows but also pan-MENAHT, as many of the entertainment types offered, as well as spectators and dancing bodies, were from throughout Egypt and the MENAHT. Calling attention to these new sites of entertainment and dancing bodies as grappling with multiple circulations of local Egyptian, pan-MENAHT, and other global flows is important in destabilizing discourse that often posits *raqs sharqi* dance and venues developed in direct response to Western or non-MENAHT demands and desires.

In addition to MENAHT, the acronyms MENAT and MENA are also frequently used in this ethnography. I try to be as precise as possible with my use of regional acronyms to contextualize my work within the heterogenous realities of these vast and complex regions, while likewise still respecting the nuanced and often marginalized influences and roles each (already blurry and complex) region has and has had on *raqs sharqi* throughout my writing. My efforts will be messy and imperfect, yet hopefully also serve to remind how fictitious nationally constructed borders are in the quest for equity, yet very real in how colonial, imperial, and orientalist violence continue to maintain their strongholds and divisiveness. Orientalism is the theory popularized by Palestinian-American scholar Edward Said to describe the dualistic relationship between the Occident and Orient as one of power, of domination, of varying degrees of a complex hegemony.[6] In other words, how that the relationship between the "East" and "West" is a constructed binary of uneven power wherein the West is centered and consequently grants itself power to define the "East" as "other" and less civilized.[7]

Due to forces of immigration, globalization, orientalism, mass media, and colonialism, as well as the ongoing violence of imperialism, *raqs sharqi* has spread all over the world from the MENAHT and is now a global dance form with a vast interpretation of styles, all particular to their cultural context and practiced under the umbrella term of belly dance. Although belly dance has become a widely recognized and popular umbrella term for this dance form in its manifold interpretations, it has a deeply problematic history and legacy. The term "belly dance" has a history steeped in colonialism. Largely translated from the French *danse du ventre*, it was used to sexualize and exotify the dance and was rife with colonial, orientalist, and patriarchal dynamics wherein abdominal dexterity was seen as primitive compared to European dances. Other practitioners find the term fetishizing for focusing on a sole body part, the belly, at the expense of calling attention to the geographic and/or cultural aspects of the dance form. Still further, many practitioners find the term orientalist for further reifying the MENAHT region as one giant homogenous zone and culture at the expense of locally derived terms for the dancing in each unique time and context. *Raqs sharqi* literally translates to "dance of the East" in Arabic.

I use the term *raqs sharqi* when referring to the professional Cairo contexts of the dance because this is the name of the dance in Egypt and in the colloquial Egyptian Arabic language (formally *al raqs al sharqi*), and the umbrella term belly dance when speaking of the dance in more general global contexts which encompasses a plethora of styles and interpretations.[8] On the one hand, Cairo is revered as a primary birthplace for the development and continued trend-setting home base of belly dance by those throughout the MENAHT, diaspora, and international community of belly dance practitioners; yet, on the other hand, it is now increasingly considered its death bed by these same communities.

Apparently, it's not only the revolution and its efforts that are woefully mourned for their apparent "death." *Raqs sharqi* is also dying, for some is already dead, in Egypt. At least, that is what's lamentably discussed not only amongst many in the global belly dance communities but also from those within and outside of the dance industry in the MENAHT, particularly the older generations. Similar to children preparing for slumber, those outside of this current site-specific work context want their favorite story read before being tucked in, the one we grew up hearing again and again. The happy, albeit clichéd ending that fits the norms already existing in society. Norms and narratives that I caution may work to put our awareness and sense of inquisitive openness and growth to sleep, not to be disturbed.

Many want to pin down, freeze in time, and transfix the dance, to make it a more tangible and singular entity, like traditional understandings of books, stories, and even grand revolutionary events. Nevertheless, with every new generation of dancers, new site-specific entertainment venue, stage, and step, *raqs sharqi* refutes and evades such capture while continually enacting change. However, not without consequence. Let's return to that lingering question asked about the arrest of dancers for their performances. Dancers are regularly arrested and policed for their performances. Although the policing of dancers has been on the rise during Sisi's presidency, the regulation and policing of *raqs sharqi* has been around as long as the dance itself and corresponds to larger socio-political dynamics that I argue are intricately entwined with the struggle for "bread, freedom, and social justice."[9]

This book will mine these connections; how the policing of the laboring female body, the blame of societal decay laid upon her bare flesh, and the sustained self-proclaimed authority to "save" an Egyptian cultural art form by Western practitioners, are all fricatively entangled within post-revolutionary politics and dominant state-sanctioned stories. Further, in circumnavigating how dancers step onto various site-specific and class-stratified stages across Cairo, as well as how they negotiate such stages with subtle winks, seismic hip shimmies, and sultry booty rotations, this book turns toward more well-rounded and fleshed-out embodied political insights rippling with revolutionary possibilities. In cultivating these connections, my ethnography argues that the core of a dancer's body engages with the gut of ongoing political transformations Egypt is experiencing in the aftermath of the revolution.

Stories We Share

This story moves. As a practitioner-scholar of *raqs sharqi*, I am committed to the understanding of dance as a form of discourse, wisdom, power, and world-shaping. With due integrity, I promise that I write from deeper than the bottom of my heart, instead pulling from the depths of my gut. The gut is not only a primary center of movement in *raqs sharqi*, but also the core of bodies, bodies that will be centralized within this book, and colloquially where moves of courage, and the seat of one's personal knowledge, are located. In other words, I refer to a more tangible and theoretical conceptualization of "gut instinct" founded on embodied knowledge. Here, gut knowledge or instinct is not based on a feminine-gendered premonition or feeling that essentializes and ties women closer to nature. Embodied knowledge is a term commonly used within dance studies referring to how we come to know things by and through our bodies with aims of disarming the fictitious Western concept of the "mind/body split."[10]

This core foundation of writing as a dedicated *raqs sharqi* practitioner-scholar, where theory and practice coalesce, allows me to distinctly honor the beauty, knowledge, and aesthetic perspectives and techniques that *raqs sharqi* embodies. Thus, I write this story intending to cultivate core connections with the potentiality and power to move us all into deeper ways of knowing and being. It's about attending to multiple movements as sources of power and subtle yet catalytic possibility, from the mobilities navigating a city, to a dancer's hip bump, to larger socio-political movements. This story makes different moves. It intends to shake up the standard ways of being and knowing, ways too often built on division, hierarchy, and linearity. It's a lesson and practice of listening. Likewise, I write this story as an artistic yet gutsy exercise in exposing and honoring the raw potentiality within a visceral vulnerability.

Sometimes, from movements as micro and fleshy as a hip bump to as sweeping and ideological as revolutions, it isn't that change has failed to occur, but rather that we refuse to see and be moved by it. Sometimes, it seems safer to stick to the dominant standards and stories, resulting in the dismissal, or even putting to death, of movements of change. This story instead follows the steps of several Cairo *raqs sharqi* dancers engaging with the visceral vulnerability demanded from exposing their flesh to choreographing moves not only with swerving significations but also manifold transformative possibilities.

I choreograph stories. My interwoven identity as a committed dance practitioner, scholar, ethnographer, and writer have shaped my life in multifaceted ways that have led me to recognize all practices (dance, fieldwork, and writing) as forms of story. While traditionally defined as accounts of people and events, here I approach stories through an embodied choreographic lens through the ways that they serve as moving forms of knowledge and power in interactive relationships with bodies, time, and space. This embodied choreographic approach also necessitates circling back and reconsidering books, writing, and other dominant forms of story in a new light; what if we understood storytelling as story sharing? In other words, story not as a unidirectional transaction with a top-down power configuration, but rather as a myriad and fluid webbed weaving of mutual interaction and spiraling exchange across an array of bodies? Story as constant states of multiple movements? This approach of fluid and ongoing exchange necessitates deep attention to relationships between bodies, space, time, and power. At the same time, it beckons shared responsibility, accountability, and agency across all bodies engaged in story, from those transmitting, transfixing, reading and listening, as well as being narrated. What if, instead of fixating on the inked letters, permanently affixed onto pages, and glued into spines until decades began to wear away their materiality, we deeply understood that the spines of books, the backbone of stories, are in fact sinuously bound to a multitude of spine and backbone having bodies that were, and are, making critical moves. What if we focused less on the materiality of ink, paper, and spinal adhesive, and more on the knowledge, emotion, relationships, and power that stories are constantly putting into motion?

This embodied choreographic approach to story does a certain kind of work. It shifts the focus and perspective. For one, it refutes the idea of a "single story," that there is ever one "pure" telling of a tale or viewpoint to take as omnipotent or "best." With full conviction I can assure readers that I have done my best in researching and writing this ethnography, but by virtue, my best cannot be enough. It's not supposed to be, and that's productive. If any ethnography were "enough," it would fall into the trappings of a "single story," wherein certain storytelling bodies, and certain storytelling formats are "most effective." This means of knowledge production and dissemination would merely continue the violence of dominant hegemonies, such as whiteness, imperialism, elitist institutions and modes of knowledge dissemination such as writing, in consolidating their power over the wondrously polyvalent ways of being in the world.

This approach also resonates with pioneering Middle Eastern feminist ethnographer Lila Abu-Lughod, who found in researching the Awlad-Ali Bedouins in Egypt that all knowledge is situated and partial and the researcher observes from a particular position.[11] Further, Abu-Lughod's work on ethnographies of connection in "Writing Against Culture" also acknowledges hierarchies and inequities perpetuated by "culture" as a tool of constructing the other; thus she urges the acknowledgment of complexity and cross-cutting of difference while being aware of when difference is used to justify domination. I resonate with her advocacy for ethnographies of connection that nuance the power and possibilities of valuing interconnections.[12]

Further, this approach pushes for perspective while carefully watching out for power, always honing in on the ways story as movement necessitates looking for those peripheralized storytellers, and modes of story sharing, such as dance, that can add nuanced complexity to the familiar narratives we grew to be comfortable with. Likewise, it demands establishing all forms of story as forms of power, power that can be oppressive or transformational, that can promote the aims of communities or reinforce their marginalization. Power that effects how we move through the current world and ripe with potentiality for how we may shape better worlds we're capable of stepping into. Finally, this understanding necessitates attending to bodies and their choreographies as core, cores of analysis, and cores of knowledge, across multiple spectrums within all more macro-political transformations.

To Close with a Beginning

To close this section on story sharing, I would like to return to a beginning: my beginning. I'll never forget stepping into my first belly dance class at just fourteen years old in my hometown of Newark, Delaware. There was a pleasure and sense of empowerment in swiveling, undulating, and circling my hips in new-to-me patterns and buttery smooth pathways. There was also an inner strength in redirecting and restructuring my body's center to be low and grounded in the pelvis, to languidly sway my hips yet still feel sturdy like an oak tree as my bare feet rooted into the dance studio floor. However, the challenge that took longer for me to embrace was to keep my upper chest and shoulder area open, with my chin slightly lifted, leaving my neck long and exposed. There was a more difficult vulnerability and openness that posture required. To move differently was only part of the work; remaining vulnerably open to connection while doing so was entirely another. It was a contradictory cocktail of strength in exposure. I had no idea back then the journey, places, and experiences my hips would roll me into, nor the life-altering connections that openness would embosom.[13]

I started dancing professionally at age seventeen, very quickly gigging in Arab-American nightclubs on the East Coast, where I received more lessons in growth. I can't forget one of my first performances as a "baby" dancer in those clubs. After what I thought was an excellent show full of explosive technique and crisp hip work, I walked briskly back toward my dressing room, gratifyingly throwing my costume cover-up around my then petite alabaster-skinned body (the main reason I was gigging in such clubs more so than "total package" dancer quality). Ziyad, a Lebanese gentleman in his mid-forties who was a club regular, cut me off in the hallway. With eyes already bloodshot from drinking, he leaned over me and gave unsolicited yet sage counsel, "If you want to be a dancer, you must be strong. Take power from your eyes, with when, where, and why you look. Stop being frantic on stage. It's the small sincere efforts that will give you the greatest reward." I shrunk beneath his penetrating gaze. Ziyad was right; I had much to learn. My dance trajectory was a constant journey in learning not only how to be strong, but also how that coincides with critically contextualized analysis of power. Moving from fifteen dollars per hour studio classes focused on self-empowerment through an embraced "sensuality" (we dare not say "sexuality") full of middle-aged white women to diasporic MENAHT performance contexts was a hands-on lesson in learning just how varied, yet overlapping, circulations of power and meanings were.[14] For example, in diasporic MENAHT contexts of dance, it was subtle interaction, charisma, and cultivating connections with the music and your audience that held far more sway than whatever range of motion I could reach with my hips.

Shortly thereafter, I began fervently scribbling observational and analytical notes as soon as I'd get home from gigs, even when I had to force my eyes to stay open at five in the morning. I wrote about interactions I had, small things commented on during the work night, on stage and off, and what deeper meaning they might hold in relation to various power dynamics surrounding gender, sexuality, race, class, and nationalism. Those scribblings became more official. I enrolled in university and became an anthropology major with an Arabic language and studies minor, eventually traveling the MENAT and earning a Ph.D. in Critical Dance Studies from the University of California Riverside. I would even argue those scribblings were the early seeds of my doctoral dissertation, an ethnography on Cairo *raqs sharqi*, which was in turn the foundation for this book. However, all of my research and writings are most deeply rooted in my desire for more profound understanding and connection, brought forth through the remarkably compelling relationships and experiences critically swiveling hips have enduringly circled, bumped, pushed, and dropped me into.

Let's pause here. I want to circle back and share with you a memory from my first Arabic story, an academic textbook, from my first year as an undergrad. I recall sitting in my Arabic language class and eagerly flipping open the cover of my *Al-Bustan* textbook. But wait—*wrong end*. Immediately, I was confronted with the reality that the moves I was comfortable with weren't always the ones I needed to make. Allow me to elaborate. As a reader, you're following me in this English language text from left to right. However, if written in Arabic script, you would approach this text from an alternate directionality; you would be reading from right to left.

Let's work with this feeling. I encourage readers to be open to dislocation as a lesson to other ways of being in the world, other paths of knowing, other directionalities, and the insight that what may seem an ending is always in some ways a new beginning. Together these encouragements weave a multiplicity and circularity in story sharing and fluid motion to be open to discomfort as a means of increasing critical awareness- an awareness that articulates that there are always more ways to move, more perspectives, relationships, and steps to consider. Likewise, this ethnography is just a few out of many.

In other words, this ethnography is not a transplantation of "what happened" in contemporary Cairo's *raqs sharqi* scene, or even my translation of what happened. Rather, this ethnography is my own choreography and staging of my experiences via my particular relationships with the people, places, and politics of contemporary Cairo's *raqs sharqi* scene. It is a few intricately and tenderly interwoven scraps of story sharing fabric from a richly colorful and perplexing tapestry that is always in process of becoming.

Recentering Cairo *Raqs Sharqi*

This ethnography is an act of recentering. During my literature review reading on belly dance scholarship as a doctoral student my project reached a turning point, and I decided my research would center Cairo. Shaking up and rounding out the scholarship on belly dance provides critical interventions and expansions. An impressive volume of academic literature has been penned about the dance form and the various significations the dance is capable of producing. In particular, the copious amount of belly dance scholarship can be configured into roughly five main, yet overlapping, classifications from discourses of feminist and gender empowerment, use-value, orientalism, MENAHT and international contexts, as well as contemporary globalization scholarship.[15]

Notwithstanding the intellectual merit of these various studies, they have predominantly been framed to center certain bodies and contexts, while marginalizing others. Specifically, an analysis of the literature reveals that predominantly Western bodies, contexts, and significations have been center-staged throughout the discourse, with the consequential effect of marginalizing non-Western subjectivities, significations, and stories. This is especially the case regarding the multiplicity of MENAHT bodies and significations elided in the literature, despite their primary role in developing and transmitting this dance form into new contexts.

Therefore, it is critical to circle-back upon the scholarship and round it out through studies of multiple centers and circulations of *raqs sharqi*. A focus on circulations of *raqs sharqi* within Cairo centered contexts especially will enable critical challenges and nuances to the MENAHT's historic and dynamic ongoing role within local and global belly dance discourse. A landmark ethnography, *Femininity and Dance in Egypt* by Noha Roushdy is one exemplary example of accomplishing such necessary work through exploring subjectivity and sociocultural meaning of Egyptian dance.[16] There is also the classic ethnography by scholar Karin Van Nieuwkerk. Her book, *A Trade Like Any Other, Female Singers and Dancers in Egypt* valuably highlights the working-class dancers of Mohamad Ali Street in Cairo through grounded ethnography.[17] In conversation with the work of these two women and expanding upon existing scholarship, my ethnography will be the first to engage in the dance-centric analysis of the research and writing of Cairo *raqs sharqi* while also exploring cutting-edge contemporary political contexts focused on intra-MENA circulations.

I recall thinking through my decision to center my study in Cairo, and in email or phone exchange with prominent belly dance scholars being told in cautionary response that, "the field has turned toward the global." As if, somehow, the bustling and dynamic city of Cairo has been left behind, or out of, global circulations. Considering Cairo's historic and on-going role as the center of pan-Middle Eastern circulations of entertainment and its leading role in pan-Middle Eastern political movements, it becomes a particularly rich site for exploring how dance shapes, and is shaped by, such dimensions—both past, present, and future.[18] Additionally, "global" can often problematically essentialize only those sites, bodies, and contexts that are either elite or accessible to the Western gaze.[19] Take, for example, our opening dance vignette around the thirty-second social media clip. These snippets of access are often solely what is used to analyze the contemporary Cairo dance scene. Such analyses reify orientalist paradigms where what exists is only grasped as what's accessible or knowable to the Western gaze.

This ethnography instead follows the dancer's lead, aiming to shatter these ideologies through deep mining of multi-sited *raqs sharqi* contexts and bodies throughout contemporary Cairo, paying acute attention to local and global class-based meanings. Even the deepest site of Cairo, the cabaret where no photo and video policies abound, will be quarried for local, intra-MENA, and global circulations. My approach is in conversation with Edward Said's later work, in which he seriously undertakes Middle Eastern feminist scholars' critiques of *Orientalism* and argues that there exists a mutually constitutive relationship between culture and imperialism. He laments the notion of totalized identity that imperialism constructed through conceptualizations of nationalism, and instead urges scholars and people to think, write, and know one another based on our inherent interconnectivity in ways that avoid dominating forms of duality and division.[20]

Through mining each of the core discursive approaches to belly dance literature in turn, I discovered that although the bulk of studies focused on orientalism, there remained a binary directional flow of studies between "East" and "West." In this unidirectional flow, the dancers problematically gained agency and complexity as they moved from Eastern sites and bodies to Western. I commend the numerous studies on orientalism and belly dance in particular for focusing on how corporeality and embodiment complicate why and how people engage with orientalism.[21] (Problematically, these representations of the "exotic Arab other" gave Western practitioners a "safety net" with which to work through their own self-fashioning and identity transformations without having to tackle the harsh political realities of being "other.") However, these studies continue to complexify non-MENAHT subjects at the expense of granting this same complexity and relationship with embodiment and corporeality to MENAHT contexts and bodies.[22]

Within Dance Studies, corporeality is a theorization relating to the lived reality of embodied experience. In other words, the body set in culture, wherein the body is understood with agency while also already interpolated by larger systems of power. My definition of corporeality pulls from those of dance scholars Cindy Garcia and Susan Foster. Foster's pioneering book, *Corporealities*, originally defines and "seeks to vivify the study of bodies through a consideration of bodily reality, not as natural or absolute given but as a tangible and substantial category of cultural experience."[23] Garcia enacts corporeality as the power-fueled relationships between salsa dancing bodies that are both performing identities while also negotiating identities already bestowed upon them by larger societal forces, complicating simplified conflations between corporeality and identity while focusing on relationships.[24] My book aims to redirect the corporeal complexity of belly dance scholarship by centralizing the Cairene dancing body as a means of knowledge production and dissemination while fleshing out nuanced portraits of the lives, stories, and embodied political insights of Middle Eastern dance and non-dance bodies.

Centering Cairo circulations of dance locally and globally is particularly necessary considering Cairo's historic role as the center of pan-MENA circulations of entertainment such as dance, and its leading role in pan-MENA nationalist and feminist movements. It is also crucial because of Cairo's position as a key center within the MENA today, with nations looking to Cairo for not only the latest trends in music and dance but also as a primary negotiator in the aftermath of the "Arab Spring," particularly Egypt's January 25, 2011 revolution. This book queries and argues for the unique insights, tactics, and corporeal knowledge a ground-level, dance-centric analysis offers to such pressing gender, economic, and state politics. Despite revolutionary ruptures and movements, Egypt, alongside many other nations involved in the Arab Spring, remains confronted with increasingly autocratic regimes and ideologies that discipline and structure bodies and systems into top-down, linear, and unidirectional ways of being.

In response to such political precarity, this ethnography asks: What does it mean to move into revolutionary new relationalities and realities? What unique insights and knowledge does a dance-centric lens offer to such politics? How is corporeality core to macro-political themes, and what tactics and embodied knowledge does centralizing corporeality offer to such pertinent politics?

This ethnography answers these inquiries through nuanced dance-centric analysis and sensitively attuned visceral and choreographic writing that embodies Cairo *raqs sharqi*'s site-specific style, structure, values, and semiotics. Altogether, the embodied knowledge within my site-specific *raqs sharqi* chapters and interim "taxi transitions" that maneuver between chapters, argue that moving into these new relationalities and realities means moving multiplicitously, multi-directionally, and meaningfully into core connection within ourselves, between one another, and amidst our communities.

My research methodology consists primarily of participant-observation fieldwork at an array of class-stratified commercial performance venues (completed within various fieldwork stays between 2015 and 2020) with a focus on choreographic analysis and embodied knowledge within these field sites.[25] I use the term choreography in reference to the foundational relationships between bodies, movement, time, and space. I consider choreography as a larger event inclusive of all the people within the dance site, analyzing not just the dancers on stages across Cairo but also the movements, interactions, and connections between audiences, musicians, wait staff, and city dwellers. Further, this ethnography highlights "taxi transitions" between site-specific chapters, in which I expand choreographic analysis to the movements going to and from my field sites using various forms of public transportation to link together larger infrastructural and intersectional city politics. I focus on how power circulates between all such entities, with each being sources of power, although the extent of which is fluidly determined depending on context and interaction. Additionally, I conduct in-depth interviews with professional dancers, audience members, managers, musicians, and others involved with the dance industry at large. This book focuses on commercial sites of *raqs sharqi* only, that is, where audiences pay to get into venues that regularly feature professional *raqs sharqi* performances. Weddings and other social-celebratory occasions across all class levels have been an enduring context of *raqs sharqi* as well, however these contexts are out of this book's scope.[26] My book's project sites include five-star cruise ships and decadent hotels studding the Nile, the elite yet controversial "new" disco-clubs whose success ironically mushroomed post-revolution during the ultra-conservative Muslim Brotherhood rule, and the smoky working-class cabarets with all-male spectators clustered along historic Pyramid Street.

As my ongoing project contributes to Dance Studies through its topic and method, it also expands upon ethnographic studies across disciplines by charting invigorating new approaches on how to do and write-up multi-sited dance ethnography that contextualizes both micro- and macro-level city dynamics through kinesthetic frameworks. I apply the Cairo-based site-specific choreographic structure, aesthetics, and values of *raqs sharqi* itself for my ethnographic research and writing models and frameworks. In other words, dance ethnography *as* embodied and contextualized *raqs sharqi*.

This approach provides a means of negotiating an enduring puzzle to my project: how to grapple with my vexed positionality as an *agnabiyya* (white female foreigner) practitioner-scholar while remaining focused on centering and mining intra-MENA contexts and meanings through a richly nuanced and sensitive dance-centric analysis.

Additionally, this ethnography also contributes to Middle Eastern Studies, through highlighting women's and other marginalized bodies' agency and corporeality. The literature in this field labors to deconstruct stereotypes of the Middle East but has yet to fully explore the agency of women's bodies, particularly professional dancing bodies, too-often relegated to the margins of "respectable" society as well as notions of "ideal" womanhood. Due to legacies of colonialism, imperialism, and interlinked waves of conservative Islamic ideology all stemming from insidiously shape-shifting patriarchy, *raqs sharqi* is devalued, considered frivolous at best, or immoral at worst.[27]

Additionally, Middle Eastern Studies scholarship follows a range of responses to orientalist approaches to belly dance. Scholars such as Amira Jamarkani and Maira Sunaina both posit that belly dance is an orientalist product that is not Arab, but a Western fantasy.[28] This is a fairly standard viewpoint from academics, and Arab dance scholar Najwa Adra intervenes in their findings by arguing that sometimes elitism, paired with *raqs sharqi*'s local (MENA) stigmatization and popularization amongst working class populations result in these attitudes.[29] The dancers in this book are real, and their danced discourse valuable, yet too often overlooked due to Western orientalism coupled with MENA classism and a mutual dismissal of dance and performance as discourse. This ethnography, which forwards choreography as a site of discourse and class analysis as vital, highlights how dance and non-dance bodies corporeally and diversely participate in Cairo's political dynamics.

This ethnography also expands upon cutting-edge theorizations on corporeality in MENAHT contexts. Too often discourse places MENAHT corporeality in an adverse light—for example, veiling, FGM, and honor killings—whereas this study centers corporeality as a complex challenge to such negatively essentializing and orientalist discourse. In doing so, my book is in conversation with inspiring emergent scholarship from Egyptian ethnographer Sherine Hafez, which also exemplifies the importance and necessity of considering corporeality, and female corporeality in particular, within Egypt's political transformations.[30] This is especially highlighted in my project's focus on choreographic analysis of multiple movements within and between larger dance events. My project not only highlights but also centralizes people and bodily realities which are often marginalized or erased within MENAHT scholarship, such as *raqs sharqi* dancers, *reklam* (hostess) cabaret workers, and taxicab drivers.[31]

During the initial stages of exploratory fieldwork, I distinctly recall a taxi driver calling me an *3abeeta* (idiot) under his breath upon hearing about my research, "the people can't afford bread here, and this idiot thinks we need research on dance." He thought I couldn't understand or catch his Arabic, but I was listening. Repeated encounters such as this have re-directed my project to focus not only on deep listening across peripheralized modes and bodies, but also to keep economic and class threads as core contours of my project. At the same time, I advocate for the undermined yet powerful meaning-making capabilities of dance as practice and academic inquiry.

Cairo Ethnography as the Foreign Dance Doctor (*Dakturat al Raqs al Agnabiyya*)

They don't know how to listen. There are far too many Egyptian dancers to name that have bluntly and exasperatedly exclaimed this to me as the biggest mistake they see non-Egyptian dancers make in *raqs sharqi*. It is exceedingly relevant here, in my ethnography, as well as to a practitioner and to a Western academic readership at large. Western practitioners and scholars do not know how to listen. Dozens of Egyptian dancers have complained to me repeatedly about how *aganib* (foreigners) are getting it wrong by not listening to the music, not listening to or understanding the lyrics, not understanding their culture, aesthetics, teachings, and values. Because *aganib* do not listen, many Egyptian artists conclude that non-MENAHT dancers have no feeling. *Ihsas*, feeling, is the vital lifeblood and soul within *raqs sharqi*, cutting across contexts from the working-class cabaret to elite five-star hotels and weddings. When mutually shared and transmitted, it cultivates a sense of togetherness and community.[32]

Taken off stage and placed within an academic or general public Western sphere, this critical mistake of not listening remains imminently relevant. Too often, Western practitioners, academics, and the general public project onto the MENAHT what we perceive to "know" about it. Within Western and MENAHT relations, *aganib* continue to take the role of the star performer who projects outward and fills up the stage, rather than that of earnest student-learner. I have well over a decade of practitioner experience in *raqs sharqi*, as a student, teacher, professional performer in a variety of U.S. venues, and as a dance scholar. For my research centered in Cairo, I found that culminating my embodied knowledge from *raqs sharqi* was most ethically beneficial when I stepped back and positioned myself as an informed learning, listening, critically self-aware, and devoted student-mentee.

While the experience of professionally performing in Cairo contexts to live music would have generated a rich perspective to inform my dance studies research, for this specific project, it was outweighed by costs. First, there is a noticeable tension and divide between many Egyptian professionals and foreigner, where many Egyptians are harmed due to foreigners coming in and stealing vital work by offering cheaper prices (or mere uncompensated "exposure") and having greater access and privilege to resources that put them ahead (such as costly plastic surgery, whiter skin, and more "open" cultural lifestyles that don't face the same stigma as Egyptians do). These dynamics are deeply entwined with histories and contemporary politics of neoliberal whiteness, imperialism, uneven economics, and colonialism, such as the common desire for lighter skinned performers and foreigners' privilege to easily garner visas and hop on a plane and afford to dance for pure limelight/ego. My goal was to gain the trust of, deeply listen to, and learn from the perspectives of intra-MENA dancers and dancing for work would have directly or indirectly made me lose a lot of the rapport and value I was otherwise able to gain. Using my embodied knowledge and privilege to be able to sit back and deeply listen to and learn from intra-MENA actors (while compensating them) was of utmost importance and value in my project. (Further, it's illegal for a foreigner to work in Cairo at venues with regular shows without proper licensing and paperwork.)

Dancing assuredly informed this project in multifaceted ways. I did perform to live orchestras in festivals, socially dance a ton, and take classes with many Egyptian dancers and musicians throughout my research project, which greatly informed and nuanced my embodied knowledge and ethnographic "deep listening" skillset. A renowned drummer Yossry was a great help to my research in allowing me to take dance lessons with up-and-coming cabaret-circuit Egyptian dancers to his live drumming and additional sociocultural instruction, and then allowing a group interview to follow in his Pyramid Street music studio. With my combined positionality and this ethnography's objectives, I found Yossry's methodological approach extremely fitting and valuable to deep listening and embodied knowledge.

It is necessary to move beyond researcher positionalities that follow an "insider/outsider" binary, as this doesn't do justice to the multiple roles of identity and relations of power within which my body, and all the other research bodies, are entangled. This will also work to disrupt dualistic understandings and move beyond narrow scopes of analysis that further reify East/West orientalist paradigms while nuancing how my positionality affects my research. The role of "the practitioner" in scholarship must be used to add more than legitimacy, authority, and "insider status" to the scholar, particularly when great modes of privilege and uneven imperialistic power relations (in terms of race, class, gender, nationality, sexuality, etc.) deeply entwine the site of my own research body to that of my fieldwork site. In particular, my approach suggests that these multiple identities and relationships must be interwoven with rich attentiveness to how these interlacing politics play out, are performed, mis/perceived, and policed both choreographically and through interactive embodiment. This focus on subtle micro-interactions on the bodily and movement level can help illuminate when larger hierarchies of power are transgressed or reified.

This choreographic attentiveness to positionality politics reminds me of continual and dynamic "weight shifts" in *raqs sharqi* movements. I bemoan the common trend of researchers stating their bullet-list "progressive performative positionality" checklist at the beginning of their scholarship and halting there, never returning to how those intersectional aspects of their identities are played out, performed, and/or policed during interactive exchanges and relationships within the doing of the research on the ground. In my experience, the power, privilege, and nuance of the variously interlinked aspects of our intersectional identities are in constant interactive motion, experiencing literal "weight" shifts of power, privilege, nuance, in the research, fieldwork, writing, and dissemination of such research across myriad audiences.

The perspective of the practitioner is indeed valuable and leads to particular knowledge and focuses that other perspectives may elide, which was often the case before the emergence of the field of Dance Studies. For example, dance was often seen as merely a reflection of culture or politics, as opposed to a force that is both shaped by, but also shaping, such loftier dynamics in complex ways. However, the caution within this approach is not just to position oneself as a practitioner in ways that garner an uncritical or singular authority, but to simultaneously situate and mine the deployment of one's practitioner status, as our identities as practitioners can perform many roles in unique connection to our myriad self-identities. In other words, my positionality as the *dakturat al raqs al agnabiyya* gestures toward a fieldwork model that retains the keen awareness and vulnerable curiosity of the student-teacher relationship wherein the researcher-student is open to and honors new knowledge and techniques transmitted from mentors, all while remaining deeply informed by her already embodied knowledge of the form.

First and foremost, this necessitates deep, visceral, and vulnerable listening, and figuring out methodologically how to do this kind of work as an *agnabiyya*. Listening in earnest to what means the most to my Egyptian participants, and what they would have this book focus on and do, as well as listening to the dance form's structure and aesthetics within site-specific Cairo contexts was central to best figuring out how to do this ethnography with integrity. This sense of deep listening has greatly informed this ethnography as a whole, from my fieldwork methodologies to the kaleidoscope of bodies and stories I highlight. From the taxi drivers that navigate the curves and congestion of Cairo city streets to the exhausted but enlightening cabaret dancers sharing their perspectives with me as they rush between gigs at daybreak, subtle and sustained listening was essential. This further extends to being aware of and listening to the kinesthetic sensation of Cairo city and dance circuitries. How are the sudden curves in the road in conversation with the dancers' languid hip curve articulations from cabarets to hotels? How are the various bodies moving throughout this city in conversation, and what are these choreographies at large saying about contemporary Cairo? While reeling with additional perplexities, one realization crystalizes; conceiving of my positionality as a puzzle doesn't pan out, because puzzles piece together perfectly in the end, and this project is far too vexed and messy of a process. Yet, as Middle Eastern feminist scholar Lila Abu-Lughod reminds us, these stories are worth telling in all their messiness and contradictions.[33]

With that said, you too play a role in responsibly cultivating the most effectual ethnography performance. I encourage you as a reader to engage with this text as an ideal *raqs sharqi* audience member. This means reading with active engagement, pausing when something resonates with you or leads to discomfort or further questioning, writing it out in the margins or on a separate notebook, and keeping that energy circulating by following through on your own reactions as you read. I ask that readers also be sensitive, vulnerable, and attuned to their emotional responses to this work. Listen, notice how the words move into you, as well as how you move after interacting with these words and engaging with these stories.

Pay attention; the richness lies in the subtleties. This also requires you to take a seat, focus, and listen as other bodies take up the stage. As a dancer, I was struck by how consistently my methodology choreographically necessitated having a seat. I sat in the back corner of cabarets, along the perimeter of stages at hotel and boat shows, and at the bar in new disco-clubs. I sat in taxis, Ubers, and many living rooms and coffee shops, listening to interviewees. As a dancer, I'm used to being center-staged and exerting myself while others sit and watch. Perhaps other dance and academic readers are as well. Thus, I invite you to have a seat as we listen to the choreographic knowledge of others. After you leave this ethnographic performance, try to engage with it in a way that nuances your own deep listening skill set. Try to engage in a way that rounds out your sense of being in the world in ways *raqs sharqi* already embodies and valorizes, by doing and being with more connective *ihsas*.

Dance-Centric Analysis: Ethnography as Embodied *Raqs Sharqi*

This book hinges upon interwoven theoretical and methodological approaches across disciplines. Theories and methods from Middle Eastern Studies, Middle Eastern Gender and Sexuality Studies, Dance Studies, ethnography, and choreographic embodied writing whirl together into an interlocking embrace in this book. These diverse theoretical and methodological entanglements supported me in grappling with the politically vexed riddle of how to do and write my ethnography, with aims of centering intra-MENA bodies and significations with my own body situated as a U.S. working-class white practitioner-scholar.

I found that the most sincere and effective way to move through my fieldwork and writing was according to how I already move, relate, and know—that is, as a dancer. The dancing body produces its own discourse; thus, it is incredibly enabling if I as a scholar am able to map and apply my dance's choreographic structure, values, and aesthetics to my ethnography. This approach to ethnographic fieldwork and writing will not only allow for what I term a deeply dance-centric analysis but will also provide a productive model of how to "do" dance ethnography, particularly when I or another practitioner-scholar is exploring a globally practiced form in new cultural contexts and on different bodies.

This dance-centric approach will help to capture the complex ground-level lived reality of dance and non-dance corporealities, as well as allow not only the dancers but also the embodied insight within their dancing, to take center stage. Highlighting choreographic analysis as method is a critical element because the microanalysis of movement and relationality within and between bodies, including my own, pointedly unites and gestures toward the larger macro dynamics of power that all our bodies are engulfed within.

As many dancers in the field have told me when attempting to define *raqs sharqi*, "dance *is* feeling." Just as the objective of cultivating connections through feeling is a pinnacle aim of Cairo *raqs sharqi* performances, so too do I aim to foster this sense of knowing and being by doing and writing this ethnography. In my fieldwork and writing, this is theorized as "multiply moving" ethnography, wherein the adverb "in a multiple manner" gestures toward an approach necessitating attendance to the multiple linguistic and physiological meanings of moving. In other words, both in centralizing mobility and motion as sites of knowledge, power, and possibility, but also to researching and writing in ways that move emotionally, stirring up poignant affect that leads to physical reaction, change and connection. In other words, moving as embodied within the core values of *raqs sharqi* aesthetics, to use movement and musicality to create connections emboldened with *ihsas* (feeling) circularly between performer, musicians, and audiences.

Additionally, this dance-centric approach necessitates circling back to my core research question. In re-theorizing revolution as a *raqs sharqi* dancer, I focus not merely on the common political understanding and movement of revolution as drastic, vast, and seemingly sudden moments of political transformation, but rather, revolution as change enacted through circular motion or revolving. This re-theorization resonates with the circular performance contexts, aesthetics, movements, and musicality in Cairo *raqs sharqi*. It turns toward a circular awareness and analytical attentiveness to more subtle, peripheral, and dynamic subjectivities and situations as significant sites of knowledge and political tactics.

When dance scholarship focuses on dance circulations, or the "movements of movement," multiple configurations of power are made visible as well as the multiple positionalities of diverse corporealities that negotiate these political circuits.[34] Larger hegemonies of power intersecting with race, class, gender, sexuality, nationality, and ethnicity are fluidly embodied and contradictorily contested upon bodies and their relationships to one another. A focus on circulations of dance is particularly enabling in centering the otherwise peripheral. This framework focuses on multi-directionality and multi-positionality of power dynamics in ways that also considers politics between variously marginalized corporealities as significant.

Why does it matter not only where we pull our ethnographic moves from, but also where such moves may reach? Because research, when understood and disseminated as facts and absolute truths, doesn't often open people's minds, hearts, or arms to multiplicity; it seldom changes the world. More often, it's used to validate dominant worlds certain groups want centralized; this contrasts with research based in body-centric relationships and revolving relationality churning with emotion. This secondary approach does a different work because, as known through my experiences of *raqs sharqi*, people may open up and come together by and through "moving" relationships—in my ethnography's case, most powerfully—when the dual understandings of "moving" coalesce. To cultivate connectivity, we have to feel something and feel something with the heightened momentum of movement, such as a sinking or swelling heart or stirring gut reaction.

This potential for core connections and subtle yet catalytic capacity within my "multiply moving" ethnography embraces visceral vulnerability and reaches all bodies involved in the research and writing as founding motive, method, and motion. What am I as ethnographer drawn toward at a gut level in the field? What causes me to pause, what peripheralized sensory modes are activated throughout the fieldwork that make me lean in, focus, and listen more deeply. Likewise, these moments of visceral vulnerability are "read" as subtle yet significant research in other bodies, the drop of sweat trickling down a dancer's brow alongside an exasperated sigh, the furtive glances with tensed musculature, knowing winks, and the moments of silence accompanying subtle, direct, or dropped eye contact. This compels me to push at the limitations of the written record, to choreograph my writing in a way that words, stories, and emotions have the sensation and potentiality of movement. This also means writing in a way that resonates physically with audiences. How can I share this story in a way that pulls you in?

Lila Abu-Lughod also prompts researchers to avoid the seductive romance of resistance. She argues that sharing a complex, intersectional, and visceral story holds more integrity and grit than crafting a happy ending superficially suited to progressive politics.[35] This is especially valuable in studies of dance, as dance is often taken up by the general public as a liberational trope. Here, dance is understood as power, power that can be wielded in enabling and hindering ways, often simultaneously. When grappled with theoretically and complexly, dance may offer caution and insight into the flesh and bones of larger political dynamics, in sinuous ways other approaches may simply scratch the surface of.

Most *raqs sharqi* performances within MENAHT contexts are structured improvisations. Structured improvisation operates betwixt and between standard notions of improvisation and choreography. Here, I refer to choreography as preset and designed movement to a particular song. In *raqs sharqi*, there is always a set structure to the movements; dancers must embody the music and the feeling, mood, and structures within the song. However, the majority of the show is not choreographed. Instead, the dancer goes with the particular event's audience, music, performance setting, and her mood and tastes in designing her show as she performs it. (I use the term "she" throughout the text referring to professional Cairo *raqs sharqi* dancers to call attention to the gender dynamics implicit in this art form in the contemporary Cairo commercial venue contexts where only women are allowed (and socially expected) to work.)[36] This structured improvisation approach grounds the performance in relationships, where all entities, audience, dancer, setting, and music or musicians, are important in shaping the most effective show. This is particularly relevant because the principal understandings of *raqs sharqi* within Cairo contexts revolves around the *tafa3ul* (interaction), *hudur* (charisma), and *ihsas* (feeling) that comes from the combined and shared relationality of the musicians, dancer, and audience.[37] Improvisation is not random and natural because there is an underlying structure to what movements are chosen and why, even if this doesn't feel like a conscious decision in the moment.

Applying structured *raqs sharqi* improvisation as an ethnographic approach demands a deep contextualization of one's show, informed by particular histories of places and bodies, with an acute awareness of gender, class, nationalist, and sexuality dynamics within such histories. A dancer must know the history of the venue, audience, music, and performance context to design the best show. She is also continually aware of how she and all others are being read through intersectional lenses. For example, interacting with a male audience one way may have a certain meaning, while interacting the same way with a mixed-gender family crowd may have an entirely different meaning. That same interaction may also signify differently on a five-star hotel stage versus in a cabaret. Meaning always depends on the context. Additionally, it's within the nuances of subtle movements and pauses, such as a sly wink or bashful shoulder roll, where the deepest power or meaning can be "read." My approach resonates with Middle Eastern feminist theories and methodologies that gesture toward non-Western-dominated forms of agency and power within MENAT women's worlds. Marnia Lazreg is one such scholar arguing that there are multiple modes of being female while presenting multiple frameworks for moving beyond the paradigms of the "oppressed 'Arab' woman". For example, Lazreg forwards that scholars need to understand the value and meaning within small gestures, seclusion, softness, and subtlety; all qualities that Western feminism may dismiss as weak or passive.[38]

I am most capable as a *raqs sharqi* dancer when I can keenly and acutely improvise within the overarching structures I find myself within, musically as well as contextually, such as knowing how to best engage and capitalize upon my audience and material surroundings in any particular, yet ever-shifting, moment. *Raqs sharqi*, like Dance Studies and MENAHT Gender Studies scholarship, all gesture toward an understanding of the body as capable of agency, yet always already interpolated and framed within various larger and overlapping hegemonies.[39] The dancer can negotiate these larger systems to her best advantage through various tactics but can never transcend them entirely. In conversation with feminist scholarship on the Egyptian revolution by ethnographer Hafez, my approach exemplifies the necessity of considering female corporeality within such political complexity.[40] Through protest stories, Hafez articulates how Egyptian female corporeality is disciplined and controlled, while simultaneously embodying possibilities of resistance and transformation. She contends that both processes are entwined and work upon the body hand-in-hand. This likewise engages with work by Abu-Lughod, whose research forwards the understanding that modernization and feminist projects in the Middle East simultaneously offered both regulation, or new forms of control, while also offering emancipation and new forms of opportunity.[41]

These negotiations and "wiggle room" within larger power structures are not solely determined by the dancer. The dancer-researcher must always be keenly aware of all bodies, particularly her own as it is employing, playing, and being read in gendered, classed, raced, and sexual lenses. All the bodies within the space, including those historical bodies that helped create the current conditions for where the dance event is now, co-constitute meanings in conjunction, and never evenly or homogenously. Like the *raqs sharqi* performance, no dancer can fully anticipate the circumstances in which she will burst onto the floor and find herself, but with utmost preparation and training she can have a foundation that enables her to do her best to most sensitively grapple with and navigate these situations.

In the immediate moment, it's about going with your gut, as there's no time for anything else. At the same time, a dancer learns to trust her own gut because that feeling is based on a depth of ever-growing experiences and preparation in dealing with various kinds of people, music, energies, and shifting contexts. In other words, the dancer's gut knowledge pulls deeper than what's commonly associated with "feminine intuition." Rather, I propose this gut knowledge moves beyond essentializing discourse of women's "innate" biological essence tying her to nature but is based on the accumulation of all her on- and off-stage experiences and negotiations with various bodies over time. It's a honed internalized analysis of her current environment—including people's behavior and verbal and nonverbal communication, in relation to how her own body is being read within larger dominating structures—that allows her to promptly choose her next best move.

Likewise, her sphere of awareness is circular and constantly on the move, whether she is at a crowded wedding party surrounded by over-enthusiastic guests or on a small stage at a hotel with a full band of male musicians behind her with her audience seated all around the stage's perimeter. The dancer knows significance comes from everywhere, and in a circle, everybody matters; there is no beginning or end. The dancer, like the ethnographer, should be continually and intensely aware of all the micro and macro interactions that are engulfing the larger dance event, and be ready to shake up her foundational theoretical and methodological techniques in order to most eloquently fit the music. First and foremost, this necessitates open and vulnerable listening, and responding earnestly to what means the most for the people you're performing for while not over-stepping the music. It further requires an understanding of the particular space you're within and knowing that there is not one set method, technique, or model that will fit and do justice to each situation. Thus, the site-specific chapters to follow each have their own unique structural approach and theoretical lens.

Cutting across Cairo contexts of dance, a successful show is about cultivating meaningful connections. The core aim of *raqs sharqi* in professional Cairo contexts is to create connections between bodies emboldened with feeling (*ihsas*). In making subtle movements and interaction, eye contact and playful or powerful gesturing with her crowd, in knowing where and when to pause, punctuate, or stretch out the emotional lyrics of a song through the lingering sinuosity of her hip work, a dancer, at some bodily level, knows that everything, and everyone, connects to everything else. Her job is to highlight and make the entire room feel that sense of connection, while also working to maintain central control over the precarious kaleidoscope of power dynamics intertwined within and between this fluid web of connectivity. As the solo female dancer, her body and choreography, while grappling with these forces, simultaneously become the pinnacle nexus of all these crisscrossing dynamics and power plays. As ethnographer, I too must learn to feel and know how everything connects to everything else, and which forces become more centered, marginalized, buttery-smooth, and disruptive throughout these tethered interplays. This leads to layered mappings of multiple rather than singular meanings, as well as research that resists linear, binary, and singular analysis within any dance event. Instead, circular awareness and movements alongside vibrant shimmies shake up and produce knowledge that rounds out analysis to center what's often marginalized.

The Maneuverings of a "Multiply Moving" Dance Ethnography

As this ethnography is my choreography, let us rehearse the sequence of chapter stagings and steps designed to parallel the structure of a *raqs sharqi* show. Chapter 1 begins the series of site-specific chapters as readers step aboard a Nile cruising tourist boat. This first site-specific chapter can be understood as a *"mejance"* or *raqs sharqi* introduction piece to begin the multisong performance. The introduction is often somewhat choreographed and serves as the musical piece that familiarizes the dancer, musicians, and audience with one another. It is akin to initial greetings and small talk when two people first meet and are trying to figure each other out to make the rest of the show more meaningful to take the audience on a deeper journey. As the show progresses, the connections between dancer, music, and audience are ideally supposed to deepen, and the creation of *ihsas* becomes heightened. In other words, these chapters start with what's likely most familiar to readers and then goes deeper into the core of Cairo as the show progresses. This decision reflects not only my own movements of accessibility into the field as an ethnographer but will also be the most "familiar" of the three sites in terms of venue, accessibility, and theoretical approaches to the largely Western audience likely to make up the readership of this book. As a dancer, I know the most effective and affectual show is one directly catered to the audience of the evening.

Following, we check-in to Chapter 2 on five-star hotels before getting "snazzed" up for a late night in the controversial yet wildly popular disco-clubs of Chapter 3. Finally, this ethnography closes with a smokey-night out in the Pyramid Street cabarets of Chapter 4. In following this trajectory, I also move the reader along my ethnographic journey, as this was the order of my own entry into these research sites. The bodies and contexts within these sites move from being more cosmopolitan and international into an increasingly intra-MENA and local Egyptian community. Additionally, this ordering reflects general non-local access to these sites, with my hope being that by the time readers arrive at the most stigmatized and marginalized site of the cabaret, readers are at the deeper point in the *raqs sharqi* structural performance that makes them more open to new understandings, connections, and maneuvers.

Note, I am speaking about accessibility from a non-Egyptian perspective, which due to my book's institutional form and publication in the English language I believe will make up the majority of my readership. As *raqs sharqi* dictates, I must cater my show toward the audience in order to create the most meaningful connections. This accessibility is not just with the physical presence of how easy it is to step into such venues in Cairo but also in terms of media, wherein video clips can more easily be found of boats, disco-clubs, and hotels, while cabarets hold a strict no photo/video policy. However, it is worth noting that this "accessibility" not only assumes a non-Egyptian body but also one that is middle class or higher, as some local working-class cabarets are the only one of these sites that is accessible from a class perspective. While I do not identify as middle class, not from when I was a grad student and not currently while writing as a part-time lecturer living in a broken-down backyard San Diego RV that I illegally rent, finding the economic resources to do this project was an intense struggle throughout my fieldwork and writing. The state of academia's exploitation of contingent faculty and graduate labor greatly contributes to this rapidly growing obstacle. However, it's also important to note how class status does, or does not, translate overseas. As I write, one U.S. dollar exchanges for eighteen Egyptian pounds, making my economic standing exceedingly privileged in Cairo circuitries.

Finally, *raqs sharqi* is ideally designed to take audiences on a journey. For academic connoisseurs aiming to skim, fervently dissect, and expeditiously jump around and extract this ethnography for "to the point" arguments, relax; enjoy the show as intended. As the dance, this ethnography's knowledge values lingering, circularity, and the savoring of subtleties; therefore, not until the conclusion will audiences be multiply moved and ready for macro-level analysis and arguments.

Now that the overall choreographic structure is rehearsed, let's take a closer look at the signification and steps within each site-specific chapter. Chapter 1, "Nile Tour Boats: Cruising the Nile while Contesting Borders, Boundaries, and Bodies" steps aboard the *Nile Maxim* five-star boat, where three different dancers' shows are compared and contrasted for the ways they construct and perform gender, sexuality, and nationalism through varied bodily, physical, and ideological borders and boundaries. This chapter will highlight how space shapes meanings but how bodies moving within such spaces choreograph significant weight in what semiotics are created, deconstructed, and exchanged. While the overall variety "packaged performance" entertainment on cruise boats is designed to "sell" an image of Egypt to locals and tourists, what exactly that package says about the female dancing body, and the nation at large, is largely dependent upon the individual dancer through her intersectionally understood identity and what she intends to say with her art. Within the four field sites explored in this book, these boats are unique and appealing to open this ethnography with because they are the most cosmopolitan and mobile site, both literally and figuratively. The boats move, cruising up and down the Nile, while the bodies on these boats are most likely to be the least anchored to Cairo, meaning that many visiting tourists make up the audiences and boats are where many transient dancers, particularly foreigners, are hired.

This chapter centralizes the peripheral through my encounters with Samia, one of Cairo's ubiquitous bathroom attendants. Samia's dance reviews frame the overall chapter analysis. Further, this chapter's writing structure is broken down into two parts to embody the common two-part *raqs sharqi* show structure on boats. *Raqs sharqi* boat shows often begin their first set with the *mejance* (entrance number), followed by one or two songs where dancers and audiences first become acquainted. The dancer then exits for a costume change into a more folklore or *sha3bi* (popular working-class urban) style costume which is followed by the "second set," which starts with a folklore-inspired *tableau* or dance, such as *raqs al 3asaaya* (stick dance) for *sa3idi*.[42] This is followed by a couple more songs and often includes dancers performing amongst the tables off-stage in order for a house photographer to take purchasable memento photos of guests with the dancer. Thus, part one opens with house dancers Safiya and Randa, both of whom choose to design their *Nile Maxim* shows as soloist dancers who remain on stage throughout their performances.[43] Part two centralizes the regular house dancer Farah Nasri. Farah chooses to design her shows collaboratively with *funun al sha3biyya* (male backup theatrical folklore dancers) and lots of off-stage audience engagement. Suitably, part two explores the tensions and possibilities opened up through the decision for female *raqs sharqi* dancers to perform either with, or without, *funun al sha3biyya* and the gendered policing and powers at play when dancers step off-stage. Finally, this chapter cruises to a conclusion with the comparative analysis of these different dancers *raqs sharqi* shows and how their insights may offer particular maneuvers into grappling with the country's larger gendered, nationalist, and economic politics.

Chapter 2, "Five-Star Hotels: Checking In, or Checking Out? Contemporary Conditions in the Revolution's Aftermath" mines the predicament of *raqs sharqi* within five-star hotels' unstable future since the 2011 revolution and the ensuing economic fallout. Historically, *raqs sharqi* performed within five-star hotels was decadent, popular, and considered the "crème de la crème." Not only was this particular venue type considered the most elite and prestigious, but these were also where the greatest star dancers would be found and featured. To be a dancer working regularly in a five-star hotel meant that you had "made it." However, in post-revolutionary Cairo, there are few five-star hotels even offering extravagant *raqs sharqi* venues and performances like decades past, and as a result the five-star "star" system has also nearly vanished. In fact, renowned Egyptian dancer Dina's show at the five-star Semiramis hotel is said to be one of the last remaining that follows in the legacy of extravagant classic five-star hotel *raqs sharqi*.

Consequently, a popular discourse within the local and global dance community, as well as amongst many everyday Egyptians, is that "*raqs sharqi* is dying." As an example, when I first met Dina as a Cairo *raqs sharqi* ethnographer, she simply stated, "but there is no dance in Egypt now."[44] Due to growing conservatism, global fashion trend changes, and changing economics within the country Dina was claimed by News Week (and many in the international belly dance community) to be the "last great Egyptian dancer."[45] However, rather than accept appearances for surface-value, this chapter delves into what I will theorize as the "appearances versus actualities" of bodily labor and explores how *raqs sharqi* remains, but differently. In other words, this chapter explores how the work is still there, but the work has changed. Considering five-star hotels' decadent past (and elite centralization within both local and global belly dance histories), how are these spaces, and the bodies within them, functioning in today's Cairo since the 2011 revolution and economic fallout? What political and economic relevance does contemporary *raqs sharqi* in these sites offer?

To meaningfully "check-in" to the core issues five-star hotel *raqs sharqi* shows and dancers are embodying, this chapter explores a fieldwork case study focused on a specific dancer performing within an established hotel site: Amina at the Marriott hotel's Empress nightclub.[46] To deeply embody the ways *raqs sharqi* is situated within five-star hotels, this chapter's research and writing centralizes the dancer's choreographic analysis as the main draw for the investigation as well as writing structure, just as audiences would typically be drawn into certain hotel shows based on who was the performing dancer. Just as staying at a hotel is bookended with the checking in and checking out processes, the choreographic analysis of Amina's show begins before she takes to the stage and wraps up with her larger hotel site exit. In doing so, my hope is that rather than seeing empty rooms, sites, and futures, Amina's show may sway us toward intersectionally understood actualities sweetened with abundance.

Chapter 3, "Discos: Risqué Moves and the Exposure of Policing Politics" scrolls, then steps into *raqs sharqi* within Cairo's controversial disco-clubs via the viral social media video clips shared from their stages as intertwined sites of policing in larger local and global dance and sociopolitical feminist and revolutionary movements. Interestingly, these "provocative" discos were popularized during the finalization of President Morsi's ultra-conservative Muslim Brotherhood rule in the wake of the 2011 revolution and remain popular to this day. This chapter zooms in and out amongst the relationships between post-revolutionary social policing of Cairo's female dancers' risqué movements across social media screens and disco stages, as well as the state's entangled policing of both micro and macro level movements of authoritarian dissent.

What possibilities, cautions, and tactics gather in moving toward more revolutionary realities, when such moves are deemed risqué? To begin, it's useful to pan out and not just analyze an uncontextualized social media post (so often the sole access point of the outside international industry of dance practitioners), but rather to gather a more well-rounded tale by tangibly leaning into the site that disco dancers embody. The choreographic writing of this chapter aims to highlight while also rectifying this issue through zooming in but then critically out from screened snippets to physically stepping into the "meaty material" of dancers on stage in the flesh. We get to choose how we engage and make connections, and this ethnography's objective is to cultivate core connections, best accomplished from the insight from the fleshed out in-site when body-centric frameworks and theory are centralized.

Pay attention, particularly in this chapter specificsite, audiences are put to work. Just as audiences within disco-club sites are the most kinesthetically active and physically involved in the show, so too do I urge readers to attune to the "greater picture" and the way seemingly separate sites and stories are interconnected. However, to best understand and embody these interconnections, we need to get with the vibe of the disco-club. I theorize vibe as an embodied environment of potential unity and possibility. When realized, vibe not only makes visible interconnections and their significations, but also cultivates an energetic environment influenced by the bodies within the shared space, environments potentially rippling with revolutionary possibilities capable of sustainable embodiment. However, as the two-part case stories suggest, this embodiment necessitates sliding into serious (and often quite scandalous) risk. However, this risk is critical in exposing the core of policing which operates as a "triple threat" intertwined within and between state, society, and self.

Chapter 4, "Pyramid Street Cabarets: Negotiating Slippery Stages and Contradictory Competitions" steps into a smokey cabaret, where we experience our final full-night ethnographic excursion. This chapter investigates how variously marginalized bodies within the cabaret site actively negotiate the increasingly slippery terrain of turbulent gender, economic, and nationalist politics. This politically vexed terrain is undermined by repressive regimes, changing notions of masculinity, the female laboring body, and the overlapping hegemonies of the local Egyptian economy as well as Arabian Gulf petrodollars tied to the oil industry. To mine the semiotics of this site in ways that embody the contours of the cabaret entertainment system, this chapter is structured by *nimar* (cabaret dancer performance sets), including the interim gap between *nimar*, when the stage is swarmed with other dancing bodies, from *reklam* (cabaret hostesses) to tipsy clientele. At the same time, while the investigation focuses on choreographic analysis of the variety of bodies that take to the stage, the writing, like the cabaret show, is constantly interspersed and paused for infamous yet abrupt *tahiyya* (microphone-reverbing formal "greetings" to well-tipping clientele).

While cabaret greetings focus on keeping money flowing, they do so by calling public attention to "bodies that matter" within the cabaret. However, in this chapter, bodies that matter are not valued due to their monetary richness, but rather for their wealth of wisdom. Therefore, interview excerpts from a vast array of peripheralized working-class cabaret characters are performatively inserted within the writing, adding powerfully punctuated interruptions to the choreographic commotion that sharply cuts into the choreographic analysis while at the same time sinuously bending toward political tactics necessitating multi-directional and multiplicitous moves.

Ultimately, the cabaret site was chosen to close this ethnography because it often requires deepest access into intra-MENA circuitries, bodies, and significations. The surface of this book started off scraping away at the often binary, stereotyped, and reductive formulations of *raqs sharqi*, predominantly understood in Western contexts and readerships through an orientalist "East-West" lens. This deep into the book, my hope is that the audience is more primed to value and deeply listen to the intra-MENA bodies, meanings, and contexts through Cairo-centric circulatory paradigms and rhythms. As the cabaret is the most locally and internationally stereotyped, de-valued, and dismissed venue, this primed listening is particularly relevant.

Yalla, let's move. We don't want to miss the opportunity. I spot one of Cairo's taxis heading this way; we'll need to catch it to head out to our first site. I offer just a gentle reminder before we embark. Lift your chin slightly, expose and expand throughout the upper chest—stay open to connection.

Taxi Transition: *Zahma* (Traffic)

I sighed in exasperation as I wiped the beads of sweat from my brow. *I really can't be late this time.* I stood on the edge of a busy street and hastily hailed a taxi; I had a Nile cruising boat performance to catch. I was worried about being late and missing the boat that sets off at 8pm sharp. Being "late" was an all too pervasive state of being in the condensed city of Cairo, well known for its gridlocked traffic (*zahma*) and other series of delaying obstacles that get in the way of any simple task involving maneuvering throughout the city. As a U.S. ethnographer, I felt sizable anxiety at the thought of being even a moment late to meet new dancers and other research collaborators. However, in this case, if you arrive late to catch a boat performance, you feel especially unprofessional, as the boat leaves the dock to cruise the Nile river. If you fail to be on board by the appointed time, your last resort is to hop onto a small speed boat and "catch up" to the cruise. Staff help you awkwardly clamber aboard while you desperately hope that you don't fall into the Nile. (Yes, I know this from personal experience.)

I snapped out of my anxiety when one of the city's black and white taxis pulled over just ahead of my position. I swiftly stepped toward the driver-side window to see if the driver would accept my destination. Despite my hurry, I stopped suddenly. Glancing at the driver, I paused to evaluate the situation. Based on my positionality, being alone as a young, white U.S. *agnabiya*, I was always vigilant about situations I was potentially putting myself into. Though catching a taxi may seem a simple enough task, I often used first impressions and gut reactions to hypothesize if this ride might result in either harassment, a terrifying Mario-kart style speed race down the jammed streets of Cairo, or most likely, enormous over-payment (i.e., the "foreigner tax"). While I've experienced an overwhelming number of positive taxi rides with professional and thoughtful drivers, my reasons for hesitating were all real concerns. At the very least, taxi riders can expect a less than comfortable ride; usually the AC is broken or not used, you spend considerable time roasting away in sun-soaked stopped traffic, the pollution and dust slaps you in the face through the open windows, and if you don't like second-hand cigarette smoke, well—tough luck.

In a city with a population of over ten million, where the average Cairene salary is around US$4,500, the uncomfortable cab conditions and chance to make extra pounds off a usually much more well-off foreigner are unpleasant but pragmatic realities. In this case, however, my pause was due to the gruff

Figure I.1 Interior of a taxi in Cairo. Credit: Peter Atkinson/Alamy Stock Photo.

and weathered male face that peered at me through the open window. Dressed in a sweat-stained *galabeya* (a robe-like garment traditional to the Nile Valley), cap, and long full beard, with stern but tired brown eyes, my impression was that this man wasn't just religious and traditional, but probably conservatively so. I wasn't sure what he'd make of a young *agnabiyya* traveling alone throughout Cairo. However, perhaps due to my rush, I leaned over slightly, my left arm lightly crossing my chest from any "immodest" views, and more timidly than I'd aimed, asked, "*Zamalek?*" He nodded abruptly, and with a mix of gratitude and hesitation, I yanked open the creaky rear door, the socially appropriate place for a single young woman to sit, and plopped onto the torn and faded leather seats. The engine rattled as we headed off into the dusty traffic; I gazed out the open rear window as a light breeze caressed my cheeks. I felt my shoulders relax.

The trip was characterized by small lurches forward constantly interspersed with pauses due to the traffic; I felt my body vibrating slightly with the excessive rattling of the engine. The constant cacophony of car horns bleating their frustrations mixed with the lurid voices and blasting radios from passing by vehicles, but this taxi's radio was playing Quran. Though the recording was scratchy, I felt it somehow mixed pleasantly with the outside *dausha* (loud noisiness) and simultaneously calmed the chaos engulfing our vehicle. As the recitation washed over me, I felt all the stress and difficulties from the long day melting from my tense muscles. On rough days, and this had surely qualified as one, living alone in Cairo as a twenty-six-year-old ethnographer who was attempting to meaningfully engage with Cairo's male-dominated nightlife entertainment industry was rife with difficulty, self-doubt, and exhaustion, to put it lightly. The poetic flow and beautiful heart-lifting words of the Quran weren't just washing over me at this point; rather I felt the words penetrating my bones and expanding throughout my body with a much-needed sense of peace and resolve. They overwhelmed me.

Without warning, I burst into tears of serenity. I scuttled for a tissue from my purse and tried to get myself under control, but quickly glancing up at the rear-view mirror, I saw the driver looking at me, his previously stern brown eyes now softened with concern. As our gazes met in the mirror, he gently asked in Arabic, "*are you okay?*" I nodded shyly, pointed toward the radio, and acknowledged in broken Arabic, "Cairo is difficult, but this is the most beautiful voice in the world, I feel relaxed." The driver beamed with a bright smile as he looked upwards and lifted both his palms up in thanks, "*Allahu Akbar*," (God is most great). He enthusiastically twisted around in his chair and exclaimed to me, "this is Quran, the words of Allah, I am so happy to have a foreigner feel Quran in my taxi. Also yes, I agree with you on these points. Where are you from?" "*Amreeka.*" "Ah, *Amreeka*. Most American people that I meet, they sit here in my taxi, they are so nice and good. But you must know, and I'm sorry, the American government is so bad for the world. But of course, the people are not the government, and the government is not the people, I hope you feel the same about Egypt. If you cross the world you will find most of the people are good, but that is the important thing, you must know the people." He stated this as his hand gestured back and forth between the two of us, referencing an additional bodily face-to-face element to his assertion. He lightheartedly concluded with a laugh as he twisted back around, "You must ride in the back of many taxis, haha!" The halted traffic subsided as the driver, Mohamed, lurched our taxi forward and we continued the ride.

My aim for this initial transition is to give a partial sense of the chaos, calamity, and "pressure cooker" density that is Cairo city life and transportation. At the same time, this experience illustrated for me just how often capacities for human connection and complexity are opened up within the bubbling chaos, in curious ways that are both hindered and enabled by that same chaos. Starting a *raqs sharqi* ethnography steeped in Cairo's nightlife, often marginalized as seedy and suspicious to the general public, with the flowy eloquence of Quran recitation might seem slightly out of place, but that's the point. Making Mohamed, the working-class, traditionally garbed, thick-bearded religious man the first character we meet in this story would seem antithetical to the sultry, sexy midriff-bearing dancers soon to take over, but that's the first step that needs to be taken. We need to break down this sense of binary being, seeing, and separation. The Middle East has long been caricatured in orientalist representation by these two figures; the lavish belly dancer available for consumption and the oppressively conservative brown Muslim patriarch.[47] The reality, moving past representational tropes, is more complex, rich, messy, and full of human capacity for more humane, dignified, and nuanced connection.

Further, while religion is often treated politically within academic discourse, it is important to know the diverse and often beautifully subtle and mundane ways it's experienced and interwoven into a multiplicity of lives. My kairotic experience also demonstrates the key importance in acts of deep listening; listening to your gut, the larger circumstances and context of the moment, as well as the subtleties and pauses in music and rhythms, whether they be in a boat, hotel, cabaret, or the city streets. At the same time, my aim is that moments of connection can exist alongside cautions against romanticizing. In other words, there were uneven power dynamics between Mohamed and me, even in our moment of connection within the shared space of the taxi. Mohamed works in uncomfortable taxi conditions, the poor and overcrowded infrastructure and cityscape of Cairo, and wears the sweat-stained *galabeya*, highlighting his working-class labor within larger structural problems that he navigates to survive and provide for his family. Through our interaction, Mohamed also teaches that rifts exist between governments, national politics, and everyday people. He advises that the best way to know others is through ground-level bodily interaction, rather than looking solely from the top-down macro-level of politics outside spheres of lived realities.

Most importantly, as Mohamed's combined verbal and kinesthetic discourse taught me, is to know people through more personal and ground-level relationships. As both *agnabiya* and back seat passenger, on the one hand, I found my responsibility was to go along for the ride while focusing on listening in more nuanced and diverse ways. On the other hand, our positionalities resist romanticizing as they point to both gender and class dynamics in our use of the taxi space. To choose to set upon this ethnographic project with the mobility afforded by my passport and the purchase of a US$1,000 dollar plane ticket differs from the driver I met in the midst of a stiflingly hot and uncomfortable workday. Further, my back-seat positionality also highlights uneven gender dynamics, as a male body would not have warranted the same expected physical distance between our bodies. Upon arriving outside the boat entrance, I exited the taxi, thanked the driver for the ride, and paid. While Mohamed and my paths have yet to cross again, and considering Cairo most likely never will, I remain thankful for the momentary connection.

1
Nile Cruising Boats

Cruising the Nile while Contesting Borders, Boundaries, and Bodies

After stepping out of the taxi, I double-checked the sign above to make sure I had arrived at the correct boat. I walked up to the two male security guards standing idly around a thin walk-through metal detector. I began to slide my purse off my shoulder for their inspection, but they waved their hands, indicating it wasn't necessary, and allowed me to pass straight through the detector. During President Mubarak's era, from the 1980s until the revolution, venues such as hotels and cruise boats responded to increasing security threats, and corresponding drops in tourism, by ramping up their security features. Mediated entrances such as I had experienced here had become the standard. Much of the extreme fundamentalist unrest that targeted Egyptian minorities, tourists, police, and government officials was attributed to President Sadat and Mubarak's neoliberal economic "opening" to the West, perceived as corrupt, alongside the deepened cleavage between rich and poor that such policies further exacerbated.[1] (Importantly, any religion can, and has, been interpreted in a grossly harmful politicized way to promote extremist agendas that the vast majority of peaceful practitioners of the faith do not consider rightful interpretations.)

I wondered what the guards' criteria were for allowing certain people to "pass through" without thorough inspection; my foreignness, gender, or was the security apparatus symbolic more than pragmatic? Nevertheless, on the one hand, their now pervasive presence warns of the tight entanglements of tourism, economic stability, and national security that engulf and mediate entrance to not only commercial sites of *raqs sharqi*, but also the country at large. On the other hand, the nonchalant hand waving me through signaled the reality that bodies embodied, or were at least mis/perceived to embody, as either a threat to the system or economic necessity. I headed down a small flight of stairs to reach the docks where the large Nile cruising boat was docked.[2]

Figure 1.1 Overlooking Cairo city at night with views of hotels and stationary boats. Credit: Sam Pollitt/Alamy Stock Photo.

The boat loomed large against the backdrop of the now darkened Nile river, the waters gently lapping against the platform I stood upon. I could see the Nile water glistening with the reflection of the numerous lights from various hotels, buildings, and giant advertisement billboards clustered together on the other side of the river. They gleamed as shining reminders of cosmopolitanism and commodification within the city. My scenic viewing was interrupted by the familiar whooshing sound of compressed air releasing from a large bus stopping outside the guarded entrance. I looked over my shoulder to see one of Cairo's large tour buses beginning to unload about a dozen or so international tourists. I briskly crossed the ramp into the boat entrance to be seated and settled before the large crowd arrived. An elderly man greeted me outside the boat while checking my reservation. He reminded me of the 350-pound minimum charge and that beverages were extra. I nodded as a suited waiter then escorted me to my table within the boat.

The boat was decorated neatly yet rather plainly. Still, the plastic chandeliers, bow-tied waiters, and slightly cigarette-burned linen table clothes all hinted at an air of elegance catering to middle- and upper-class tastes. The tables were seated in a general "U" pattern around a small square dance floor with a keyboard and drum set sitting preparedly behind it. A medium-sized buffet with an assortment of mediocre-quality Middle Eastern and international food was set up in front of the stairs that would take you either to the second floor or the open-air deck above that. I headed upstairs for some fresh air before the night began. As I walked across the upper deck, it felt like a domino-style procession of eyes looking me up and down from the mainly Gulf and Egyptian men smoking and drinking tea and coffee sitting along the deck's perimeter. I often went to boat shows alone; I faced the least harassment in these sites, and they weren't quite as suspicious toward a young foreign woman on her own in comparison to my other research sites. I thought I'd find a quiet spot to gaze upon the Nile at the end of the deck. However, once there, I was greeted with bartering attempts by a local tradesman with two tables set up full of typical Egyptian tourist trinkets of little pyramid, Pharaoh, and Bastet figurines. I picked up a Bastet figurine and flipped it over and translated the Arabic sticker on the bottom, *san3a fi seen* (manufactured in China). "Everything hand made from Egypt," the man retorted in English as he gestured to the rest of his wares.

His display of cliché tourist trinkets alongside his masking of the paraphernalia's manufacturing origins demonstrates not only the significant touristic nature of boat cruises but also the particular tourist relationship between Westerners and Egyptians. The tradesman cleverly marketed his stock in an "authentic" way that often appeals to Western tourists and their imperialist nostalgia. In other words, marketing appealed toward the Western longing steeped in racial domination for a pure "ancient" Egypt unaffected by modernization. Likewise, his marketing also camouflaged uneven globalized economic flows that have made it cheaper to import tourist goods from China rather than make them locally. I sighed and leaned over the railing at the farthest end of the open-air deck; I could see the forefront of the boat down below where two middle-aged men in *galabeyas* were settling in before the cruise set off. One was sitting on a plastic chair taking a cigarette break while the other man was performing his prayers using a large towel as a prayer mat. After spending some time above deck, I headed back down to the first-floor restaurant to make observations as the boat was starting to fill up.

During my fieldwork, most boat cruises were relatively filled with customers, unlike some of the hotel shows, which might just have a scattering of guests throughout the room. Tonight's mix appeared to be a standard cosmopolitan blend, about half of whom were from throughout the MENA, particularly Egypt and the Arabian Gulf (*khaleeg*), with the other half being from India, China, Japan, Europe, and South America. Family crowds were most likely to be found in boats as well as some hotel shows, hardly in cabarets. The audience tonight was a mix of couples, large tour groups herded in like sheep, and individual families. I learned to tell those coming off the tourist buses not only from their large group size but usually because they looked the most exhausted and starved. After all, tonight's cruise was one of the last stops after a day-long series of excursions throughout Greater Cairo. I smirked at the exhausted and sunburnt faces finding their seats as my mind wandered to re-cap the contexts of boats. (Perhaps the reminiscing would block out my growling stomach, it too eagerly awaiting the buffet.)

Hiring professional dancers for tour boat cruises for both locals and tourists wasn't new; it's been an Egyptian staple since the colonial era, when orientalist travelers such as Flaubert and others documented such occurrences.[3] However, beginning in Nasser's presidential era and crystallizing during the Sadat and Mubarak eras, *raqs sharqi* on boats became popularized and standardized in a similar fashion to that experienced today. These two-hour cruising boats were retired ships that could no longer reliably make the longer cruises between Cairo to Luxor and Aswan, so they were transformed to offer lucrative evening cruises. This current cruise structure featuring standardized variety entertainment was shaped due to broader economic, professionalization, and globalization shifts. For example, it was during the entertainment business and professionalization switch from female-entertainer led *awalim* to *raqs sharqi* dancers working under male *impresarios* that began in Nasser's era that boat entertainment switched to the current system that was standardized and popularized in the Sadat and Mubarak eras.[4]

As a dancer, I'm aware of how these venues are viewed within the current Cairo dance industry. Within each category of site there exists a hierarchy of class and prestige levels, as well as a hierarchy amongst the site types themselves. At the top tier of standard cruise boats, you have the *Nile Maxim* and *Nile Pharaohs*. The *Pharaohs* was the first boat of this kind in Cairo to start having the packaged deal variety entertainment show with musicians, dancers, buffet, and *tanoura*.[5] *Tanoura* refers to a male-dominated Egyptian movement practice, often used for secular entertainment purposes, that involves whirling in a heavy colorful skirt adapted from *Sufi* practices. In these boat performances, *tanoura* is explicitly entertainment (i.e. not for spiritual purposes) and often includes other "tricks" such as adding LED lights, balancing various objects while whirling, and so on. *Tanoura* is accepted as a cultural heritage of Egypt, and the *El-Wikala tanoura* troupe performs weekly and benefits from state support. There is likewise a plethora of cheaper boats that also carry less reputable status throughout Greater Cairo.[6]

Most of the clients had finished spilling into the boat at this point, and the two-man team of musicians began taking their places just behind the square

NILE CRUISING BOATS 45

Figure 1.2 A *tanoura* performance on the Nile Maxim. Credit: Tracey Gibbs www.traceygibbs.co.uk

dance floor, as wails of instruments tuning called for attention. The variety entertainment show was about to commence.

The standard variety entertainment includes an Egyptian house band playing MENA and international music (at this point, I'll never get Frank Sinatra out of my head), with open-floor social dancing. This entertainment is followed by a two-part *raqs sharqi* show with a *tanoura* performance before or between the dancer's sets, separated by her costume changing, then back to the house band. The boats are the main *raqs sharqi* commercial venues in which to find regular *tanoura* performances.[7] Everything is scaled down to the smaller size of the boat and particularly the boat's stage, so there are fewer musicians than a dancer may bring to a wedding or hotel, and the show is also truncated compared to how long a wedding or hotel show might be. Consequently, the pay is also significantly less for entertainers than what they'd likely make at a wedding, hotel, or more upscale cabaret. Most boats have a minimum charge for dinner, but boats are still not nearly as expensive as five-star hotel venues or the new disco-clubs. However, the minimum price is still about a few weeks of salary for an average Egyptian, so for local audiences, these trips are often saved for special occasions for the middle and upper classes. Additionally, because the tours have set times in the early evening, usually between 8 and 10 pm, it is easier to find musicians to hire for boats because venues and dancers are not competing with the often more lucrative hotel and cabaret jobs occurring later in the night. This earlier time also results in a more family-friendly atmosphere, since families can go out and celebrate a nice evening, possibly with children, while still getting to bed in plenty of time for work in the morning.

Many boats, unlike cabarets and hotel shows, work with tourist companies to create package deals and are the most common venue for international tourists to have access, affordability, and interest to go to. Boat venues are known within the industry to be the most touristy of my four field sites due to the idea that dancers are just one of a handful of elements drawing tourists in (in addition to the Nile cruise, buffet, and *tanoura*). As such, boats have a lower reputation for star dancers than hotels and weddings. Many in the industry have explained that tourist boats are for the mediocre dancers who can get away with putting on less of a wonderful show because they "just dance for tourists" who aren't as analytical about the art form (implying non-MENA), and foreigners looking for a "clean" place to dance. However, most boat dancers and staff will tell you that audiences are typically half MENA and Egyptian, with the remaining half being non-Arab tourists from across the globe.[8] (Catering to such a diverse audience is a note-worthy skill in and of itself.)

To elaborate on these two interconnected points, tourists often come expecting to see "any belly dancer" rather than a dancer known by name like in five-star hotels. Also, here "clean" refers to the job being less likely to involve sexual harassment toward the dancer by audience members and staff/management alike, as well as there not being significant numbers of sex workers in the audience. Returning to foreign dancers, the boats are currently and historically one of the most common sites for foreign dancers to work. I state this for a variety of reasons. While many foreign dancers and Egyptian talent and boat management have rather harshly stated that foreigners train harder, are reliable with putting in effort and being on time, and are "better dancers," compared to their Egyptian counterparts, deeper mining would argue that it is a combination of factors, and such critiques are imbued with orientalism and imperialism. For example, the desire for lighter-skinned dancers with body types and overall aesthetic looks that fall into globalized Western beauty standards are prominent amongst boat management and their elite MENA and global audiences. Also, the "in betweenness" of foreign dancers that dance *raqs sharqi* with more Western-imbued techniques and looks cater toward orientalism's desire for what Edward Said calls the "familiar in the exotic."[9] Further, stating that foreign dancers prefer the safety net of the clean reputation and environment boats implies that intra-MENA dancers are more likely to engage in "non-clean" activities and solicitation for work. This critique is also imbued with moral superiority toward non-MENA women.

In lived reality, economic necessity is a larger factor weighing toward how dancers from all backgrounds approach their work. Further, Egyptian dancers having grown up in the culture, are more equipped with tactics and approaches for grappling with more dubious advances and offers that most foreigners don't have the same culminated experience, and thus tactics, for negotiating. (This is not to imply that *raqs sharqi* in Cairo is unique for female laborers having to deal with sexual harassment and advances, as this is common throughout the globe in all professions, particular gendered entertainment industries. However, I am suggesting that how these dynamics manifest is situated within particular sociocultural contexts in ways wherein a foreign U.S. dancer's toolkit of anti-harassment tactics may not be as effective in Cairo as a Cairene dancer who has grown up negotiating these in-situ intricacies). As well, most professional working Egyptian dancers are not working with the fantasy idea of "having danced in Egypt" and the stardom of the international belly dance market in mind; rather, they are working primarily to make economic ends meet. Thus, for Egyptian dancers the low pay of boat work and at least two hours wasted aboard while cruising are not as economically feasible as working in other sites, whereas for foreigners, the fame, fantasy, and experience of working in Egypt can override economics. This is especially true as most foreign dancers are not coming from the same economic backgrounds as most Egyptian performers.

The more accessible nature and affordability of boats, as well as different reasons audiences choose to partake in a Nile cruising entertainment package, results in boats being one of the more stable and reliable sites of *raqs sharqi*. Patrons attend the boat for special occasions and a decadent night out, as well as for dual strains of "Egypt tourism." Ethnographer L. Wynn succinctly elaborates upon this stability factor in her work on Western tourism, which focuses on the ancient ideas of Egypt, verse the Arabian Gulf's contemporary entertainment tourism in Egypt. She states, "The difference between Arab and Western tourism is literally night and day: the pyramid tours (for Westerners) start early in the morning to beat the midday heat, while nightclub evenings (for Arabs) don't come to an end until the early-morning light."[10] The way boats navigate between both strands of tourism and local patronage allow boats to stay afloat while other dips in tourism, the economy, and political stability more gravely effect other sites of dance.

For example, while numerous *raqs sharqi* performances occurred throughout Cairo on the eve of January 25, 2011, on the day of the revolution dance work grounded to a halt. A number of foreign dancers left the country as business tanked. Their embassies assisted them in leaving the country and returning to their home countries, where they performed and taught on the local teaching and performance circuit. Most Egyptian dancers, and musicians that depended on dancers for work, suffered a crushing blow as their jobs were either lost or greatly diminished in quantity. The *Nile Maxim* stopped working for about a month, then resumed with fewer cruises (down from two to three pre-revolution to one to two post-revolution) as well as a cut in entertainers' pay. Not only did many dancers suffer deep pay cuts, but because they pay their band members from their pay, many male musicians also found themselves cut from the band entirely as groups became smaller due to economic necessity. Those that remained hired were paid significantly less. Many dancers reported that their pay was slashed in half after January

25. Still, in comparison, many hotels and cabarets never reopened their venues for *raqs sharqi* post-revolution.

Bearing all this in mind, it seemed perplexing to me that boats were often dismissed for being simply "touristy" and "mediocre," particularly the *Maxim*, which at the time featured multiple powerhouse dancers of MENA-heritage. I wondered what knowledge centralizing the danced discourse itself would set sail to—*Oh drat*. My eyes closed as I let out a bemoaned grumble, *I hate when this happens* . . . I had to use the bathroom.

Different Dancers, Different Shows

Samia held the tail ends of my dangling scarf back as I washed my hands in the bathroom sink. I forced a slight smile toward her; goodness this felt awkward. I always wondered how someone as introverted and shy as myself wound up researching a dance ethnography in the bustling nightlife of Cairo. I especially wondered this whenever I had the misfortune of needing to use the restroom at one of my field sites. While a brief escape to a public bathroom may seem to offer a few precious moments of solitude, this was not the case in Cairo. I shut the sink water off as Samia, the bathroom attendant, offered me a clumped handful of tissues to dry my hands. I tried to force a slightly bigger smile toward her as I clumsily attempted drying my hands with the tissues. Rather than absorb water, they just seemed to break off into a ton of sticky smithereens, creating a bigger mess than what I'd started with.

Samia was a congenial-looking woman in her fifties, dressed in a plain name-tagged uniform, black *hijab*, and without makeup. She was the *Nile Maxim*'s long-standing bathroom attendant, having worked there for the past seven years. Bathroom attendants were common in my field sites. In middle- and upper-class venues, they added a familiar touch of elegance and service to the environment. In other cases, they were just making the most out of another possible job opportunity. As a foreigner, it astounded me how there was a job for every simple task in Cairo that at least required tipping, *baqsheesh*; from the woman that points to the open toilet stalls and offers tissues, to the men that help you pull your car in and out of well-open parking spots. Regardless, I always felt awkward having someone standing around while I was just trying to use the bathroom. I especially felt awkward when they engaged in these small acts of service. Acts such as pointing to the open stalls and wiping down the toilet seat before I went in, handing out little scraps of toilet paper to use, and in this particular case, unnecessarily holding back my scarf from the sink water as I washed my hands.

I was reminded of dance scholar Cindy Garcia's work and how the bathroom attendant in L.A. salsa nightclubs signified an unwelcome reminder to many Latina dancers of the working-class body they were trying to disguise.[11] However, aboard Cairo's *Nile Maxim*, I was struck by how Samia, along with the dancer, were the only visible female employees on the boat, compared to the dozen or so men currently spread out throughout the ballroom. The ways they negotiated their gendered bodies as workers intrigued me. One was covered modestly and plainly, the other exposed and adorned elaboratively. One was tucked away into a gender-segregated space while the other would be center-staged, both highlighting the varied ways female bodies intelligently adapt to their particular male-dominated contexts to best capitalize upon them. However, in many ways, Samia embodied the culturally idealized working woman, from kissing and then holding up her tips in thanks to God, to her primarily women-only interactions; she clothed her working-class body with idealized piety and modesty. Thus, though her laboring body remained slipped away at the margins of the boat site, her location worked to center her working body within morally acceptable terms. I wondered what her thoughts on the other working women of the boat might be, those that strutted on the spotlighted stage, adorned in elaborate makeup and gem-encrusted *badlat raqs* (dance costumes). What unique insight might her particular positioning within this field site offer to *raqs sharqi* discourse?

I introduced myself to Samia and asked more about her life; she was enthusiastic about sharing. She didn't enjoy her work per se but was helping to support her family. As she talked, she showed me pictures of her children on her cellphone while she beamed with the smile of a proud mother. She said that to work well in Cairo you have to have a good education and have the right connections. She stated that she had neither, so she felt lucky to have this job on the *Nile Maxim*. She asked me why I came here so regularly alone, and I explained my research on dancing. She lit up with a mixture of amusement and enthusiasm. She thought it was interesting (okay, quite peculiar) to be able to get a Ph.D. in not only dance but in *raqs sharqi* specifically; she gushed about how much she loved dancing. She started dancing in the restroom, gracefully swiveling her hips in a figure-eight pattern as her hands lightly floated in the air with elegant soft waves. She said she loved to dance but only at weddings and family parties, her contextual amendment articulating the socially sanctioned contexts for dancing without stigma, as well as reifying her own modest identity. "You must learn a lot about dancers from the Golden Era, the past, like Tahiya Carioca, Samia Gamal, Naima Akef . . . I love them all, they danced so light, *raqs sharqi* was more elegant back then, everything was more elegant back then."[12]

The term "Golden Era" is often used to refer to the period of Egyptian cinema beginning in the early-mid through the middle of the twentieth century. During this period, many actresses/dancers became popular, not only in Egypt and the Middle East but around the world. Many of these dancers are still recognized as the greatest stars and are still a source for inspiration for belly dance enthusiasts today. During this time Egypt was the central hub of films throughout the MENA world. This new medium not only further disseminated dance locally and globally but became an alternative to the "live" cabaret performance scene, so as time passed star performers could work within the more socially "respectable" medium of films as dancers and actresses. Contemporaneously, the Golden Era is often looked back upon nostalgically.[13]

I asked Samia if she often watched the main dancers on the *Nile Maxim* boat and what she thought of their dancing. She held my shoulder, lowered her gaze, and winked at me knowingly.

First Show: Safiya

International Egyptian *raqs sharqi fannana* (artist) Safiya spun onto the stage with infectious energy in a classic two-piece bra and skirt style Egyptian costume with a pink silk veil flowing behind her.[14] Her long and thick dark brown hair cascaded down her back as she circled the stage for her *mejance* (entrance song). She smiled sweetly at the surrounding tables full of clientele from Egypt, the Gulf, and around the world as she sashayed across the stage. After circling the stage twice, she tossed the veil behind her as the rhythm changed, and she went into a series of hip drops accented with light shimmies on the downbeat. She threw her head back and seemed to laugh with joy as the percussion picked up. Safiya was one of those dancers who had excellent musicality and movements, but it was her charisma that made you fall for her. Whenever she looked in my general direction, I couldn't help but smile back at her as her sweet smile and bright eyes made me feel like we were seasoned friends sharing a secret.

She remained on the stage throughout the first part of her show and embodied the melody with flowing gentle arm work and wrist flourishes while her intricate hip work captured the percussion. Her movements were diverse and juicy. She had a wonderful mix of both percussive and serpentine accents and technique. She often tossed her long locks forward and back or from side to side, accenting her movements and the heavy *dum* drumbeats with that sweet feminine *dalla3* quality through her hair tosses or cheeky shoulder lifts. *Dalla3* is reminiscent of that sweet coquettish type of femininity that you often see, for example, in Egyptian romantic pop music videos where the male singer is chasing the affections of the shy girl next door, or more often, above on the balcony. It was that elusive quality of *hadur* (charisma) that drew me into Safiya's show. I could feel the energy exchange and circulation between her musicians, singer, and the audience as interpolated through her sincere love of the dance and music.

After her entrance, Safiya performed to a popular pop song and then grabbed an *3asaya*, or cane, from her assistant and performed a *sa3idi* song with the stick, referencing the *Sa3id* region of upper Egypt through softer folklore movements and gestures. After a costume change, she came back and did *sha3bi* Egyptian music and dancing as well as Iraqi and *khaleegy*. She did a lot of *khaleegy*-style dancing, even including a section in her *mejance* opening, despite there not being a dominance of Gulf clientele in this venue, unlike what one would likely find in elite hotels or cabarets. She was confident in her movements but still relaxed and playful, often looking back over one shoulder while lifting it slightly to give a coquettish smile to a client when they weren't expecting the connection because of her otherwise forward focus. It was Safiya's consistently playful and unexpected exchange of joyous teasing facial expressions and body angles that highlighted her charisma and strong audience connection.

Safiya was an amazing performer and extremely skilled. She used her entire stage space but never crossed the stage's border, even though it was just a small dance floor and not a raised stage. She only crossed it to enter and exit the main room for costume changes throughout her show. I was sitting perhaps twenty feet away from her, but I felt she was mouthing the lyrics and making jubilant and coquettish expressions just for me at several points throughout her show. Her contagious charisma was further amplified with her musicality; as the lyrics would start a new verse, she richly articulated the emotion of the song, whether joyous or full of longing, with her facial expression and movements. For example, when the singer's voice trembled and extended the ends of a verse, Safiya's brow would squinch as she burst into voluminous loose hip shimmies, her hands pressing out and downwards to her sides as if pressing into the surge of intense emotion.

Safiya's energy was contagious. Her lead drummer would often feed off her dance and start adding in wilder head tosses and percussive tilts of his own head as he dutifully followed the directives of Safiya's hips for accents and riffs. Likewise, her male singer often matched her emotive movements, both swaying with elongated and soulful lyrics followed by both bobbing their heads enthusiastically with the beats. The audience, too, was part of the energy circulation, particularly among its enculturated MENA members, many of whom were singing along with the lyrics and waving their hands in the air to help feel the music and keep the energy cyclical. A table of Egyptian men frequently shouted out encouragement to the dancer, praising her for her playful yet powerful interpretation of the popular songs.

Back in the bathroom, Samia was artfully giving me a French braid after that night's entertainment show, as she said my hair looked bad that night. At this point, we both looked forward to our regular meetings in the bathroom. I always tipped her generously—I can't omit the economic aspect of our relationship—but we'd also formed a serendipitous bond despite my then shaky conversational Arabic. She finished my hair and took a few cellphone photos to show her friends. Samia was well versed on the boat's regular performers and had strong thoughts on each that she was more than happy to spill to a curious researcher. Through an astute mix of miming and conversation, Samia would give me her assessment of each dancer after their show that night. She straightened her tan uniform shirt and checked to make sure the outer bathroom door was closed before she began. "I love Safiya. Safiya is so sexy and such a woman. Safiya is a real woman." She repeated these words as she imitated Safiya's dancing. Samia boldly stepped forward, claiming the small interior restroom floor as I automatically stepped back to give her more room, as she demonstrated soft, internalized, and sinuating full-body undulations, hip infinities, and tight smooth circles. Her arms were relaxed and curved as they softly framed her hips. "Safiya is a real woman, a full woman! Safiya is a soft dancer, and because of this, she is sexy. She can be alone on the stage, and you still feel her. She is incredibly sexy as a woman with her dance."[15]

Samia's choreographic and verbal analysis calls attention to important aspects of meaning-making in Safiya's *raqs sharqi* show. The first is how a woman moves her body and performs her personality. This combination embodies and performs a particular type of gender construct. Further, Samia's approval or lack thereof, of such gender performativity highlights how various types of gender constructions may either be centered or marginalized within larger Egyptian cultural norms. The second revolves around how Safiya's use of the stage space and interaction between her body and the others within the space also constructs effective *ihsas* as well as power relations and boundaries.

For example, I recall stepping back as Samia boldly commanded the small space of the bathroom to mimic Safiya's style of dancing. Similarly, Safiya commands the stage space without robust aggression or direct confrontation, a stage that just previously had been open-floor social dancing for diverse clientele from across the world. It is not a raised stage at all, but rather just a square of dance floor material that then proceeds into the carpeted floor the tables are on. Rather, in entering and circling the stage energetically with swaying hips and her veil flowing behind her, a *mejance* prop more common on the global belly dance stage than the local Cairo circuit, Safiya commanded the space through a strong sense of presence. This presence embodies dance scholar Melissa Blanco Borelli's corporeal theory of hip(g)nosis. Hip(g)nosis theory insinuates that a dancer that knows the multiple ways her body, particularly swiveling hips, are read as racially and sexually marked by multiple hegemonic audiences can manipulate these power dynamics through carving out her own agency, identity, and power.[16] Safiya accomplished this while remaining anchored in exaggerated, enchanting, and a local and global desirability through her performativity of confident and self-assured "*dalla3*."

After the night's cruise had finished and the boat returned to port, I was fortunate to be able to sit down with Safiya inside the now empty banquet room to interview her about her dance life and perspectives. The same sweet enthusiastic smile and animated story sharing peppered our conversation as much as it spiced up Safiya's show. She started by explaining how she got started in her dancing career. She began with ballet classes when she was little and then performed with the national folklore troupe, *firqa komiyya*, before venturing out as a solo *raqs sharqi* dancer under the tutelage of legendary Mona Said (renowned for her emotive performances in earlier decades). She noted that while each of these dance teachers and forms imprinted on her style, she created her own unique *raqs sharqi* style through her personality and life experiences. I couldn't help beaming beside her as she shared; she was so genuinely in love with dancing, and her performance energy still seemed to be radiating off her. Her insights nuance the following choreographic analyses.[17]

While much contemporary *raqs sharqi* within Cairo has become highly focused on the percussion, rhythm, and punctuated accents, Safiya keeps a balance of percussive accents, shimmies, and melodic circles, undulations, and sways without over-privileging the drums. The percussion-heavy and rhythmic focused dancing of contemporary Cairo is often posited in comparison to the "softer" and more melodic styling of the Golden Age dancers of the past, who Samia nostalgically yearned for as exemplifying *raqs sharqi*. This change in dance style is largely due to changes in the musical styles, which are tethered to larger economic, fashion, and globalization trends occurring since President Sadat's era. To begin with, the percussion section, not including lead drummers, are often the cheaper musicians to hire, so you can fill up your band more and add more energy without spending as much. Further, percussion-heavy music in general is fashionable, but particularly *sha3bi* music, which originated in the working classes and has continued to permeate the dancing scene with fervor since Sadat's era as it speaks to and resonates with the population's social issues and lives.

Sha3bi refers to a popular working-class musical genre that incorporates instrumentation of Upper Egypt alongside new instrumentation such as the accordion that is associated with working-class sentiments and vernacular.[18] Ahmed Adaweya was the first to become a famous star singer from this genre from Mohamed Ali Street. His upbeat and fast music extolled the conditions of working-class lovers, life, and witty criticism of the establishment.[19] Adaweya's duets with many star dancers led to the popular incorporation of *sha3bi* aesthetics, music, and styling into *raqs sharqi* shows across venues. *Raqs sharqi* necessitates embodying the music. Thus, the pace, gesturing, technique, and attitude of performers embodied aesthetics and movements from working-class vernacular. *Sha3bi* technique and stylization is often heavier, more grounded, and derived from a low center as compared to classical *raqs sharqi* which can, at times, have a higher center or more lifted aesthetic. *Sha3bi* incorporates gestures found in working-class vernacular and social dance, while often being performed in a *baladi* dress or *galabeya*.[20] At the same time, the *sha3bi* style embodied in gesture, dress, and persona the ever-growing reality of middle- and working-class Egyptian women who must take on more socially constructed "male" attributes such as working outside the home, and featured lyrics that resonated across such audiences.

Turning away from Nasser's socialist economic ties with the USSR, Sadat opened up to the United States and capitalism with economic policies and political alliances that encouraged investments locally and globally into the private sector. Unfortunately, his was a failed economic liberalization. Welcoming neoliberalist capitalism only served to drastically increase the ranks of those already rich, particularly allies within the regime, while further marginalizing the middle class and poor. This marginalization remains relevant as the gap between the rich and poor has only continued to widen post-revolution.[21]

Safiya touches on this important economic resonance, still increasingly reverberating in Cairo since the *infitah* "open door" policies. While *sha3bi* and percussion-heavy music takes over stages, for certain bodies, not so much. "A big problem we have in Egypt now is that you find the stage empty from great Egyptian performers like myself and Randa. The drop in the economy affected the whole world, but not evenly, so the top Egyptians prefer to teach outside to foreigners, to teach them the right way in this art and earn better money. Our work here depends on tourism so much, but any foreigner can come and quickly take the spotlight here because our circumstances and resources are not the same."[22] My heart sank as I remembered being waved through the metal detector, also entangled in this same perplex web of uneven economic, nationalist, and gendered dynamics.

The politics of my own foreign resources allowed me to stroll quickly and easily into one country whereas certain Egyptian bodies find it necessary, and difficult, to sashay in labor outside of *watinuhum*—their homeland. After all, my own ethnographic positioning wasn't all that different from the professional foreign dancers that Safiya was referring to. These foreign professionals are often critiqued for undercutting gigs because the "dream" of working in Cairo is more of a priority for them as opposed to financial stability and restraints.

I noticed my ears were still slightly ringing from the boisterous percussion. Perhaps Safiya's choreography offers insight into more than just aesthetic musicality in not over privileging the drums. She is likewise cautioning how a political over-privileging of the neoliberal global capitalist "dream" sets the stage for a drastically globally uneven entering and exiting of corporealities across national, gender, and class lines.

On top of Safiya's adept musicality, she is also enabled with this rich balance of movement and style in her dancing due to her particular identity, positionality, and background. Having a background in theatrical folklore dancing adds both a heightened sense of hyper-femininity to her dance as well as expanded staging elements more familiar to cosmopolitan audiences such as larger use of stage space and floor patterns. Theatrical folklore from Egyptian Reda and *Komiyya* troupes both implement notions of hyper hetero-gender identification and space to exemplify idealized state-sanctioned Egyptian gender identities and create stage personae.[23] Safiya's training also included working with star dancer Mona Said, well known for her feeling in the dance, as well as looking for inspiration from Golden Age dancers who performed with more melodic music. This training aligns with her *dalla3* personality, which appears with her subtle use of shoulder gesturing, sweet and innocent facial expressions, smiles, and the use of her long hair. This "mix" resonates across various local and global cultural audiences. While the *raqs sharqi* body is denigrated for publicly performing a powerful, sexually embracing identity outside of acceptable familial contexts for money, the performance and embodiment of this type of *dalla3* is both idealized and romanticized within larger Egyptian culture, particularly the middle and upper classes.

From her cocktail of a silk veil entrance to the large dose of *khaleegy* dancing as well as *sha3bi* and classics, Safiya caters to a wide range of audience preferences, locally, across the MENA, and globally. The combination of these bodily and aesthetic constructs work to make Safiya appealing to a wide range of audiences and particularly elite and cosmopolitan sites of performance such as the *Nile Maxim* and international belly dance festival circuits. Being aware of these mixed patterns, and able to articulate her hips accordingly in them, allows her to successfully perform hip(g)nosis for a wide array of spectators. Like the Nile cruising boat venues themselves, her simultaneous catering across multiple audiences keeps her dancing career afloat, locally and abroad, despite continuous rough economic and sociopolitical waters.

Safiya's story also provides further context for how she actively negotiates with the performance space to create layered power dynamics, boundaries, and meaningful interaction, especially concerning the border separating her stage from the audience. The site of the tour boat, particularly a five-star boat such as the *Nile Maxim*, has the aim of providing cultural and family-friendly entertainment to a local and cosmopolitan audience of the middle classes and up. Likewise, *raqs sharqi* in elite venues such as boats and hotels since the time of President Nasser and onward has been straddled with regulations and rules that both keep the dance economically productive to the state but also maintain a sense of state control, morality, and nationalism through policing and other regulations.[24] The dancer must negotiate all these physical, legal, and corporeal boundaries and regulations.

For example, in the multiple attempts to eradicate the practice of *fath*, or sitting and drinking with customers by female dancers (a practice considered a moral vice and pervasive in *raqs sharqi* entertainment halls since their inception), additional regulations were that dancers couldn't cross the boundary of the stage, drink, dance, or talk with patrons.[25] In 1973 the *musannafat*, a government organization established toward the end of Nasser's era and in charge of licensing and regulations for *raqs sharqi* professionals, successfully prohibited the practice of *fath* under President Sadat. The crackdown was more intense than previous attempts to eradicate the practice, and enhanced policing and regulation of dancers continued to increase from the Presidencies of Nasser and Sadat up until the current day.

For example, the dancer was not supposed to go off from the stage during her performance or interact with customers at their tables, before or after her show, as the she could be charged with delinquencies such as "soliciting prostitution." Today, dancers continue to be policed and regulated for their movements, costuming, suspect sexuality, and use of space/audience interaction in performances. Of course, the extent to which these stipulations were enforced varied widely across sites, bodies, and time.

On contemporary boats, these regulations are often not enforced, but their histories still carry weight in setting boundaries between the body of the dancer and those of the audience. Further, the fact that boats are smaller-scale and more intimate environments, along with the fact that they do not have raised stages, and these stages are often social-spaces for clientele to dance before and after the dancer's show, make the boundary of this border permeable and fluid. It is from knowing the historical politics embedded in dance sites, as well as their corresponding cultural and state meanings and policing, that Safiya, as an Egyptian performer, is able to efficiently play with this boundary and her gender embodiment with such force. She knows class politics and state policing are held somewhat at bay when performing within the stage's border. This border afford her protection to fully commit to the vulnerability of her feelings, physicalized through movements of her often primarily gendered and sexually read and policed body.

But, at the same time, she also reifies her desired class identity, respectable *fannana* status, and sense of power as an Egyptian female performer by choosing to maintain that boundary. This reification is demonstrated through not crossing her stage's border as well as through the romanticized and ideal *dalla3* gender identity she performs. As she states, "I have only ever danced in classy five-star hotels and other elegant places, like the *Maxim*, where I've been a house dancer for a long time. Here in Egypt, people can think very poorly about dancers, but not me. People cannot judge me harshly after they see my show, maybe if they see a bad dancer in a local cabaret without training, they can think this, sure, but with me? No" (2017). Instead, she lets her feelings as expressed through *hadur*, *ihsas*, and *harakat* (movements) cross over and circulate amongst the clientele.

Notably, these spatial regulations and policing of *raqs sharqi* performances were constructed as necessary, in part, to control and contain the unruly marginalized body of the dancer and the *fitna* (social disorder related to sexual power) she may elicit.[26] At the same time, these physical and legal boundaries have contradictorily enabled the dancer to gain power in expressing and embodying a deeper range of her feelings and artistry. This power is in direct relationship with fully embracing the spectrum of gender performativity available to her marginalized body. Or, in Safiya's words, "the stage pushes me to have more character and interaction, more of myself, but still natural. The stage and experience are growing the dancer." Of the dual restriction and yet freedom offered by the regulated site of the stage, Safiya says, "It makes me brave all the time, and I do what I want. My depth of experience with the stage allows me to get better at dealing with all kinds of different people, situations, and moods. I become more honest with myself and trust myself. I come onto the stage and say *ana hina*—I'm here."[27]

Second Show: Randa

Surprisingly, I could hear Randa, also an internationally famous Egyptian dancer, before I could see her. The long duration of a *mejance*'s introduction is supposed to build up drama, energy, and add esteem to the performer before she enters the stage. Typically, the heightened music booms from the live band, usually as soon as they set up and take their seats on stage, and this is when guests start twisting in their chairs and turning their necks in anticipation of the dancer's arrival. However, in this case, Randa herself was backstage with a microphone singing the opening lyrics for her own *mejance*—which usually contains praises of the dancer—catching me off guard. I nodded

Figure 1.3 Randa's Nile Maxim performance with her band. Credit: Tracey Gibbs www.traceygibbs.co.uk

my head in approval; she must have a lot of self-confidence to pull that off. Further, I recognized her decent singing voice.

Soon, Randa charged onto the stage with a burst of energy. Her intense outward-focused energy immediately hit me as she pivoted in a circle throughout the stage area with strong linear "windmill" arms framing her movements. Visually, she wore the standard two-piece bra and tight-fitting skirt costume, but her muscular and toned athletic body, particularly her abdominal muscles, caught my attention. Her entrance number was full of outward-directed movements, drama, and power, as she spun and pivoted around the stage with crisp and strong stops and punctuated accents. She would catch the percussion with outward pops from her lower belly, accompanied by striking linear arm punctuations or percussively bumping her hip out to the side as she crisscrossed the stage with her arms raised straight up toward the sky.

Bold linear lines, seismic earthquake shimmies, and sharp punctuated accents marked Randa's dance style. Her expressions changed with the mood of the music, but rather than emanating a circular exchange of energy and charisma like Safiya, Randa's energy was more directed outward, and she seemed to take most of her power from the music and from within herself rather than feeding off the audience's energy. Her percussive hip accents, strong turns, and tightly internal and muscular small hip circles all pointed to her extensive training and dedication to the form, and her explosive delivery of this technique and powerful and linear arm framing highlighted her signature stylistic interpretation of *raqs sharqi*.

Randa stays on stage intentionally. She wants to deliver a strong solo show as *fannana* (artist). She performs a classic song next, which is only slightly softer in interpretation due to a greater focus on dynamic facial expressions, singing along, and gesturing to interpret the lyrics and feeling of the song as opposed to powerhouse technique. Like Safiya, Randa doesn't cross the boundary separating the stage from the guests' seating area of the ballroom. However, in contrast to Safiya, Randa reaches her audience more directly through her dynamo technique. Her feeling and personality are also strong, but not as predominantly as her physical technique.

I became startled at one point during her show. As Randa was dancing across the stage, taking up the full range of space with rapid three-quarter turns, a male musician, in his rightful place on the stage's back perimeter beside the percussionists, was in the line of her path. I held my breath as Randa came hurling toward him. The drummer's eyes widened as he quickly clambered out of her way, momentarily losing his place within the music. Randa showed no sign of the possible collision's effect. Whirling on, headstrong as a hurricane—it was clearly other people's responsibility to avoid her path of destruction. This cycloning calls attention to power hierarchies on stage wherein the dancer holds power over her all-male band, including the singer.

Randa later did a bit of a singing and dancing duet during her *baladi* song, where she interacted with her young singer Hisham, as each sang the corresponding male and female lyrical exchanges. Hisham seemed completely comfortable with the duet, smiling at Randa and making eye contact while singing, even stepping back and forth lightly while bobbing his head to the music. The male singer with female dancer duet was a common part of many dance shows in Cairo, the exception here being the wildly contrasting age difference. Hisham seemed very much in the prime of his youth, while Randa was a well-seasoned and mature dancer. Typically, this age contrast is swapped, with the male singer likely to be or appear older than the dancers, who often appear in their twenties and thirties. Here, the gendered age difference granted Randa another heightened sense of authority.

Returning to the restroom, Samia stiffened up and took on a grave expression of disapproval. "Randa—no. Randa no, no, no." She wagged her finger and shook her head repeatedly. "Randa is too much strong, too much, too much! Always strong, all the time! She has no *dalla3*. She makes dance like a man makes karate! This is not a dancer! She has the stage, but she refuses to make dance, just karate!" This time, I deliberately stepped back as Samia extended her palm assertively out, facing me with direct physical aggression. She demonstrated karate-esque movements such as multiple chops and forward power kicks as she held her hands close to her face in fists. She laughed at herself and then leaned in toward me, "maybe I can make like a man, but . . . ." She opened her palms to the small sparkling clean restroom we were sharing space in. "Randa does not need," she concluded as she gestured toward the stage and live music reverberating from outside the restroom confines.[28]

Again, Samia highlights key areas of significance within Randa's *raqs sharqi* show. First, she points out how Randa's construction of a powerful, direct, and strong woman can be threatening or marginalized within larger Egyptian cultural norms, particularly due to the contexts she embodies this form of womanhood within. By noting that Randa "has the stage," Samia argues that gender constructions and embodiments can either enable or

Figure 1.4 Randa performs aboard the Nile Maxim boat. Credit: Tracey Gibbs www.traceygibbs.co.uk

hinder depending on their specific contexts. Further, the comparison of Samia's workspace and conditions to Randa's highlights class and labor dynamics as they intersect with site-specific gender performativity and effectiveness. Finally, her demonstrations of karate as "making like a man" and refusal to acknowledge Randa as a *raqs sharqi* dancer point to how deeply gender is embedded not only within a binary system, but also a kinesthetic corpus, within Egyptian culture.

I also had the chance to sit down and interview with Randa later in my fieldwork. The interview occurred in the hotel lobby where Randa and internationally acclaimed male dancer Tito were teaching at Randa's international belly dance festival, "*Raqs*, Of Course," to about fifty foreign women from across the globe. Randa, Tito, and I held the interview all together on lounge couches outside the ballroom, where Tito had just finished teaching a workshop.[29] After telling me about how she got started in *raqs sharqi*, Randa made sure that I recognized the power the dancer holds in Cairo. She talked about how she controls her all-male band, how she creates the overall program of song sequences for their shows together, and how her musicians must follow every directive emanating from her word or her waist. She also let me know that while she had briefly worked with male managers in the past (a norm in Cairo since Nasser's era and particularly prolific post-revolution), she now does everything on her own. The *Nile Maxim* just gives her the dates to show up (she rarely works on the boat these days with her busy international teaching schedule), and she handles everything else her way.

She earnestly explained to me how difficult life is for Egyptian dancers working in Cairo, that the suffering they experience is a real consequence of following their love for the dance. She told me about her childhood growing up in the conservative area of Mansoura, how from her earliest beginnings, she knew suffering, but love even more so. She remembered how she would run away to dance at all the extended family's weddings and any neighbors' parties; with any chance to dance (socially) she would run. However, her family would beat her when they found out. Yet she still could not quell her love for dance, and to this day, she told me how awfully society would speak about a dancer behind her back as if she is a prostitute. Finally, she gazed over at her youthful son playing down the hallway. She sighed heavily. She said the worst suffering was yet to come, and that it would be when her son wanted to marry while having a mom as a ra2asa (dancer). She said that despite the suffering, nothing makes her a human, and especially nothing makes her a woman, as much as dancing. She said because of all the societal suffering she wants to have family in this art and to be close with all the festival dancers around the world. I nodded empathetically. I remembered being too shy to remind her of our interview upon my initial arrival at the festival because Randa looked so "at home" chatting and sharing advice with other festival students.

Combining the choreographic analysis of Randa's show, her perspectives on dance and Samia's comparative critiques lends a layered and rich exploration to Randa's danced discourse. Randa is interesting for two reasons. First, she honestly admits to starting her career in the stigmatized Cairo cabarets and then moving up to the international teaching festival circuit.

> I started in cabarets and then progressed to big hotels, but only for a little while, the Sheraton shut down because of money in the early 2000s recession, so I had to move to the Maxim but mostly outside festivals. On the Maxim and in hotels they're looking for a 'show-show,' but in cabaret, you just start a short sentence, then you're just looking for the money. It is quite different, nobody cares about my art in cabarets, because it's not a place for art but rather just cheap drunk men. I hated working there and wouldn't do this teasing way catered to men as they expect from dancers, so I moved up quickly because I had the talent and feeling for art.[30]

Second, Randa is known to dancers for the fact that she is a successful Egyptian dancer who is known to be more loved outside of Egypt than within. From my research and interviews I am confident in asserting that a significant number of dancers start working in cabarets (of all calibers) and then move up in terms of social mobility. However, most will do their best to completely bury their cabaret work history as soon as they've moved up.[31] In other words, many move from cabarets to more elite five-star hotels and nightclubs. In contemporary Cairo during the time of my fieldwork, many dancers were working across venues, often working in cabarets, boats, weddings of all levels, and hotels. Consequently, the *raqs sharqi* venue system embodies the strict social class hierarchy of Egyptian society. However, in the past, specialization in one type of venue was the norm.

In Cairene society, it is incredibly difficult for social mobility to occur; you are known for the combined socioeconomic status of not only your beginnings but also those of your family. For example, even if one were to gain immense wealth, the social class is harder to transition because you are where you came from. Within the contemporary *raqs sharqi* gig circuit, most cabarets are considered the bottom of the barrel in terms of social and class status for dancers and the clientele that frequent them. Boats are often regarded as mid-level but family-friendly, and five-star hotels are the cream of the crop. Of course, hierarchies existed within each of these strata; for example, the *Nile Maxim* is considered a five-star boat.

Due to the way sociocultural class functions in Cairene society, many dancers that start in cabarets and then move up the social ladder will diligently mask their beginnings. For example, dancers may state that they only ever danced in elite venues and would never be caught dead in a cabaret. (This is also true for workers of all genders in general that begin their careers in cabarets and then move up to more socially palatable venues, including entertainers such as singers but also regular servers, managers, and wait staff.[32] However, the stigma is certainly heavier for female entertainers.) A famous director of one of the prestigious belly dance festivals in Cairo frequently talks down cabaret dancers. She tells the local and foreign dancers she trains never to step foot in a cabaret because it will sabotage their careers. Yet, at the same time, she often finds new local dance teachers for her festival from various cabarets across Cairo to market as "authentic rising stars" to foreign dance clients. Admittingly, she has stated to me that they are nothing but "cabaret cats" that, like the Cairo street cats, cannot stand to be in any clean, elegant place. She knows that they will eventually leave her and return to the "garbage" (cabaret work circuit) from which they came.[33] Thus, the fact that Randa openly admits to starting work in cabarets with honesty about her discomfort with the realities of the work is refreshing but unusual. It is also more understandable, considering the bulk of her work and status now comes from outside Egypt, where this narrative of the "rags to riches" parallels illusory constructed notions of the "American dream," often met with open arms. This narrative is not the case within Cairo, where Randa's cabaret beginnings would likely be met with harsh opposition and a blockade to social mobility.

Randa's mobility as a dance teacher and performer has also led her to *raqs sharqi* circuits outside of Egyptian and intra-MENA flows. She has found her home on the globalized belly dance festival circuits, which while centered in Cairo, have international flows throughout Asia, Europe, and North and South America. Her intense, strong, and outward energy are not as marketable or successful within the Cairo circuits; for example, Randa was never very popular as a wedding dancer and mostly performs on the *Maxim* when foreign dancers request her. Still, she has strategically been able to enter the global belly dance circuit in ways that allow her dancing to do a particular kind of work.

As Randa enthusiastically elaborates, "outside (Egypt), I feel it is completely art! Foreigners want to catch every moment of my technique, my feeling, everything! They look at me every second and cheer, they care, and they want to catch every bit of technique."[34] On the global festival stage, her large windmill arms and strong outward energy and focus on intensive techniques are celebrated and more familiar to foreign audiences. This acceptance is because of the often larger proscenium style stage formats, but also due to the ways belly dance in Western contexts has changed to embody the strong outward feminine archetypes of Western feminism. These archetypes kinesthetically resonate with powerful punctuated accents and grand, full-body movements.

From the opening notes of her own voiced *mejance*, Randa makes a statement about being a dancer and an Egyptian woman. Before any audience eyes can judge her dancing, looks, or interaction, audiences instead hear Randa singing her own praises, making it clear from off-stage that she is already certain of herself and what her work is about. As she clarifies, "In this dance you show yourself, you show who you really are. It makes you feel you are female, that you don't need men to tell you 'oh, you are beautiful' or anything, no! Because you *know*. You know yourself, and you trust yourself."

This meaning not only circulates because of Randa choosing to sing her own praises. It is also created because the character of a dancer that is also a talented singer refers back to the pre and early *raqs sharqi* age of the *awalim*. The *awalim* were groups of esteemed female entertainers colloquially considered a 'grandparent" of contemporary *raqs sharqi*. In these communities, a dancer was considered *shamla* (complete or whole) because she was multi-talented in dance, singing, and reciting poetry.[35] The *awalim* were also a female-dominated community that was strong before the male-dominated impresario business system took over, which is also referenced in Randa's choice not to have a male manager.

As Samia notes, Randa's bold gender performativity and embodiment on stage are almost too boundary-pushing for many Cairo contexts of *raqs sharqi*. Randa herself uses Samia's same phrase of "making like a man" to define her work and gender relationships.

> If you dance in Cairo, you will become clever and strong because you work amongst men that want to *eat* you in our mentality! Every man wants some

part of you—money, body, power, love! Dance teaches you how to deal with each one on his own level, to take what you want and make them respect you. As a dancer, you make yourself like a man, talk, and act like them. Be strong!

However, Randa has quite successfully channeled these gender semiotics into more Western and internationally palatable frameworks and contexts that have helped her dominate the global belly dance festival circuit in ways that deeply resonate with her own sense of Self. Importantly, she is not catering to the Western market as some dancers criticize her for doing. Rather, Randa has tactfully and engaged with it and made a home out of this particular circuit while remaining true to her own core values and objectives within dance as an Egyptian woman.

At the same time, it is important to call attention to the overlapping ways in which Randa has and continues to perform within normative Cairo circuits of class, gender, and nationalism. She also talked to me about the financially well-off husband she had to help her start her career when she was still working on stepping up from cabarets to five-star venues. Thus, she and her husband's pooled economic backgrounds and resources worked to both start Randa in the cabaret circuit as well as aid in her social mobility from such stages.

While *raqs sharqi* as a profession is highly marginalized within Egyptian society, normative heterosexual marriage relationships are often enabling ways for dancers to gain safety, respectability, and social mobility in their dance careers and everyday lives. Though Randa's performative focus on powerful outward-directed technique, energy, and physical strength alone on the stage cultivate a strong sense of womanhood that resists the binary *dalla3* or femme fatale expectation, her off-stage life narrative highlights normative constructions of gender and sexuality.

She proclaims, "Believe me, my work is on the stage only, I never go off stage and make teasing guest interactions! I make art to prove to everyone I am an artist, not something else, many hide another profession behind dancing. I do my show then I go home! I'm a married woman, a mother, a respectful person. I want to show that this dance is work, talent, and art. I did change the social stigma around this for myself, that not all dancers are prostitutes. I'm a normal person with a family and husband. But, in these times especially, one woman is not enough; we all have to be together." She shakes her head and looks down before continuing, "Two is not enough! We, all dancers, have to be together to prove something, change something! I did, but one woman is not enough, not now."

In defending her respectability and self-identity, Randa identifies multiple times as a wife and mother. Thus, while Randa pushes on the boundaries of normative gender embodiment and performativity through her performance and dance career on stage, she simultaneously reifies the respected gendered and hetero-norms of identifying as a wife and mother off-stage. On stage, Randa's intensely robust hip locks, bumps, and shimmies present a strong woman who can stand alone not only on stage but also in life, not needing to depend on a man to define her sense of beauty or worth. Men, like her musicians, remain as background, there to follow the lead of her waist.

At the same time, Randa chooses to keep her dancing within the state-sanctioned border of the stage in ways that also call attention to how her gender resistance simultaneously reifies state and class signifiers and constraints. For example, since the Sadat era, *musannafat* regulations have deemed it inappropriate for female dancers to leave the stage and intermingle with the audience as a way of eradicating *fath*.[36] By not crossing her stage border, Randa gains power not just by denying physical "teasing" interaction with men but also by perpetuating a fictitiously constructed gendered dichotomy of moralized labor between the regulated and proper "artist" versus the illicit and unruly prostitute.

Balanced Landscapes or Strong Solos? Farah Nasri and her *Funun al Sha3biyya*

I was particularly curious about what Samia thought about French-Algerian dancer Farah Nasri. Farah, though she identifies as mixed race and multicultural, is still "not Egyptian," and therefore considered an *agnabiyya* by the Egyptian boat staff and the general public. The *Nile Maxim* staff also prefer to market, promote, and identify Farah as French rather than French-Algerian. Farah had been contracted with the *Nile Maxim* for the past three years when I met her and was the main dancer working the boat cruises every day throughout my early fieldwork. Previously, she was a sought-after professional working in London, but after coming to Randa's international festival, she decided to test the waters of working in Cairo.

The two most obvious aspects of Farah's *Nile Maxim* shows that set her apart from the other featured dancers are that she has decided to create her show with *funun al sha3biyya*, backup male theatrical folk dancers, whom she endearingly calls her "*shabab*" (younger men). *Funun al sha3biyya* refers to popular performing artists, and specifically in this case study to the predominantly male theatrical folklore dancers from, or following in, the lineage of the Reda Troupe created by Mahmoud Reda and Farida Fahmy in the 1950s in Egypt, as well as the *firqa komiyya* (national troupe). As I refer to them in this chapter, I refer specifically to the backup male theatrical folk dancers that work with *raqs sharqi* dancers either to create spectacle for *mejance* entrances and/or to create a fuller show with theatrical folklore inspired *tableaus*.[37] Secondly, Farah spends much of the latter part of her show off-stage interacting with guests around their tables. (These two aspects also allow her show to fittingly meld into the "second set" writing structure of this chapter.)

Tonight, Samia immediately flung the main bathroom door shut then bounced over to deliver the next dance analysis. Samia had the strongest feelings about Farah's dancing. "Farah, no. I do not like Farah at all! Never! Farah is not a dancer; Farah is only for men! Farah goes around and around in circles running for men, and this is not dance!" She demonstrated sharp, punctuated, and hard-hitting percussive hip and chest accents to go along with her disapproval of Farah's use of the total performance space. She shook her head then paused in introspection while finalizing, "Yes! Farah cannot even be alone on the stage, she even has to bring the men on stage with her to make her show!"[38]

Samia strongly felt that the two aspects of Farah's show that set her apart from the other *Nile Maxim* dancers—her use of backup male folklore dancers and her heavy off-stage interaction—didn't mesh with the ideals and values she felt embodied *raqs sharqi*. Following Samia's lead, this section seeks to explore two questions. First, what significations does the packaging and framing of hyper-gendered and nationalized performing bodies have on this site when dancers incorporate *funun al sha3biyya*? Second, what meanings are created through Farah's decision to perform a large portion of her show off-stage interacting with the audience? To better understand these dynamics, it is valuable to trace the history of how *funun al sha3biyya* and *raqs sharqi* dancers began performing live shows together in Cairo. The *funun al sha3biyya* and *raqs sharqi* pairings seen contemporaneously are closely tied to innovations forwarded by Mahmoud Reda's *Reda* troupe, deeply in conversation with nationalist state politics of President Nasser's era, as well as 1970's *raqs sharqi* star innovator Nagwa Fouad.[39]

In 1952, The Free Officers, an Egyptian group of military soldiers, overthrew the Egyptian monarchy, which was still heavily tied to the British. Shortly thereafter, one of the officers, Gamal Abdel Nasser, became the president of fully independent Republic of Egypt. During Nasser's almost twenty-year rule, Egypt was characterized by strong Arab nationalism, secularism, state socialist ideology, and a tightening grip of the militarized state authoritarian system. The bourgeois class slowly diminished under state socialism, and foreign presence greatly and forcefully diminished. Meanwhile, women's self-image refashioned toward their deepened roles as mothers and daughters not only within the home but also of the nation, now constructed as a family.[40]

Women were constructed as mothers and daughters of Egypt, and they believed their efforts in raising citizens and participating as dutiful family members amidst the zeal of Arab nationalism was critical to Egypt's independence from the British and continuing independent success. Women's liberation expanded due to increased job and labor opportunities outside of the home under increased industrialization which led to greatly amplified public visibility and acceptance. Further, women were granted the right to vote and granted equal access to state resources of social welfare, education, and other health and government services. However, though women's responsibilities and duties were expanded, their private family relations scarcely changed. Women were still expected to carry out patriarchal subordinate roles within the family, gained few legal rights within personal status laws, and participated in building a new republic that was entrenched in the male dominated perspectives and ideology of a military autocracy. As scholar Sherine Hafez elaborates, "Once again, state governments chose fraternity over equality and women paid the price. Once again, women's bodies were claimed by domestic laws that precluded their full participation in the public sphere."[41] In other words, though women's bodies swelled in the public sphere with regard to their labor and education opportunities, they were more deeply tied to the patriarchal state under a military autocracy that wasn't concerned with women's rights and legal equality in the domestic sphere.

Likewise, Nasser's government realized the potential dance and cultural performance arts hold within political projects of nationalism, and traditional heritage arts flourished. Early in Nasser's presidency, Mahmoud Reda and Farida Fahmy, elite and educated Egyptians, pioneered the *firqa Reda*, or Reda Troupe. Their troupe was soon after state-sponsored. This theatricalized dance form was a blend of the popular Soviet-style state troupes of the time, with theatrical dancing and staging from ballroom and other international concert-dance forms, as well as featuring a core grounding in stylized regional folk and character dances from across Egypt.[42] Politics of representation performed by state folk dance ensembles, with the Reda Troupe as the emblematic Egyptian example, participated productively within Nasser's political project of nationalism. Politics of representation include performative power, the power to define who and what the nation is, and maybe even more importantly, who and what the nation is not. The Reda Troupe was founded on its reputation for being clean theatrical folk-inspired dance, performed on reputable state-sanctioned stages and by educated middle-class and up men and women from "good families."[43]

Funun al sha3biyya are a related off-shoot to the theatrically staged folk dancing Mahmoud Reda and Farida Fahmy pioneered in Cairo. The shared repertoire, step combinations, and aesthetics *funun al sha3biyya* use in their shows with dancers still largely stems from Reda Troupe work. However, the form also incorporates such aspects from other major theatrical folklore troupes that followed in the Reda Troupe's wake, including a second national troupe, *firqa komiyya*, that was spearheaded in the Soviet Moiseyev Dance Company character dance style. This innovative dance genre largely aligned with Nasserist era politics and thus came to represent Egypt, often displacing, or at least competing with, *raqs sharqi* soloists that had previously been seen similarly to "cultural ambassadors" of the dance at home and abroad.

This representational "exchange" presented a cleaner (less sexually stigmatized), and more middle- and upper-class masculine vision of Egypt that didn't have to contend with the gendered working-class and sex work connotations *raqs sharqi* wrestled with. The Reda Troupe presented Egypt as a family nation wherein heterosexuality and idealized state-sanctioned gender roles were the norm. Regarding male dancers, Reda legitimated the professional male dancing body on stage. Still, he did so through hyper-gendering the masculine body through trained athleticism and technique, which suited masculine nationalist, and heterosexual constructions.[44] For example, one aspect of achieving male performer's legitimacy was to erase any traces of men's playful social *baladi* hip-articulated dancing that may mimic *raqs sharqi* movements seen socially by both genders without stigma at urban weddings. These performances further solidified idealized heterosexual constructions of gender and sexuality for men and women as demonstrated between male-female staged pairings. Men performed hyper-masculine large and athletic movements, and erased the serpentine and shimmying *baladi* hip work from their repertoires, while women performed a "cleaned up" version of hip work and coquetry that erased the sexuality from their movements.[45]

However, it was star dancer Nagwa Fouad (an Egyptian-Palestinian artist performing in the 1960–90s), who spearheaded the popularity and fashion trend of incorporating *funun al sha3biyya* into otherwise live solo *raqs sharqi* stage shows. Nagwa was a show woman and desired to add more spectacle and prestige to her grand stage shows. She married and collaborated artistically with Mohammed Khalil for many years starting in the 1970s. Khalil had been the director of the *komiyya* troupe and worked in high positions with theatre and culture palaces under the Ministry of Culture.[46] Khalil and Nagwa both shared a desire for *raqs sharqi* to be elevated to the point where it was not only loved, but also respected, and performed within a dignified context.

Together, they thought this could be achieved through more elaborate stage show productions featuring costume changes, composed musical and choreographed stage numbers, the incorporation of narrative storylines, and robust folkloric *tableaus* with male and female backup dancers from the national troupes.[47] Khalil argued that *raqs sharqi* never reached its full potential, as it was still being reduced to "sexy movement" that is not taken easily because it is by a solo woman. Therefore, adding a framework through nationalist storylines that incorporate dancers of both genders would create a more dignified, balanced, and respected containment for the dance.[48] Notably, this framework stands in direct conflict with what Samia states makes *raqs sharqi* so powerful and unique: the ability of a moving, solo, and center-staged woman to express herself, create art, and share feelings.

Reaching further, working with, or without, *funun al sha3biyya* becomes more complex. In an interview, the dance ethnologist Sahra C. Kent, who also performed in a five-star Cairo hotel during the 1990s, elaborates:

> Well, excluding Nagwa, it became almost impossible to find women to work these backup dancing gigs for dancers, so it largely just became men doing it because the women's families were concerned with their being out at night. If they were going to do all that, they would just be belly dancers to make a lot more money, but anyway, you can find hundreds of trained Reda and *Komiyya* men. When I was here, it was incredibly fashionable to use the guys. I used them. Now evidently, when Nagwa had guys and girls, she had

paid chaperones and drivers for them, and it was Nagwa, so that's how it was all right for her to have men and "good girls" in her group.[49]

Kent further explained how huge Nagwa was at the time, and how competition between dancers has always been fierce in Cairo. She stated that while not every dancer could afford to hire a fifty-piece orchestra, they could for sure afford to hire a couple of backup men and suddenly make their show appear bigger. As she explains,

> If you've got an hour to yourself and don't use dance props as we do in the United States, the guys help to fill in space during costume changes and make *tableaus*. People like it, and it's not expensive, so it stuck. But if you don't have regular work, it's hard to keep them, because like musicians they'll just go wherever they're getting paid, so when a lot of the regular work dropped so did those job collaborations.

Finally, I thought hearing the opinions of a principal female dancer for the Reda Troupe, Farida Fahmy, on *funun al sha3biyya* with *raqs sharqi* dancers would be enlightening. Particularly as Farida was able to achieve a famous and respected role in Egyptian performing arts that deemed her the "daughter of Egypt." I sat with her in her apartment as she petted one of her many lap dogs and gave me her side of the story.

> I'll tell you how it happened. When Reda Troupe started and became so popular, it's very interesting, the belly dancers at this time got very nervous, especially an influential big star. Hence, she said she wanted to have some people dancing around her and thought this would add prestige with spectacle. So, then this started with these boys in these golden suits going around doing this rubbish thing. The first thing they started doing, which was ridiculous, was she would come and dance, and then she'd go out. We'd sit for a few minutes listening to the music, then she'd come out with another costume or a stick or something, but then she'd do practically the same movement as before! So, she had a small set movement vocabulary, and that's it! So, she needed more spectacle to make up for it. As for the guys, they just imitate, nothing original, they just do what Reda troupe does, well they try to, so it's a knock off of a knock off of the original Reda troupe, without the basic foundation that makes a dancer in the Reda Troupe stand out, get it?

Most of these boys became after that free-lance, because they're just interested in following the easy money, it's not usually about art.⁵⁰

I asked how she thought *raqs sharqi* dancers working with backup dancers might be enabling to *raqs sharqi* shows.

If she, the dancer, stands there and does her homework well, and seriously performs what her own dance form is, and she has her own unique thing to say, she doesn't need any of this. But, to have people just running around her, it became a trend. They wear tacky clothes, really shiny stuff, and she's standing there doing her own little movements. It's taking a vision of the Reda Troupe that was . . . well look, most people watching dancers now are drunk anyway, so. To dance for people who are eating and drinking at the same time, it's degrading anyway. The people that go on boats and to nightclubs and eat and drink, they don't care anyway, it's not respectful. If she thinks this makes her look cleaner, she's deceiving herself.

Other performers I talked to stated that *funun al sha3biyya* used to be much more common on boats even though the space was small, but most boats have done away with them because of the budget cuts that started during President Mubarak's era pre-revolution and continued post-revolution.⁵¹ Another U.S.-based Cairo dancer, Vanessa Friedman, who works closely with various folklore troupes, touched on the entwined stigma and financial aspects of *funun al sha3biyya* in an interview. "I knew *funun al sha3biyya* guys that would never work with a dancer because they'd think it's not nice. Others think hey, it's night orders, I get paid extra. The problem is the scarcity of work, there hasn't been a lot of work, a lot of them have other jobs to make ends meet, many have kids to feed, so they'll take gigs with dancers for extra money, not for prestige. I'm sure they don't feel it's the epitome of their careers just doing 'sashay sashay, pivot turn.' Remember the boats are trying to have entertainment for the whole thing and some people don't like the dancer so much so adding folklore makes up for that a little bit."⁵² Having a brief historical contextualization for *funun al sha3biyya*, I move into the choreographic analysis of Farah and her *shabab*'s shows on the Maxim.

. . . "Excuse me, where are you from?" I was trying to take mental notes of Farah's band set-up as well as survey the audience before Farah's show commenced. "Hello, excuse me, I said, where are you from, what is your name?" I thought maybe if I pretended not to hear the *khaleegy* man from the table next to mine, he would stop interrupting my mental preparation for the show. I was wrong. A large middle-aged man with a protruding belly pulling at the seams of his suit, he now started waving his hand in my direction. He was sitting with five other men at a table center-stage in front of the dance floor. In other words, his group was given the unofficial "VIP" seating for the show. It wasn't a busy night, and the boat staff all knew about my ethnographic research, so I sat alone at the table beside the Gulf men's.

"The show is about to start," I replied to him, trying to defuse any chance of conversation. "Yes, but where are you from? What is your name? My friends and I are all wondering what a pretty young lady like you is doing here all alone? You know I can be the best tour guide if you want to see the best nightlife in Cairo. We are from the UAE." I replied curtly to him that I was not in need of a tour guide, I was here working on a book, and I was just there to watch the show.

I pulled out the small notebook I kept tucked away in my purse and pretended to occupy myself re-reading old field notes, but he persisted to his friends' amusement. He quickly escalated to asking me on dates and assuring me he could provide the best experience of Cairo nights that I would never forget, along with other propositions full of thinly veiled innuendo. I never wanted a band to set up so fast. I found myself glancing out toward the large wooden and glass doors that Farah would soon emerge from. I turned around after a light tap on my shoulder. It was Hamid, one of the older male waitstaff on the boat that knew I was there for my research. "Christine, are you okay?" He seemed genuinely concerned for me, and his soft eyes made me feel more comfortable. "If these guys are bothering you, just tell me because I can move your seat to back there." He pointed to a far-off table almost completely behind the band, where I would inevitably get a horrible view of the show. I assured him I was fine where I was but thanked him for his concern as he left to return to other business.

I tried to cover the frown that crept across my face when his concerned solution was that I be displaced, as opposed to chastising or re-locating the VIPs. I took a deep exhale. I reminded myself that my solo presence was at odds with the cultural gender norms, that I was already "out of place" being alone late at night in an entertainment venue. I also reminded myself that as much as the Egyptian male waitstaff probably desired to put these VIPs and other wealthy entitled guests in their place, their paychecks depended on catering to their satisfaction. Due to the immense rift in economic privilege and dependency between the two regions since the oil economies took off in the Gulf, Hamid was reacting in a paternalist protective way. I felt his actions offered him a sense of control over larger uneven economic flows between Egypt and the Arabian Gulf countries, as well as reified his sense of Egyptian masculinity. Interruptions such as these are constant and exhausting, but revealing for how micro-level bodily interactions in contextualized space gesture toward the negotiation of larger macro-politics.

Quickly after setting up their instruments on stage, Farah Nasri's band began to play the energetic opening notes of her *mejance*. While Farah waited in her sparkly two-piece bra and skirt costume outside, four fresh and joyful looking men in shiny and sparkly embellished suit pants and button-up shirts sashayed onto the small square stage. They performed jazz-esque steps to the opening beats of the music. Their four beaming bodies took up position on the four corners of the square stage. In utilizing pivot spins, basic step-together-steps, and with large grandeur arm flourishes and reaches the crew conveyed the sense that a star was preparing to ascend the center of the stage that the four of them were framing with their bodies. Suddenly, they all paused with proud upright posture as they reached their left arms up and toward the left, their heads also tilting to look out toward the large wooden and glass doors of the Maxim's banquet room entrance. Two male staff workers opened the doors as Farah came running out in a light blue flowery costume. The large flower decals and the use of a large flowing chiffon skirt with open leg-slits, as opposed to the common tight-fitting lycra skirt, added an extra air of charming femininity to her look.

As she ascended onto the stage with a fresh vitality and robust yet still "girl next door" demeanor, her backup dancers dutifully held their pose with only the exertion of their chests pumping up and down disrupting their otherwise stillness. Farah's light olive-skinned body was slim and fit, her petite sizing only making her robust breast enhancements all the more eye-catching. She was wearing hair extensions or a wig, and her long and full black curls spiraled out and then gently caressed the top of her flowery hip belt as she spun across the stage with eyes wide in excitement. She had long thin arms and fingers, and she used them beautifully to add flowery flourishes to frame her spins and highly punctuated hip and chest accents. Her percussive and accented style reminded me somewhat of Randa due to her sharp use of power moves, but her aesthetic look with her costuming, hair, make up, and jubilant sweet energy came across more like a sweet girl next door who had just received a basket full of puppies. Her enthusiasm was infectious, and she often shouted encouragement to rile up the crowd, such as *"Yalla!" "Aiwa"*

Figure 1.5 Farah Nasri and her *funun al sha3biyya* (Ahmed, Wael, Salah, and Mahdy) on the Nile Maxim 2014–2018. Credit: Farah Nasri, MA GK Photography

"*Yalla b2a!*" Just as the audience became acquainted with Farah's appearance, her *funun al sha3biyya* proudly strutted off the stage to allow her to finish her *mejance* as a solo artist.

There was little softness or subtlety in her opening. Rather, Farah favored powerful and staccato hip movements and a faster pace in her style, and she also seemed to constantly want to cover large amounts of the stage area in her show. She resisted keeping both her feet planted for more than a fleeting moment. Her pace, punctuations, constant maneuvering around the stage, and wide-eyed expression helped me to share in her jubilee and exhilaration. A few moments before the conclusion of her *mejance*, her *shabab* returned to the stage and engaged in more theatrical but simple steps, turns, and arm swoops and frames to heighten the energy and drama for the end of Farah's first number.

Suddenly, they all spun in unison, and then the four men on all corners of the stage leaned in toward the center, all positioning their bodies and extended arms toward Farah, who spun into a dramatic end pose in the stage's front-center. The audience cheered and clapped as genuine grins grew on all the performer's faces. They bowed and thanked the audience and then quickly exited the banquet room for costume changes.

Farah's young male singer Mohamed took a few more steps onto the stage, taking up more ground than when the dancer was performing. He was wearing jeans, a suit jacket, and a button-up. He started with a well-known classic song, after the first few notes, one of the Gulf men from the VIP table strutted directly across the stage to approach him. I didn't catch any communication between them. All I saw was the Gulf man snatch the microphone out of Mohamed's hand as he was singing and start to sing himself. He was no professional singer. Mohamed paused, stunned for a moment, I felt my heart rise in my chest. *What a jerk*, I thought. Meanwhile, the remaining friends at his table erupted in applause and encouraging cheers to their already tipsy comrade who had just committed the insolent mic-grab.

The rest of us squirmed under his harsh voice. Mohamed, hands still lifted as if holding a ghost microphone, broke from his freeze as a forced grin crossed his face. He nodded and gave a few slow handclaps. His tight grin after the frozen pause demonstrated his displeasure and surprise at the mic-grabbing maneuver. Still, he chose to respond by catering to the table's enjoyment, even at the expense of the rest of the audience's listening pleasure. He began to sing along with the man for a moment, also reaching out to share the microphone, which he slowly took back from the guest as he used his other arm to offer a slight bow and gesture him back toward his table.

Smooth move, I thought. Mohamed managed to quickly defuse the situation without allowing the nastiness of the moment to transmit to the rest of the clientele and sour the atmosphere. Rather, Mohamed made it seem like it was all done in good fun. Aided by the fact that the Gulf man was already tipsy, his own excess made it easier to manipulate him swiftly, and without any fluster, back to his seat. Mohamed glanced toward the large banquet doors with an expression I, too, had just been giving toward the dancer's entryway. It seemed we were both awaiting the dancer's strong presence to lock down the unruly *khaleegy* men. Our mutual waiting was highlighting how the dancer, more so than any other professional on stage, becomes the centrifugal force in balancing all these uneasy power dynamics at a corporeal level.

Rather than enjoy the *tanoura* show or the singer for a couple of songs between costume changes, soon after Farah exited the banquet hall, the straining voice of the *mizmar* piercing the hall.[53] Ahmed, the leader of Farah's male backup dancers, came out proudly wielding double *Sa3idi 3asaya*, two thick staffs, in a *galabeya*. Ahmed held the strong, proud, and erect posture signature to the *Sa3id* region of Egypt, known as a traditional area of *fellaheen* (farmers). At the same time, his proud grin and bright eyes highlighted his genuine love of performing arts and this solo section in particular. *Sa3idi*-inspired folklore with sticks is the most commonly performed folk-inspired dance of Egypt across both local and global professional stages since the popularity of the Reda Troupe. It represents Egypt in a proud, masculine, and traditional light. Ahmed strutted to the center of the stage. He immediately burst into a display of his technical skill and mastery over double-stick dancing based in the theatrical folklore style of the national troupes but with the added spectacle of including a lot more tricks such as stick flips, catches, and balanced strikes. He struck the sticks on the ground, spun them forward and backward, and made them flip in the air, expertly catching them while simultaneously twirling in a way that caused his dark blue *galabeya* to spin out and grant him a larger-than-life grandiosity.

The powerful strikes, posture, and laborsome turns Ahmed engaged in marked his solo with both the skill of a hard-working professional dedicated to his craft, as well as the performative masculinity that the Reda Troupe popularized throughout Egypt. Particularly in contemporary times, with the dire economy having eradicated many regular job opportunities for *funun al sha3biyya*, finding a dancer who was as skillful and dedicated to a professional performance as Ahmed was invigorating. Furthermore, the strength, virtuosic skill, and lack of any hip movement within his national troupe-based repertoire reflects how Mahmoud Reda used hyper-masculinity to legitimate the male dancing body on the middle- and upper-class Cairo stage in the time of Nasser. The precision and well-rehearsed nature of Ahmed's show reflected two important characteristics. On the one hand, Ahmed's performance highlighted his character and dancing talents. On the other hand, it showed how the *Nile Maxim*, as an elite site, can sustain regular employment opportunities for the *funun al sha3biyya*, particularly at a time when many boats had their dancers cut their theatrical folklore performances due to budget slashes.

After a few moments of Ahmed's solo stage show, he was joined by the other three crew members who were holding their sticks upright in matching

Figure 1.6 Farah Nasri and her *funun al sha3biyya* (Ahmed, Wael, Salah, and Mahdy) perform on the Nile Maxim 2014–2018. Credit: Farah Nasri, Ahmed Karem Photography

galabayas. Meanwhile, Farah brandished a sparkly-embellished thinner stick and wore a *baladi* dress with a bra cut-out to show her crystal-emblazoned push-up underneath. Farah led the remaining dancers on stage as they fanned out to create a frame for her performance on the front-center of the stage. They all did traditional *Sa3idi* steps together in unison based on the national troupe repertoires. At other times, the men engaged in simple patterned hop-steps and *3asaya* air-strikes and spins while Farah layered more *raqs sharqi* movement on top of and intermingling with the basic *sa3idi* steps. For example, she would break from the side-step hops to shimmy her hips from side to side while holding the stick horizontally above her head to help frame her isolated hip shimmy-slides. She often incorporated chest and hip shimmies on top of the basic steps and used her sparkly stick more for framing movements as opposed to spins and martial arts-like strike imitations.

During folkloric *tableaus* such as this, the group's side-by-side dancing highlighted the gender distinct norms in dance. The men would only appear for the *mejance* entrance doing pseudo-international dance moves such as jazz and ballroom steps in sparkly-belted suits, reappearing only for male roles within regional theatrical folklore-inspired numbers also in shiny but traditional male garb. The framing *funun al sha3biyya* made it clear that Farah was the star performer: they all faced her as they kneeled on the ground, one hand covering their chests while the other would spin the stick overhead and then pause as if striking in Farah's direction. As a dancer, I was impressed by how she managed the tightened space, framed by moving sticks, with her own sparkly *3asaya*. Her movements, and particularly stick movements, were more precarious and limited because of the condensed space, but I never saw a nervous expression or darting eyes from her. Nothing physically indicated she was at all phased by the constricted conditions. It was clear from the ways the five of them worked together so cohesively and creatively that they were well-rehearsed. Notably, these were rehearsals Farah would demand, as well as pay each of her *shabab* for.

For a significant duration of the second part of her *tableau*, Farah and her "guys" weaved in and out between the audiences' tables, parading right amongst the crowd while pumping their sticks in the air and making merriment through more direct audience-performer interaction. The majority of the international clientele seemed to get a real kick out of this interactive aspect of her show. This enjoyment was evident not only by how they'd twist in their chairs to keep their focus on her as she moved amongst the large banquet dining room, but also through the plethora of cellphones whipped out to capture the more personalized interaction. The *funun al sha3biyya* stayed close to Farah while she made the rounds; they pumped up the energy and encouraged female guests to get up to dance, while repeatedly glancing over at Farah protectively to make sure the male guest interaction was staying family-friendly.

The music shifted to become popular high-energy *sha3bi* as the crew continued to work the crowd. Going off stage for a female dancer can be precarious for a few reasons. One is that going off stage can be considered illegal for eliciting prostitution; another is related to overall energy for the ways going off stage limits a lot of visibility. At the same time, this loss of visibility may and some privacy and sense of intimacy or personalized audience attention to this off-stage aspect of her performance. Notably, such direct off-stage audience engagement by the professional dancer is typical in weddings but not too many other contexts in Cairo. It's expected for the star to remain on the stage for her show.[54] However, for myself as a U.S. dancer (and for Farah—having worked in Europe), this off-stage interactive element was extremely familiar. Getting audiences up to dance and performing amongst tables was standard fare in most Western restaurant entertainment venue settings.

Elements of subversive play and humor that cleverly teased sexuality and gender norms and mores were evident in Farah's off-stage interaction. She got a few white European men up to dance: she pulled them up by the hand, bouncing in excitement and shouting encouragement at them in Arabic that they probably couldn't understand. She brought one of them onto the perimeter of the stage and had him mimic her movements, a request he instantly complied with, and one she need not verbalize. In other words, with a direct gaze, Farah quickly gestured back and forth between their hips. Because this was toward the end of her show when she was thoroughly steeped in the accumulated stage power solidifying her position as the leader, this "follow along" dynamic was readily, and unquestionably, understood and complied with. Farah shimmied her chest with fervor, the man attempted to follow, albeit with more of an awkward shoulder shake and butt wiggle (as he couldn't master the upper body verse lower body isolations). He and the closest sectors of the audience erupted in laughter. Farah held her long locks coyly to the side of her face while lifting and dropping her left hip up and down, layering on a coquettish facial expression. The man in jeans and sweater again imitated her, pretending to hold back his own imaginary long locks while bumping his hip out to the side, still not quite capturing the correct movement to fits of laughter.

He automatically followed her lead without words or a second thought. From my own decade-plus of U.S. experience, and even longer watching other performances, this is usually the case in these off-stage interactions, even from men who might otherwise never allow themselves to be foolishly laughed at in front of a huge crowd. Whatever sexual male gaze or power Western and non-MENA audiences may think they hold over the dancer while they smugly watch her hip articulations from their seats is challenged when confronted with the prowess of her stage command. In other words, a dancer who understands and employs her sexually gender-marked yet center-staged body can temporarily contort the gender and racialized hierarchy of bodies. Most of the guests laugh at the man's ill attempt to follow Farah's technique.

On the one hand, these miming interactions are humorous because a non-MENA man is so obviously doing something "unmanly" in imitating this overtly feminized woman. This interaction would appear, on the surface, to reify gender norms. On the other hand, there's a deeper layer of power in wielding these stark gender and sexuality roles in a way that hypnotizes and transforms the man into a jestering puppet. At the same time, the dancer accumulates more power through her marginalized yet potent moving body. The stage is hers. When she decides to let a man enter, a man that may otherwise have far more racial, gender, and class power and privilege than her, she turns the show into a performance of her hip(g)nosis powers by using the same system of normalized gender and sexuality but in a twisted spellbinding way.

Farah demonstrated this several times through the lighthearted banter of subversive play, using entertaining humor layered upon deeper levels of gendered significations. As she continued performing amongst the tables, Farah enthusiastically pulled several women up to dance on the stage with her. Holding their hands high, she had them follow her in percussive hip drops and full-body undulations to the encouraging applause of the audience. This applause, however, was without the same comical air, as these bodies were following within normative gender constructs. Men, she messed with. At one point, she jiggled her large breasts behind a man's head. The remainder of his table erupted in laughter as he turned around with a shocked expression, leading to another burst of laughter. Again, subverting the male gaze through her direct, non-passive, and quite literally "in your face" brazen sexuality, while at the same time, following within and reifying the male gaze's sexualized structure. After all, large breast enhancement surgeries and other modifications have become almost a requirement to get paid work in the worldwide belly dance industry. While catching the man off guard, her reverberating breasts in his face still employed tactics wherein females cater to the assumed commercialized male heterosexual desire for their bodies.[55] While a significant number of professional Cairo dancers have had breast and other surgical/cosmetic enhancements to become more marketable in *raqs sharqi*, it's important to note that this is following a globalized trend from the cosmetic and plastic surgery industries.

Farah smiled and then briskly bounced off to a bald, middle-aged white European man. She leaned over him from behind, delicately but humorously placing her long curly black hair extensions over his bare head to make him look like a woman. Meanwhile, she leaned her head against his while making exaggerated "kissy" faces. The other family members at the table giggled and took a barrage of cell phone pictures. She then pinched his cheek playfully like he was a cute little boy. She was both infantilizing him while poking fun at his baldness, again seizing the opportunity to remind the audience who held power and prestige in the room by highlighting her desirable and healthy long locks as opposed to his baldness. At the same time, Farah was making a joke of the performance of femininity... fake hair on him that was actually also fake hair for her. The whole show was a charade of sorts, in the fact that it emphasized how gender and sexuality were constructions played out across bodies through appearance, movements, and performance.

Farah and her crew seemed to be steering relatively clear of the VIP table, despite their prominent ballroom positioning and the enthusiastic cheers from the men beckoning for Farah to come their way. Her *funun al sha3biyya* hawked over her as she finally sashayed over to their table. Multiple men rose from their chairs, hoping to interact a bit with Farah as well as snap photos with her. Again, photo opportunities are often a highlight of boat shows when dancers choose to engage in off-stage interaction during the second set of the show.[56] Being more enculturated with intra-MENA understandings and history of *raqs sharqi* shows, it became clear that the Gulf men were reading Farah's off-stage interaction differently than those outside of an intra-MENA social sphere. This reading, alongside the tipsy men's sense of entitlement to all the excess Egypt had to offer them on their vacation, led to another power struggle over bodily boundaries between the men and performers.

One man tried wrapping his arm around the back of the dancer's bare waist as he did a few social dancing steps with her, a move that may be read innocently from a Western perspective. However, in the Cairo context, it is inappropriate to expect such intimate physical contact between a strange man and woman. However, because Farah was crossing into more volatile territory, leaving the safety net of the Cairo stage, combined with the man's drunken sense of entitlement due to his perceived class, nationality, and gender privilege, he thought he could further push on her bodily boundaries. Farah quickly grabbed his hand to try and keep his arm from making physical contact with her back or waist. She tried dancing with him and using their arms to maintain an appropriate distance between their two bodies, but he kept attempting closeness with her.

Then, a second man got up and tried to pull her in for a kiss on her cheek while his other companion stood at the ready for the photo opportunity. Again, this is clearly inappropriate behavior in this Cairo context, and Farah immediately grabbed his face with her hand and pushed him away, giving the rest of her audience an "is this guy crazy?!" exaggerated facial expression and hand twist. Still, the transgression had already occurred. The surrounding audience laughed, unaware of the depth of the cultural transgression.

However, they also laughed due to how Farah, like her singer Mohamed, reacted in a way that made the interaction seem funny, when, in actuality, she was kinesthetically setting boundaries between the two, while maintaining the enjoyable atmosphere for the rest of the crowd. She deployed a clever and necessary tactic of all Cairo performers, but also an exhausting labor that unevenly accumulates upon working female and other marginalized corporealities.

This interaction highlights an important split in the myriad ways Farah's off-stage interaction is mined for meaning depending on the particular positionality and contextualized relationship of the dancer, space, and audience member. While the historically regulated site of the stage can offer a dancer power when she is able to transmit *ihsas* and *hudur* from within the state-sanctioned stage's perimeter, when her body crosses that stage boundary, however, those historic bodily choreographies of *fath* and subsequent state policing shadow the dancer in a more precarious and suspect sexuality, class-positionality, and morality. When the dancer leaves the stage and is positioned anywhere amongst the tables, she can be charged with eliciting prostitution, thus pitting the responsibility, policing, and precarity on the female dancer as opposed to the audience.[57]

Farah's marginalized gender, sexuality, and economic labor become capable of accumulating power on stage due to their intertwined relegation to larger nationalist state policing. However, once those boundaries are crossed, her gender, sexuality, and economic labor go from being powerful but marginalized to potentially illicit. Intra-MENA audiences are more adept at reading the depth of suspect sexual meanings in a dancer's use of on- and off-stage space because of how these gendered regulations embed within normative gender and spatial constructs, and *raqs sharqi* dance, within intra-MENA cultures. Also, in this particular instance, the table of Gulf men utilized a suspect reading of Farah's off-stage dancing to grant themselves more self-entitlement to all the excess the *Nile Maxim* site had to offer, including these corporeal attempts to demonstrate their economic, gender, and nationalist prowess through crossing Farah's personal body boundaries. Although the *funun al sha3biyya* hovered more closely over Farah, highlighting a sense of protection warranted over female corporeality against threatening outside forces, it was still Farah, centralized within all this drama, who had to think on her feet and go with her gut to diffuse and control the situation.

It was time for the finale of her show. Farah and her crew returned to the stage, the men flanking her on every corner while she undulated center-stage. After doing a few typical *sa3idi* hop steps in unison, the male dancers suddenly swarmed Farah, two of them kneeling on either side of her and grabbing the opposite ends of each other's sticks so that Farah was constrained and literally boxed-in between their large wooden staffs. They moved their sticks up and down as Farah feigned shock at her entrapment, holding both hands against her open mouth in an "oh my god!" expression. Suddenly, she smiled brightly as she burst into a strong hip shimmy followed with aggressive, wide, and forceful hip bumps from side-side while she held her arms up over her head. With great force, she threw her hips to the right and then to the left, over and over, her energy only seeming to accumulate with each hip bump.

Drastically and unexpectedly, Farah changed the direction of her hip articulations, suddenly throwing her hips straight back as she twisted them at an angle, then, with the right hip leading, thrust her hip directly forward against the front stick. The forceful blow sent the men flying backward as their stick-trap burst open with her hip's might. As the men feigned recovery from the explosion of power, Farah joyfully danced as a soloist, shaking and shimmying her hips with renewed vigor and a bright smile. Her four *funun al sha3biyya* formed a formation behind her, and Farah began spinning. One by one, the men followed in pivot spins behind her until they were all five spinning together. As the music came to a crescendo, they stopped on a dime for the final pose. Farah stood in a typical super-model stance, sinking into one hip with one hand on her cheek and the other on the extended hip, while her *funun al sha3biyya* all directed their extended arms and posture toward Farah. The crowd erupted with cheering and robust applause as the performers bowed in thanks to the audience and musicians.

After observing Farah's shows with rapture, I couldn't wait to finally interview her and her crew to gain additional insight into their dance knowledge and perspectives. I bounded down the spiral steps leading to the lower deck of the *Nile Maxim*, which held the worker's dressing and waiting rooms. However, my bubbly enthusiasm froze upon arriving below deck; I could quite easily overhear the heated confrontation blasting between Farah and staff from the boat. Apparently, someone from the boat staff had stolen all the workers' pay from Farah's gig bag (pay for her, her musicians, and her *funun al sha3biyya*). It was not the first time something like this had happened. (It's also worth mentioning that this wasn't a situation unique to Farah; most dancers I spoke with were familiar with this scenario.) Musicians sipping hot tea assuredly waved me into Farah's quarters. They seemed disgruntled but not surprised. I was taken aback by Farah, the sweet gorgeous woman I'd observed dancing so many nights now standing her ground brazenly with a no-nonsense demeanor. Her intense glare melted into her familiar pleasant smile as she turned to greet me. She assured me we were still fine to do the interview; she said if I rescheduled, there would just be a new drama the next week. She offered me a chair and began by telling me about her dance life with genuine honesty and deep appreciation of her learning experiences. I appreciated hearing Farah's perspectives and stories, and we agreed for me to return during one of the rehearsals to set up paid interviews with her musicians and *funun al sha3biyya*.[58] Farah has worked with this same crew for over two years. She doesn't rotate out her crew like many *raqs sharqi* dancers would, she deeply values their contributions and livelihood, and works hard to keep them as a family. Farah's *funun al sha3biyya* crew includes Ahmed, Wael, Salah, and Mahdy.

It was important to hear the dancers' perspectives on their work. It was also evident that dancers in Egypt tend to have strong opinions on whether dancing with *funun al sha3biyya* adds to, or takes away from, a *raqs sharqi* dancer's show. For example, after interviewing Safiya, she called me as I was hailing a taxi to go home outside the venue to add a final point that she felt strongly about. She stated that dancers who worked without *funun al sha3biyya* were stronger because they were *shamla* (complete), in that they could stay captivating in all aspects and musical styles of their show without needing help from men. She added that men were only useful as background to make a folklore-inspired *tableau* or for weddings when the couple requests it to add more atmosphere and show off the money they're spending on entertainment. Other dancers such as Randa and Egyptian star dancer Dina intentionally do not work with *funun al sha3biyya* because they want their strong solo dancing to be a testament to their strength, talent, and stardom as Egyptian women. Overall, the main critiques of *funun al sha3biyya* tended to center around the ways their presence didn't mesh with the idea, expectations, and values of a strong solo woman doing her own *raqs sharqi* show.

Further, a dancer should be *shamla* enough in all aspects of dance and music styles, charisma, and interaction, to not need any assistance in holding an audience's attention throughout her solo show. Additionally, by comparing the three dancers' case studies, it becomes clear that the meaning and use-value of *raqs sharqi* also shifts when incorporating *funun al sha3biyya*. Working with *funun al sha3biyya* transfers the focus of the show from creating connections in feelings and embodied charisma to more spectacle and theatrical entertainment. However, Farah, her crew, and the innovators of *funun al sha3biyya* and *raqs sharqi* collaborations, legendary Nagwa Fouad, and her then-husband Mohamed Khalil, argue that working with *funun al sha3biyya* presents a balanced landscape. This balance adds different dynamics to a dancer's show that complement *raqs sharqi*. Rather than decide which is better, I find it more productive to delve into the sociopolitical tensions and possibilities opened up through incorporating *funun al sha3biyya* into an otherwise solo female *raqs sharqi* performance.

I agree with Randa, Safiya, and Samia that an immense part of what makes a female *raqs sharqi* dancer in Cairo so strong is how she is *shamla* in captivating an entire crowd through her intertwined movements, feeling, and interaction through her charisma.[59] It is the tantalizing mix of simultaneously being both strong and vulnerable, as such a marginalized yet "sure of herself" figure spotlighted on the stage, to be able to dance out her emotions and life experiences in ways earnest enough to transmit throughout the audience. However, as Randa points out, this strength in being a working woman is deeply tied to how you learn to deal with all kinds of men in a kaleidoscope of contexts in ways that result in you getting what you want. Thus, in some ways, stating that *raqs sharqi* is a "solo" form is hindering in that it can elide just how strongly and complexly the female dancer is bounded by male relationships both on and off stage. As observed and stated in interviews, dancers must maintain control of their all-male bands, often male singers, managers, and venue staff, as well as audience members and their complicated off-stage marriages to men as working women in a highly stigmatized yet economically productive job.

However, what dancers such as Randa and Safiya state with their solo shows is that they love themselves enough, and trust themselves enough— really understand themselves and what they want from life enough—to make a statement with their dancing that they are what audiences are getting and they are just that: enough. They are enough in their own fully embraced, dynamic, and confident corporealized womanhood. Further, they and other dancers are successful in accomplishing this because they pull from a movement and musical foundation that is rich and dynamic. These dancers have unique movements, energy, feeling, and aesthetics for each different aspect of the multi-faceted *raqs sharqi* show, from the *mejance* to *sha3bi*, *baladi*, classical, *sa3idi*, and so on.

On the other hand, dancers such as Farah that regularly work with *funun al sha3biyya* can be criticized for not having this layered and dynamic foundation to be considered *shamla* artists. Due to the intersecting gendered and economic dynamics of the *funun al sha3biyya* entertainment trade, the dancer comes not only to collaborate with other dancers to aid her show in success, she also comes specifically to work with male dancers primarily from lower socioeconomic backgrounds. While the overall power hierarchies remain intact for the dancer, she being considered the lead power figure above her primarily male musicians, and the musicians considered above the male *funun al sha3biyya*, she still tacks on more male employees to deal with professionally, artistically, and corporeally. Innovators Nagwa Fouad and Mohamed Khalil contend that these collaborations create "balanced landscapes" through incorporating both genders and more overt nationalist signifiers through the regionally inspired folkloric *tableaus* that worked to desexualize and thus "elevate" the context of *raqs sharqi* to the Egyptian public.[60]

This containment and balancing of the solo dancer's powerful sexuality can be seen through the more obvious framing containment of the dancer, as she is often "boxed in" or flanked by multiple male *funun al sha3biyya* while performing her show. In addition to just containing and balancing her sexuality through their physical bodies adorned in traditionally regionally specific costuming and the larger nationalist staging, framing, and narratives their bodies all perform within, these configurations also reify a woman's sexuality within state-sanctioned gender norms. As mentioned by Ahmed, "We follow her around and help keep the atmosphere. Also, if someone is drunk, we might have to protect her, or maybe they are sexually excited people, and we need to watch after her. Look, if anyone ever tries anything with Farah, I will hurt him!"[61]

The men often take on a protective role over the dancer, particularly in cases where they feel unruliness or danger from drunken clients or instances of *fitna*—social chaos as related to her sexuality—may pose a threat. Additionally, the interaction between the dancer and her *funun al sha3biyya* often embodies joyful folkloric numbers that mask the political strife different ethnicities and regions in Egypt face under the state, as well as include flirtatious interaction that reifies the male and female dancer's sexuality within heteronormativity.

For example, when her crew was discussing the flirtatious fun of off-stage interaction with Farah, I asked them if they were ever flirted with by women. They all burst into laughter by the flipped suggestion of their male bodies being the sites of displayed sexuality. "Women like us, of course, but she is the sexy one, not me, haha."[62] The female *raqs sharqi* dancer's marginalized sexuality is thus constrained and contained representationally through the framing male figures representing clean and dominating Egyptian nationalism, particularly state-aligned masculine and heterosexual normativity. Thus, Nagwa Fouad's innovative folkloric collaborations are tied to women's projects in Egypt at large, wherein as women endeavor to create more space, opportunities, and potential for themselves, they simultaneously create or comply with new forms of control and surveillance.[63]

However, at the same time, this combination results in aspects of the show that rely less on *ihsas* (feeling) to create power and success, and more on spectacle and entertainment. As such, contradictorily, it's the very mixture of vulnerability and strength through a dynamic and wholeheartedly embodied sense of her embraced sexuality that a dancer creates transmittable art and feeling. When this vulnerability is traded for a more contained, relegated, and protected "balance" of gender and consequential patriarchal state guardianship of sexuality, the significations of the dance shift. *Raqs sharqi* then becomes more about spectacle and less about *ihsas*, the very quality that so many Cairo dancers posit is what sets *raqs sharqi* apart from any other dance in the world—notably, the main quality that made them fall in love with the art form.

In contrast, Farah Nasri and her crew focus on the dynamics working with *funun al sha3biyya* creates from the perspective of the labor and doing of the dance itself. While touching on the representational politics of "balanced landscapes" as related to gender and sexuality, Farah and her crew exemplify more the kinesthetic negotiations and challenges wrestled with by the performers who choose to collaborate in this way. Looking at the performances from this other perspective offers new insight that might otherwise be overlooked from an outside perspective. For example, Farah and her crew posit that working with *funun al sha3biyya* provides different challenges to work around. Such challenges include small boat stages that become even more condensed and constrained for the *raqs sharqi* dancer because she has physically less space in which to move. Additionally, the dancer must now negotiate her own use of cramped space with other close-by moving bodies. While still needing to project strong energy to the audience seated throughout the large ballroom, Farah must also work harder, yet more carefully, to claim her space on the shrunken stage.

As Farah exclaims, "To handle four men with you, if you're not a great dancer, they'll eat you alive! You see the energy and strength they have, so I also have to be so strong and have a lot of charisma. People won't watch you if you don't have a lot of charisma in the midst of all them!"[64] Not only this, but Farah explained how a dancer must also be aware of the male theatrical folklore repertoires and steps as well as skillfully be able to layer the expected feminine *raqs sharqi* techniques and aesthetics on top of, and in addition to, the steps constructed as masculine.

All this has to be done while now working to stay in synchronization with her crew, as mistakes become all the more obvious when the dancer is no longer a solo body on stage. Ahmed states, "The clever one dances with or without *shabab* any time and any place! A bad dancer will be scared she can't steal the spotlight from us because we'll do so many difficult, strong steps that she can't keep up. Also, teamwork is more difficult. To move as one unit at the same time, if you mess up in a group, you can't hide your mistake from the guests like a soloist can."[65] As the *shabab* note, the dancer now must compete and labor to keep and maintain the spotlight from the multiple men surrounding her. She must know their steps, be aware of their movements around her, and be able to layer her own charisma, technique, and musicality on top of, and in excess to, all these other factors to make it evident that the audience focuses on her as the star. While the men stick to basic Reda repertoire combinations, the fact that they greatly outnumber the dancer on stage makes their show have a more physical presence. Farah is thus charged with needing to "make like a man," while also having to always put out more than the multiple men around her in artistry and personality to reify her position at the top of the power hierarchy.

On the other hand, the men are able to do more basic steps and combinations since their gender is already the largest presence on stage, as well as the fact that they depend upon, and expect, the dancer to be doing the most unique and exceptional labor to lead and carry the show. At one point, Farah turned to her crew and asked why she can dance their steps, but they refuse to dance hers (*raqs sharqi*). Ahmed immediately retorted, "Look, if you see a woman move like a man you think 'wow, impressive,' but if you see a man move like a woman, you think, 'this is terrible.' It shows a woman's talent if she can move like a man because what we do is so strong and difficult." Samah added, "Egyptian culture does not accept for men to dance with their waists like in *raqs sharqi*; he can only dance like a man."[66]

Therefore, while Farah must be able to "impress" the crowd by embodying the "difficult" masculine movements and steps, the men refuse to return the favor. Rather, they find it shameful, forbidden, and unnatural to perform any movements that would be read as *raqs sharqi* (implying feminine) on stage. I remember swapping knowing glances with Farah during this exchange, and she elaborated through a story about when she wanted to have her crew do the opening notes of "Shik Shak Shok" (a traditional *raqs sharqi* song) for her. She told me that, for sure, they all knew how to do the movements, but they simply refused to do them publicly on stage, even just the opening notes before she came on stage. She said the men threw a fuss about it being *raqs sharqi* music, and they would never do it. It was one of her creative artistic visions that never came to light.

I then took my turn to ask the crew why Farah can do their repertoire, but they can't do hers. I hadn't finished my question before Ahmed interrupted, "*3aeeb!* (Shame!) It's a shame for a man to do *raqs sharqi*, we only do folklore like *Sa3idi*. *Raqs sharqi* is only for women. It's a feminine dance—this will never happen." Samah elaborated, "*Raqs sharqi* is for girls, for a working male dancer he can do folklore, so we merge these parts in the show. From the beginning until now, this is the relationship, the main portrait [Farah], and the background landscape. It's a nice balance when we work together."

He further explained that historically, belly dancing came from the Pharaonic times, that it was a training doctors prescribed women to make birthing easier. Later on, men observed this and found it appealing sexually, so the practice continued outside of just giving birth. He used this proposed biological determinism to drive home his point, "That's it, dancing is for women, pregnant women! Men cannot be pregnant, so they cannot be dancing *raqs sharqi*!" He then contradicted his own claims, "Well, sometimes in wedding parties you see men dancing *raqs sharqi* the same as women socially, but it's not for paid professional work. It's not his job. It's just for fun; he's not wearing a costume and taking money! We have our steps, and she has hers."[67]

Importantly, Samah's account is one of many cultural myths amongst some Egyptians (and the international belly dance community) about the origins of *raqs sharqi*. There is no historical basis for these claims, but they are fascinating for the ways these "origin stories" embed and naturalize political discourses on gender and sexuality.[68] In this case, there is a biological determination that *raqs sharqi* is for women only, a determination Samah himself immediately undermined with the lived realities of how men dance socially at weddings.

Thus, while trying to create new work with "Shik Shak Shok," Farah is limited artistically by her crew's stiff gender constructs. At the same time, her own body is laboriously stretched to make up for this stiffness through her own gender flexibility and performativity. While it impresses people if she can pick up the difficult kinesthetic labor attributed to men (because she is read as the weaker gender), she's dually constrained by the fact that the *funun al sha3biyya* have no pressure or expectation to take on typically female-gendered steps, roles, and aesthetics, and see no potential in doing so. Equally, the typical audience shows no desire to watch female-gendered technique or aesthetics performed by *funun al sha3biyya*.

While Farah's *raqs sharqi* body labors at the margins of acceptability in society due to her particular profession, her work dynamics are akin to larger struggles other working women are negotiating, particularly within difficult economic times. As Middle Eastern Gender Studies scholars Botman and Hafez argue, though the terms of women's citizenship and rights have changed over time since independence from British rule, citizenship continues to be defined within patriarchal terms, and the domestic family laws have largely been left unreformed.[69] On the ground, this refers to how women are increasingly taking on responsibilities and roles normatively deemed "masculine" in the public realm, such as the labor force, without any relief of pressure, roles, or duties in the domestic family spheres. While women across classes, though particularly those in the working and shrinking middle classes, are taking on more roles and labor, men are not reciprocating this growth by taking on more roles and duties normatively assigned to women.

As Farah's story highlights, this stunts creative growth and capacities, as well as puts an immense and exhausting pressure upon the female laboring body. As Botman contends, gender hierarchies have been created both in the family and in society that have resulted in inequality for women in politics, the workplace, and social life. As a result, she urges for a rearticulating of gender relations that can only be achieved through full democratization in both the family and in the state.[70]

Working with *funun al sha3biyya* doesn't necessarily make a dancer any less. Yet it certainly does make her work and approaches different. For one thing, this artistic choice, alongside making the choice of using 'on' verse 'off'-stage interaction, relates to where individual dancers are coming from and what statement they intend to make with their show through their boundaries, borders, and bodies. As Farah explained,

> What I learned quickly here is that you need to put boundaries and barriers as a dancer, woman, and worker. As for Randa and Safiya, yes, we are all different. It is boundaries again. Randa and Safiya are coming from backgrounds where the dancer is *fannana* [artist] and must remain on stage. Randa doesn't want to be thought of as a *sharmuta* [whore]. She must intentionally perform *fannana* only because that's the cultural understanding of her job and self, and she must be direct in challenging it. I can go around the tables and off-stage act like a sweet 3*abeeta* [idiot] sometimes and get away with it, they cannot, they must be *mi3allima* [strong boss-lady persona] all the time. It's not fair, but as Egyptians and foreigners, we're not judged the same. You have to account for the different cultures, standards, and individual goals in drawing your borders.[71]

In addition to boundaries, finding and tracing the power within these differing work and performative conditions is important due to the myriad constraints and capabilities different dancers have to negotiate depending on their backgrounds and performative contexts. In Farah's case, she and her *shabab* crew are successful because they work collaboratively and creatively together in ways that interweave their hybrid understandings of dance and art as well as their cultural backgrounds. Significantly, these relationships are built upon trust- trust in each other as individuals, but also within each artist's approach to creating dance for the stage. It's the trust that you can see between the crew in their dressing rooms below deck as they joke and laugh together, as well as their genuine expressions of joy and dedication on stage, that result in sustainable success.

At the same time, though they work collaboratively, Farah and her crew are always aware that Farah must hold the reins, artistically and professionally, while they remain as background allies. As Farah affirms, "They, my *shabab*, are all my brothers, but still, they know if I get angry, I'm employing them." On the other hand, the main cause of their sustainable success is due to economic stability and resources that are not common conditions for most *funun al sha3biyya* and dancer collaborations across post-revolutionary Cairo. The local and cosmopolitan site of the Nile cruising boat, alongside the myriad appeal of dance shows with *funun al sha3biyya*, and the five-star *Nile Maxim* in particular, result in steady and reliable job opportunities for

Farah and her crew. Farah earns enough income from dancing for the middle and upper classes to make paid rehearsals to keep her crew sharp, synchronized, and motivated. This resource is a privilege most *funun al sha3biyya* aren't currently experiencing, but Farah utilizes it well to strengthen their shows and thus career sustainability. Due to the economy, most stages require strong female solos, significantly because they cannot afford to have it any other way.

At the same time, Farah and her crew, as well as Randa and Safiya, also reaffirm their professional and successful status by perpetuating and further cleaving divisions between classes. In particular, the working-class dancers (*funun al sha3biyya* and *raqs sharqi* performers) working in cabarets across Shari3a Haram (Pyramid Street) are denigrated in all three dancers' accounts and marked in ways that reify class hierarchies within the dance industry. In this hierarchy, cabarets are classified as the low class sites of performance, and work within the industry for performers to add respectability and status to their own bodies at the expense of denigrating and devaluing the sites, bodies, and significations of cabarets and their employees. Farah is unique because she keeps her *shabab* with her for a lot more of her show than typical *raqs sharqi* and *funun al sha3biyya* collaborations. She believes they are not valued enough in Egypt and have a lot more to add to the performance arts. This materializes in Farah's decisions to "modernize" her *shabab* while also dressing and moving them in ways that would set them apart from a typical Shari3a Haram street dancer, who she claims simply serve as undervalued "space warmers" for the soloist.[72] (Farah, like Farida Fahmy, noted a typical Shari3a Haram male backup dancer will wear super shiny somewhat tacky costuming and do simplistic often unrehearsed steps.) Farah outfits her crew in fitted shirts with ties and hats. She also refers to modernizing the cuts in music and arrangement of steps adding in more complex patterning.

Likewise, Randa and Safiya both assert how cabarets are not sites for art or even dancing, diminishing the use-values of dancers in these contexts. Importantly, the economy and societal gender shifts are contradictorily necessitating both scenarios. On the one hand, strong female solos are necessary because there just isn't the capital to add male labor on *raqs sharqi* stages. On the other hand, these same conditions are also necessitating *funun al sha3biyya* to take on less prestigious night work with *raqs sharqi* dancers when available, wherein they'll be under the charge of a strong female lead and must learn to accept a background position.

Conclusion: Pulling into Port

I lingered at my table. The *Nile Maxim* had docked, and the audience began steadily streaming out of the boat. The stage was now empty except for Ahmed, the musical technician who was busy wrapping up musical cords and stowing away equipment from the evening's entertainment. He must have noticed my contemplative delay and walked over to ask how my research was moving along. I told him I was just thinking about the different dancers' shows that I'd seen recently and asked what his thoughts were. He replied thoughtfully, "Look, the important thing about this kind of dancing is that each woman must come to it and create her own style with it. Everyone says her own special thing with this dance. Every woman is different than the other, so every dancer in this dance must have a different style. This is what makes you interested in her as a dancer, through what she is coming to the stage to say by her body language."[73]

Ahmed simply states a vital component of *raqs sharqi* within Cairo contexts—that successful and captivating dancers become such due to the ways they embody and perform their unique sense of self. Further, he highlights how although the dance's form and structure is shaped by the space it occurs within, it is the bodies within those spaces that have the ultimate power in creating meanings. Thus, different dancers create different shows with differing semiotics, even while sharing the same stage space. As such, dismissing Nile boats as sites of "mediocre dancing" for "tourists" does an extreme disservice in grappling with the complex, and largely MENA-centric globalization and intra-MENA circulations of dance dynamics the sites embody.

Taxi Transition: 3*aeesh* (Life-Bread)

I'm savoring the scent of freshly baked bread with deep inhalations as my friend Wael and I walk past a bakery outside of downtown Cairo. Meanwhile, a jam-packed herd of people impatiently wait to purchase the fresh goods. Between the mixture of sewage, car exhaust, and pollution, most large cities don't have the most pleasant of smells, and Cairo is no exception. However, part of any city's charm is when you're walking about and get those whiffs of pleasurable scents that momentarily override the rancid, serving as reminders of the enriching multitude of people, places, and opportunities a crowded city space offers. I slow my pace to take in a few more breaths, the scent offering me a brief respite from the everyday city hustle. With a jolt, I realize my companion isn't sharing this sensation.

Wael stops suddenly and taps me on the shoulder, roughly shaking his head in frustration. "So get this, my dad is always complaining to me about why I don't have a better job and make more money with my education . . . he's always pushing me to go work overseas in the Gulf, or at least to have tried to become something in the military. Haha, but get this, I tell him OK *baba*, I'll work so hard in the military and for what? To put on my flowery apron and bake sugar cookies?! Can you believe this?!" I'm confused; the coupling of military soldiers and baking in aprons doesn't fit together in my mind. Wael notices my obliviousness and elaborates. "The military's really expanding into the economy, everything's coming under military-state control now, even the bread and bakeries—seriously! You cannot imagine how many sectors of the economy the military has taken over. Ha, you look super confused, that's *just* the thing, it doesn't make any sense! Can you imagine a military officer spending his time baking cookies and sweets, when supposedly we're being plagued by terrorists from every corner of the country?!" He shakes his head in bewildered exasperation. We continue onward.

With this exchange, yet another seemingly pleasurable and innocent sensation of my own ethnographic venture crumbles before me. Though I shared the same street and scents with my comrade, our experiences of these sensations starkly contrasted. Confronted with the reality of my own romanticism, countered by the real-life struggles of someone I deeply cared for, I question again how much impact my research could possibly have. We continue walking, now more sluggishly, alongside the city streets. I cast my gaze down upon our trekking feet, only hoping that in the sustained sharing of these streets, the sharing of our struggles, joys, and stories, visceral and valuable pathways may unfold.

A Couple of Weeks Later . . .

"*Ma3alesh*," our Uber driver apologizes again as we back out of another dead-end road the GPS had led us onto. I offer a sympathetic smile from the back seat. For once, I am not in a hurry. Wael and I had planned on making an interview with a cabaret manager before catching performances later on in the evening, but our interview was rescheduled at the last minute (an extremely common research occurrence!). Instead, we decide to relax at a coffee shop by the Nile until it is time for the evening's dancing shows. Still, the driver seems surprisingly flustered by the constant misleading directions of the GPS. He is much older than most of the youthful Uber drivers I encountered during my stay in Cairo. The driver then turns right onto a main street and Wael, having worked nearby the area, politely tells him that he should have gone left. The driver grimaces and quickly wipes a few beads of sweat from his brow.

I realize he must be nervous. We are in a nice Uber, and the car is in good condition with the air condition blowing full blast; a welcome treat from roasting away in old smoky taxis. Wael offers the driver a cigarette to help him relax. He refuses but takes the consoling gesture as an opportunity to share a bit of his own story. His name is Ahmed, and he is new to Uber. He tells us that as an older established husband and father, he never thought he would end up in this position. Yet, finding himself thrown into the midst of unemployment, he figured, since his car is still in good condition from his previous career, that he could take up Uber to help make ends meet. He is doing fine—not wealthy, but all his family's needs are being met. He is the proud father of three girls. He was established and respected in his community, he tells us. He pulls the photo of his three smiling daughters off from his dashboard to show Wael, who is sitting beside him in the front passenger seat.

He used to own a bakery. He loved his job; he was highly experienced and skilled at his trade. However, with all the problems in the political and economic sphere, from the government's continuous cutting of subsidies, the flotation of the Egyptian pound, and the military increasingly taking over state-owned bakeries, he couldn't compete, he just couldn't make it, and suddenly he lost everything. He sold the building, and that money helped for a little while, but now here he is, lost and meandering in a city he used to have a permanent place in, a real sense of belonging. He worries for his daughters' futures, rather than his own. He boasts to us about what bright and clever girls they are, with strong moral compasses. He wants them to feel secure and provided for. "I hope these dead ends are just on the road, and not in my life." He jokes, yet he too shakes his head in bewilderment.

3aeesh: Life Bread

The colloquial Egyptian Arabic word for bread is the same as life—*3aeesh*. The struggle for bread is deeply entangled with larger economic and political struggles in Egypt, harkening back to the "bread riots" of 1977, when then-President Anwar Sadat cut bread subsidies as part of a World Bank loan measure, and thousands of working-class Egyptians protested. Though their protests were ultimately successful in reversing the subsidy cuts, they were first met with army tanks.[74] Echoes of these riots resurfaced again in Tahrir Square in 2011, as the revolutionary chanting for "bread, freedom, and social justice" highlights the drastic ways basic life needs, the economy, and the neoliberalized state entwine. More recent echoes include President El-Sisi's 12 billion-dollar IMF loan, which once again included measures related to slashing foodstuff subsidies, and the ever-increasing grip of the military over the economy, particularly in ways the military unevenly reaps benefits from.[75]

In these "bread riots" largely working-class citizens courageously put their protesting bodies at risk throughout the country over bread, a basic but powerful metaphor for, and necessity of, *3aeesh*—life. Since the ousting of President Morsi in 2013 the regime has put in place strict anti-protesting laws, and the state of emergency has placed added precarity on these protesting bodies who can be arrested and detained without due process.[76] At the same time, these larger IMF loans, military government controls, and rising inflation with slashed subsidies have more mundane, yet still meaningful, corporeal consequences.

In the narrations above, bread viscerally ties into the sense of masculinity of two previously middle-class men, both now struggling since the drop in the economy that started around 2008 and continued after the revolution. Whereas for me, the wafting smell of freshly baked bread may bring back memories of home, family meals, and comfort, for Wael it immediately brought up feelings of frustration over a lack of control over his career options in a stifled economy over which he was increasingly witnessing the military-government regime taking more and more of an autocratic grip. For Ahmed, our Uber driver, it resulted in a physical displacement. Steering from his established life as an economically providing father with his bakery to an overwhelming sense of up-rootedness and dislocation, he now continues trying to carve out a new path for himself while still dependent upon economic opportunities that seem to suddenly careen into dead ends and wrong turns.

Due to his older age, and as his furrowed sweaty brow reveals, for Ahmed to find himself dislocated from his previously solid identity as a stable and knowledgeable father and worker is a threat to his role of provider. Yet at the same time, his tensed knuckles, which grip the steering wheel and turn sharply in and out of dead ends and wrong turns, highlight his resilience in the face of a repressive regime and dire economic woes. Instead, his laboring body, though lost more often than not amidst the city streets and chaos, continues to keep moving forward. Despite the tangible obstacles at every wrong turn or cut off, what remains at the forefront of his labor and vision, is the dashboard photograph of his three grinning girls. Thus, Ahmed maneuvers not merely amidst the shattered economy and patronizing political sphere, but more strongly within his kindred love for his daughters. Moving from this foundation, of sincere love and hope for a better future for more than just oneself, therein he finds a source of sustainable strength that fuels his persevering present and *inshallah* (God willing) fruitful future.

2
Five-Star Hotels

Checking in, or Checking out? Contemporary Conditions in the Revolution's Aftermath

My steps slowed as I approached the main entrance of the Cairo Marriott Hotel on Gezira Island, a well-off area of Zamalak. The hotel was only a short stroll from a coffee shop where I had just been typing up interview transcripts, and because of the upscale area, I felt perfectly safe walking alone despite the late hour. My pace slowed further upon my arrival at the hotel's main entrance due to its elaborate opulence. The entrance was bedecked in shiny tiled flooring, while dignified lion statues flanked the main doors, and golden architecture and columns spread out amidst the large open entrance area. The architecture's neoclassical decadence and layered historic décor fascinated the academic in me. At the same time, the extent of its elegance struck the part of me that was trying to pull off this level of fieldwork on a minuscule, self-funded, graduate student (and later part-time lecturer) budget. It was clear from first impressions that the Marriott had a rich history as well as continued extravagant appeal. As I entered the main doors, I could hear car doors slamming shut behind me announcing other guests' arrival.

I bypassed the first level of security for vehicles entering the Marriott because I was a pedestrian. As mentioned, this first outdoor security measure has become standard throughout five-star hotels in Cairo following a series of terrorist incidents in the 1990s. Here, cars are stopped at a guarded gate outside the hotel's entrance, drivers must hand over their identification, and a guard must inspect their vehicles and trunks with a sniffer dog before guests are granted entry to the hotel grounds. As I passed inside the large entrance doors I was greeted by two more male workers supervising the next level of standardized security. Next, I walked through a metal detector and used a conveyer belt inspector for my purse. After passing through this final level of security, I immediately headed toward the grand historic staircase that would lead me down to the Empress nightclub.

The majestic staircase was part of the original restored historic palace of Khedive Ismail that was built in 1869 and that existed before the site was transformed into a luxury hotel.[1] Khedive Ismail commissioned the Gezirah Palace to host the French emperor Napoleon III and his wife Empress Eugenie during the celebrations for the opening of the Suez Canal in 1869. The palace was designed by Carl von Diebitsch to resemble France's Palace of Versailles. In the 1880s the site was seized by Ismail's creditors and eventually leased to hotel companies. In 1919, the site was sold again to Syrian businessman Habib Lotfallah as a private residence. In 1952 it was nationalized (that is, forcefully taken) under Nasser and eventually returned to serving as a hotel venue. In the late 1970s the entire hotel was rebuilt. In 1983 the site had its grand reopening as the Cairo Marriott hotel, with President Mubarak presided over the reopening event.[2]

I spotted the nightclub's entrance and took a seat on a lounge couch outside the venue in the lobby area and waited for my companions for the evening to arrive. Meanwhile, I savored the views of the restored architecture, furniture, and décor reminiscent of the original palace. The nightclub was tucked away

Figure 2.1 The 6th of October bridge over the Nile River and the Semiramis Intercontinental Hotel at Dusk. Credit: agefotostock/Alamy Stock Photo

in a bottom section of the hotel amidst the historically restored part of the Marriott that used to be Khedive Ismail's royal palace. This historic Marriott site has absorbed class markers from its connection to the Khediviate and its identity as a past palace, and performances that take place in venues like this are considered to be the most "artistic" and elite of *raqs sharqi* work. Amidst the material and performance history, my thoughts also ruminated on the predicament of *raqs sharqi* within the unstable future of five-star hotels since the 2011 revolution and economic fallout. I sank into the velvety cushioned couch as my thoughts and memories swirled.

A Week Earlier . . .

As my Uber driver handed over his identification to the security guard at the InterContinental Semiramis hotel's entrance gate, I couldn't help but peer out the window. The other security guard had his sniffing guard dog encircle our vehicle while stopping us to inspect our vehicle's trunk. I missed my dog Tucker back home but was well aware this dog was on the job, making sure that there were no security threats from vehicles dropping off passengers. The Semiramis was another elite five-star hotel, particularly known as a hotspot for *khaleegy* guests. As it was the "Arab season" months of the sweltering summer, I expected the hotel to be crowded with Saudi Arabian families and solo male travelers alongside a smattering of wealthy businessmen and international tourists.

Arab season is known within the industry as the time during the summer months of vast *khaleegy* tourist vacationing. The Arab season is one of the greatest sources of income for regular *raqs sharqi* entertainment venues throughout Cairo. Arab tourists typically spend much more money on their vacations in Cairo, and stay for longer periods, than other nationalities.[3] In the critical years bracketing the revolution, the economic gains of the Arab season were threatened (from roughly 2008 up until 2016) when the holy month of Ramadan cut directly across the time frame of the tourist season, adding to the economic precarity of the *raqs sharqi* industry.[4] Notably, it was during the time of my fieldwork that the Arab season finally returned in full force to Cairo for the first time since the revolution, making this a rich time to investigate the local, intra-MENA, and global forces at work in the city.

The Semiramis was one of the first hotels to be built along the Nile by a Swiss hotelier in the early 1900s. Ever since, the hotel has remained a decadent spot for Egyptian and international high society. The original hotel was rebuilt in the same location in the 1970s as the InterContinental Semiramis hotel. It is now owned by the Egyptian Hotels Company and a group of Saudi investors.[5] Since its beginnings, the hotel has loomed large against the Nile with a commanding presence over the city. However, today the skyscraper hotel is just one of many studding the Nile. Its design, with neat square architecture and large glass windows, gestures more toward an air of simple modern elegance and architectural taste than the historic glamor of the Marriott's main entrance.

Entering hotels felt routine, going through the site-mediating procedure of paying for the Uber and then passing through the interior security metal detector while waiting for my purse to slowly make its way along the conveyer belt. The dual security checks at any elite hotel entrance always made me feel a bit as if I was entering an airport or even another country. Additionally, the glitz, glam, and comfortable amenities of these five-star hotels were far from my everyday life in an apartment with consistently unreliable hot water, air-conditioning, and elevator service. Dokki, where I rented my furnished apartment, was considered a relatively well-off area in Cairo. Still, it was a far cry from the overpowering citrusy scent of cleaning products, twinkling chandeliers, and expensive espressos found in the five-star hotels. It was this combination of elitism with the multi-layered security entrances to these sites that created a sense of separation from the everyday. Curiously, a thick wallet and a non-Egyptian passport could offer a sense of security and comfort in a country my government deemed throughout my fieldwork as "politically unstable." I also ask, what is the systematic valuation of which bodies matter? Compared to the often unsupervised and shoddy walk-through metal detectors of tourist boats, it was evident that tourist bodies increasingly mattered as their wallets thickened. At the same time, while tourists have been targeted by violent extremism in Egypt, the numbers highlight that Egyptians themselves are the primary bodies at risk, particularly minority and marginalized Egyptian bodies such as Egyptian Coptic Christians, or bodies that resist the state's authoritarian system such as protesting or dissenting bodies.[6] Thus, these elite protected sites within Cairo point locally and globally to hierarchies and strata of which bodies mattered. They also mark how protecting economic flows within a country desperate for U.S. and petrodollars, as opposed to local currency, becomes embedded within the exchange and circulation value of bodies.

I was still relatively zoned out and going through the motions of brushing my long hair out of my way to re-position my handbag on my shoulder as my heels clicked on the shiny tiled floor. My face squinched up, and my nostrils flared as the intense citrusy scent of cleaning products overwhelmed my senses. I felt a deep chill surge through my body, and I froze in my tracks like a startled deer caught in the blinding haze of headlights. I'd looked up to discover a dozen or more eyes deeply penetrating my own. An assortment of single or paired *khaleegy* men sat in the lounges and coffee shops by the lobby entrance, staring at me hungrily with cigarettes and empty cups of espresso in their hands. *Ah, right, gendered bodies are on the market in even more complex ways*, I thought. As an American working belly dancer, I'd had offers made to me several times in various Arab-American nightclubs from patrons assuming I was advertising sex work. However, to be so starkly caught off guard by the profuse intensity of glares sizing me up as if a purchasable and consumable *shawarma* was unsettling. I glanced at my cell phone; I was supposed to meet an Egyptian male friend for coffee before attending legendary star dancer Dina's *raqs sharqi* show in the hotel's Harun al Rashid nightclub. My friend's presence would undoubtedly dissipate my currently suspect position— alone in the hotel lobby area at such a late hour—but there was no word from him. I thought if I sat near the reception area, I'd be okay. Still, almost immediately, men started walking by or sitting a few feet away from me, muttering prices under their breath with discreet but purposeful eye contact.

Prostitution is illegal in Egypt but has been noted to be on the rise since the revolution and ensuing economic fallout.[7] Though it takes two to tango, only one body will pay the harsh legal penalties. Like most areas around the world, the criminalization of sex work unevenly falls upon the laboring body of the sex worker, who is predominantly female, as opposed to that of the purchaser.[8] (It is important to note that Egypt's legislation on sexual practices is a product of the country's secular law system and directly stems from codes imposed during colonial rule.) Again, the bodies that are privileged in these exchanges are wealthy and male; in the five-star hotels, this primarily means *khaleegy* and other non-Egyptian men. I found myself anxiously glancing at the police standing idly about the hotel's entrance. I wasn't looking for any trouble and the nightclub wasn't going to be open for at least another hour. Being a lone woman in the elite space put me on the alert. I found my left hand double-checking that I had my U.S. passport in my bag, unconsciously reassuring myself of the shielding my nationality may afford, a benefit many working women sharing the space with me would not be entitled

FIVE-STAR HOTELS 107

Figure 2.2 Entrance of Cairo Marriott Hotel in Zamalak. Credit: travelpixs/ Alamy Stock Photo

to. Simultaneously, my other hand pulled at the hem of my long dress, trying to better camouflage my curvy body into a shapeless lump. "We take a photo." A younger man sat beside me and began to pull out his phone for a selfie, "No, I do not want" I replied curtly. He stood up, and as he walked away turned around to make sure he had the final word—"Bitch."

There seemed to be a tension in five-star hotels, a kaleidoscope of hypocrisy and contradiction between appearances and actualities that demanded deeper dissection. The space and design of the hotel sites coordinated well enough with the price tags. The expensive lobby espressos and 1,000 pound-and-up minimum entrance fees for nightclub shows paralleled the sparkling clean chandeliers, suited wait staff, and squeaky-clean tiled floors with red-carpet staircases. However, it was what, why, and how various bodies moved within these elite spaces that marked their changing functions and contradictory collisions.

Five-star hotels, and the upper-class bodies that can afford them, circulate discourse about upper-class bodies and sites being more elite, family-friendly, "clean," and "artistic" (wherein such adjectives are referred to in opposition to the drunken, debaucheries, and sexual desires associated with more "entertainment"-based cabaret sites). Yet the traditionally *dishdasha*-dressed Saudi sheikh planted within the sparkling clean lobby nursing his espresso as he surveyed the scattering of numerous sex workers for his evening "holiday" served to chisel away at the elaborate displays made to maintain class and moral appearances. In other words, it revealed the hypocrisy of sites that cater to rich clientele who denigrate sites catering to poorer people, while at the same time enjoy access to poorer bodies and their labor.

Five-star hotels became a popular site for decadent five-star dancers—*fannaneen* (artists)—and extravagant *raqs sharqi* shows. These hotel shows particularly boomed after Sadat's opening-up of the economy. Yet their numbers and extravagances were already dissipating with the economic woes and increasing conservatism of the Mubarak years, grinding to a temporary halt with the 2011 revolution. Within Cairo dance circuits, as well as within the international belly dance community, an established performer at a five-star hotel in Cairo is understood to be the "cream of the crop" of elite stardom, the ultimate dream. As different established sites for *raqs sharqi* performances, such as cabarets, boats, and five-star hotels, became standardized within Cairo, a hierarchal categorization was constructed in the minds of dancers (and the general public alike) that relegated certain sites, and the bodies within them, as low versus high class.

Cabarets and similar entertainment hall venues were the original sites that housed *raqs sharqi*. From the early 1900s through to the Mubarak era there existed strata of cabarets considered elite and extravagant, often those visited by world leaders, celebrities, and dignitaries locally and internationally. These cabarets also hosted top *raqs sharqi* artists. However, particularly since the 1960–70s and the influx of *khaleegy* tourists and monied Libyans who began throwing money as tips (see Chapter 4), and the increasingly negative depiction of *raqs sharqi* nightclub dancers in the media, cabarets became stigmatized. This stigmatization was relational. Cabarets were morally stigmatized as sites of debauchery, sexual excitement, and alcohol.[9] However, as *raqs sharqi* became established in five-star hotels (popularized during the Sadat era), these hotels came to be seen as the highest caliber of *raqs sharqi* venue on the scale of low class versus artistic entertainment venues outside of the smattering of elite cabarets that still existed due to the elite bodies that circulated within them as performers and audiences.[10]

Additionally, the rubric for cleanliness, sexual promiscuity, morality, and "entertainment versus art," also grew as sites for dance were ranked higher up on the hierarchical scale. Though a hierarchy of status levels exists within each type of *raqs sharqi* site in Cairo, the emergence of *raqs sharqi* within five-star hotels came at a time when there already existed a stark split between popular class *awalim* and *raqs sharqi* "*fannaneen.*" *Awalim* were deliberately kept out of five-star hotel *raqs sharqi* shows, due to their popular class connotations. However, there were of course *awalim* performing in these hotels, just under the radar, and they were also dancing in the now well-defined *raqs sharqi* style, aesthetic, and costuming.

During Nasser's time came a split in the business systems used for dance performance bookings and operations. The popular classes and wedding circuits continued to operate largely in the traditional *awalim* style, with a female-led *usta* system and informal word of mouth or colloquial contracts.[11] On the other hand, with the opening of the economy toward the international market, newly owned and operated hotels and boats began utilizing the male impresario system, which remains dominant today. Nasser introduced many new regulations and laws to further regulate and monitor *raqs sharqi*. These new regulations alongside international business dealings made written contracts and bilingual and bicultural work procedures standard fare for conducting entertainment business in these newly popular sites, marginalizing the *awalim* system.

Nasser's increased licensing, regulation, and monitoring of *raqs sharqi* had dual objectives. First, *raqs sharqi* would continue to contribute to the economy, a main motive for regulation and policing throughout the dance's history. Secondly, these regulations also worked to steer the infamous image of the "dancer—ra2asa" further away from his conceptualization of Egypt as a nation, and more specifically, the ideal of Egyptian womanhood as a dutiful mother or daughter to the nation.[12]

Five-star hotel nightclubs for *raqs sharqi* were considered elite, extravagant, and by and for the well-to-do of Egyptian, intra-MENAHT, and international high society. This hierarchal dynamic also links to the "cosmopolitan" branding of international hotels as opposed to other more local (*baladi*) sites. As professional dance mentor and Cairo resident, Sara Farouk Ahmed stated in an interview at Eman's costume atelier:

> When people are spending their money, they want to see it. Five-star hotel shows they want to see a "show-show." They want to see costume changes, large extravagant orchestras, expensive dinners and drinks, and audiences used to come to see a star dancer with a good reputation. It was the specific star dancer that was the draw. It's not like a boat where you just want to see the Nile, *tanoura*, and any "belly dancing," no, in the past you go to a five-star hotel to see a specific dancer, like Fifi Abdo, Soheir Zaki, or Dina. As for the minimum charges, those were in place to keep certain people out. For the average Egyptian middle-class bank teller, a night out would cost you a good month's salary or more.[13]

Since the blossoming of five-star hotels in the Nasser era, business owners wanted to find more ways to keep hotel guests and wealthy locals spending within the hotels, rather than outside of them, and international variety dance shows and *raqs sharqi* performances proved to be a productive means of doing so. In hotels, you would have more upper-class, family, and mixed-gender audiences. At the same time, five-star hotel audiences are dominated by upper-class Egyptian and intra-MENA, particularly *khaleegy*, audiences with a smattering of international tourists (including the occasional table full of foreign belly dancers on vacation).

Raqs sharqi shows in five-star hotels are typically much longer than in other sites, often including three costume changes and a forty-five to an hour-and-a-half-long set that includes a three-part show. For dancers, they are the most lucratively paid site-specific gig. The show is largely under the artistic discretion of the dancer, more-so than any other established site of *raqs sharqi* within Cairo. However, the dancer chooses her music and dance selection based upon her audience. For example, perhaps the dancer will incorporate older classics with an older Egyptian audience, or a *khaleegy* or Iraqi number for mostly Arabian Gulf clientele. The show begins with a *mejance*, the standard entrance-piece often individually crafted by the dancer and her band. The dancer has her own regular band, and the band is often larger in hotel shows.

Following the *mejance,* the dancer often performs a couple of songs of her choosing, then changes costume for a second more folklore-tableau-inspired set such as *sa3idi*; the third part is totally up to the dancer. In decades past, the five-star hotel shows were packed with entertainment. Often multiple bands and popular singers came on between 10pm and 2am with the dancer and her show remaining one of the key highlights. Now, there is often just an opening band or singer, the dance show, and another singer and band to conclude the entertainment.

Even discernable within these generalized descriptions, there is an obvious cleavage between "back then," what was standard within five-star hotel shows when they were a more prosperous staple of *raqs sharqi* entertainment,

Figure 2.3 Fifi Abdou, famous Egyptian dancer at the Cairo Sheraton hotel. Credit: Christine Osbourne Pictures/Alamy Stock Photo

and the contemporary contexts of dancing within these sites since the 2011 revolution. Many hotels have only recently begun reopening their interior nightclubs and fancy restaurants for *raqs sharqi* shows after periods—ranging from months to years—of being closed since around the time of the revolution. Many hotels are not a far stroll from Tahrir Square, thus during the months following the 2011 revolution they were closed, and many boarded up to protect from vandalism and looting.

However, to understand the contemporary conditions in five-star hotels and among star Egyptian dancers, we need to step farther back once again. Extravagant hotel shows have dwindled since the economic decline of the Mubarak years. Multiple forces played a role in the state of *raqs sharqi* and star Egyptian dancers in five-star hotels. During the Mubarak era there was a flood of foreign *raqs sharqi* dancers competing on the professional Cairo market for hotel and boat venue dance jobs. Globalization, spurred on by cheaper air travel and the established immigration and subsequent cultural production of Middle Easterners across the globe, led to a deeper dissemination and popularization of belly dance that markedly circled back to Cairo during the 1980s and after. Foreign dancers, particularly from the United States, Europe, South America, and Russia, sought for work opportunities in Cairo, the heartland and cultural hub of belly dance locally and globally, for in-depth performing experience, money, and a rise to fame both transnationally and in their own home countries.[14]

Just as larger economic and cultural dynamics destabilized the long-held monopoly of Mohamed Ali Street entertainers in Sadat's time, the influx of foreigners without in situ knowledge of the Cairo dance business and culture led to a rift in the market for local Egyptian dancers. Tied into this factor, a greater number of male impresarios and businessmen also entered this growing market opportunity, hungry to seize upon the economic benefits of these new job opportunities. However, this wave of new food and beverage managers and impresarios predominantly comprised businessmen who often didn't have the connoisseur tastes of their predecessors when it came to *raqs sharqi* aesthetics and history. Many of the new foreign dancers worked under these new businessmen for less than their Egyptian counterparts and didn't have to reconcile the same cultural stigma and societal expectations.[15]

Further economic and religious conservatism was related to the state of hotels and star Egyptian dancers. Mubarak continued the failed economic liberalization policies of Sadat, and the gap between the rich and poor continued to grow as the middle class drastically disappeared. Allegations of corruption ran high, and alongside the vast economic disparities between the wealthy and the poor, further conservative Islamization grew. Although Egypt's aid in the Gulf War of 1991 granted the country major debt relief, it wasn't enough to stop the continued deterioration of government services and extreme poverty among the lower classes. Religious revivals and piety movements were common in this era, and by the 1990s had even spread to certain sectors of the upper classes as well as performance arts.[16] Many public entertainers and professional women retired and took on the veil during this time, and a new genre of pious entertainment was created. All these entwined factors placed a far heavier burden upon local Egyptians in navigating the *raqs sharqi* industry, factors that simultaneously paved a smoother route for non-Egyptians.

Changes in global fashion trends, the rise of DJs and recorded music technology, musical changes, dire economics, and increasing conservatism, along with the fallout of the Gulf War, resulted in a dearth of elite nightclub patrons and many hotel nightclubs shut their doors. All of these entangled circumstances affected the extravagant five-star hotel shows, making it no longer fashionable, nor economically feasible, to carry on in the tradition of hour-long shows with twenty-plus orchestras in decadent hotel nightclubs. Throughout the 1990s and early 2000s, many famous star Egyptian dancers and hotel clubs retired or shut their doors.

In relation to these changes to sites where *raqs sharqi* was regularly performed, as well as by whom, a popular discourse within the local and global dance community, and among everyday Egyptians, has emerged that bemoans that "*raqs sharqi* is dying." However, since President Sisi came to power in 2014 with claims to improve the downtrodden economy, as well as the return of full-swing Arab seasons to Cairo, locals and dancers alike have ruminated on the future of such elite sites of *raqs sharqi*. Many dancers and Egyptian businessmen in the industry are hopeful that five-star hotels will kick back into action.

Many believe that such hotels will be the last spaces to recover from the revolution and its economic fallout because of how costly the shows are. However, what I found is that *raqs sharqi* is not "dying" in Cairo, and I caution against the classist and orientalist politics embedded within such phrasing. Rather, I propose that the work of *raqs sharqi* is changing. In other words, not only is the site-specific professional work of *raqs sharqi* changing within contemporary Cairo, but also the political work the dance is doing to larger class and nationalist politics.

Furthermore, that intense citrusy-cleaning product smell, or rather what it represents, theoretically permeates this chapter just as it overwhelmed and permeated my senses within extravagant hotel lobbies, restrooms, and elevators. Ostensibly, it is a difficult and pressing labor to keep up appearances when they contradict lived actualities. In other words, this chapter purposefully fluctuates between the ideological surface-level appearances such elite site-specific structures work to construct, and the actual bodily labor—what I refer to as the "actualities" of various bodies moving within and amidst such larger situating structures. This fluctuation aims to capture a rich and corporeal level of meaning-making and knowledge.

This is also accomplished at a structural writing scale. This chapter's case study follows Amina, a working-class cabaret dancer from Alexandria who has recently arrived in Cairo to try to become a more established and economically successful working dancer.[17] While the Marriott hotel's Empress nightclub has been graced with famous greats like Nagwa Fouad and Fifi Abdou, it has scarcely operated since the revolution, is currently only open one night a week. Even this one night is for a mere handful of tables sprinkled throughout the large nightclub. Thus, this case study reflects the contemporary tension and uncertain future of *raqs sharqi* within five-star hotels, where both Amina and the Marriott are struggling to survive and rebuild. Thus, while popular discourse circulates the "dying legacy" of *raqs sharqi* on a surface level; is there more to the physical actualities than meets the eye? As my nostrils flared from inhaling another overwhelming explosion of citrusy cleaning product from a long-gone housekeeping worker, my body, and this chapter's argument, sensitively listening across multiple modes, assured me: *yes*.

As my gut productively tangled in response to the sensory information from the glistening sheen of golden framed mirrors, the décor and the powerful lemony-fresh scents, it would tangle again, months later and more than an ocean away from these sites, with tense contradiction as I sat down to type up this chapter. Sure, these words being read are fixed now, organized, and tidy. But what if I scrub away at their neat and clean exterior to highlight my own experience as I write them, try to make visible both my own labor's limitations and enablement? My objective is to choreograph the writing based on the site-specific *raqs sharqi*'s form and structure. As I have listed, this includes a deep mining focused on individual dancers as the draw to these sites. I planned on my case study focusing on the individual dancer's life story, including a full-length interview paired with rich choreographic analysis. Most of my interviews were long and drawn-out sit-down affairs, and I have hours' worth of interviews with a handful of other hotel dancers in Cairo. There were other hotel shows I was able to visit much more frequently than the Empress nightclub's because they didn't have as staggering high of a minimum charge.

But in my gut, I was still drawn to write about Amina. Despite not being able to secure an interview with her and having more resources and access to other hotel sites and dancers because of the cheaper costs, my raw field notes exploded with insight, excitement, and fine details when I discussed encounters and shows with Amina at the Marriott. I felt torn. It didn't initially appear to mesh with the choreography of writing I envisioned as best suited to this chapter to end up writing about the only hotel dancer I was not able to secure an interview with. *But the dancer is the draw. You go to that space largely because you are drawn to her, what she has to offer, and say with her dance.* My gut was certainly drawn to Amina, and every time I tried to find a different angle to present other hotel sites and dancers, I just kept being pulled back to her.

I reflected on my failure to secure the interview, and in doing so, came to realize that my own bodily labor (in the many "failed" processes of trying to get the interview as well as continued site access) was directly tied into the danced discourse I learned from Amina. Trying to hide my own discouraging labor in the ethnographic process by going against the draw in my gut would be to provide a polished product that was more superficial, at the expense of focusing on the messier and more uncertain actualities of my own ethnographic experiences. I failed to secure the sit-down interview I so desired because I simply didn't have the purchasing power that was essential to entering these sites, not just as an audience member, but also as a researcher.

My limitations in doing this site-specific research were attuned to the contemporary contours of *raqs sharqi* within five-star hotels, where the greater the net worth, the greater the accessibility. After all, those steep price tags and minimum charges are designed to keep certain bodies out. These barriers are further enforced by the multi-layered male management business system that oversees elite venues and star dancers. As with Hollywood celebrities, there are multiple walls one must go through before being able to speak directly with the artist. At these sites those barriers were predominantly male staff and management working for either the dancer or the hotel venue. Like the heavier security upon entering these sites, these barrier systems, physical and corporeal, are set up not only to protect and ensure the safety of certain bodies but also to ensure their paid-for privileged privacy.

My access to these particular sites and dancers was intricately dependent upon not only my own intersectional classed, gendered, nationalist, and racialized positionality. My access was also interwoven within the entanglements of how my positionality tied into those of my research collaborators and other bodies within the sites. Sometimes the ways our identities synced together were enabling, and at other times hindering, but the interlinking relationalities were the primary key to unlocking both limiting and enabling power dynamics. To elaborate: unlike boat cruises, five-star hotels were sites I did not feel comfortable attending alone. As my entrance into the site demonstrates, my place there is read as suspect and leads to unwanted attention. Furthermore, I'm granted more authority and respectability if I follow the cultural codes for gendered bodies in these sites, which is helpful when trying to break through the multiple layers of the male management system.

However, most of my research collaborators in Cairo were lower middle-class Cairene men. These collaborators couldn't afford to come with me to these sites, and the late hours didn't mesh with their often twelve-plus hour workdays in the summer heat. I couldn't afford to cover both of our entrance fees to these sites, and more often, my male companions weren't comfortable letting me do so as a woman in an elite site in which they already felt out of place.[18] Thus, I found myself waiting outside nightclubs for someone, such as the dancer's male manager or male technical assistant to arrive to let me in without having to pay. In exchange for this service, they often tried to hold my hand or link arms as we entered together. If that were subtly declined, they would at least jokingly flirt with me, my youthful, white-skinned foreign body adding to their social capital and appearances of robust heterosexual masculinity.

In the end, Amina remained the dancer I was drawn to, and just as a captivated audience member would follow this resonance into the dancer's corresponding hotel show, I followed my gut to write about Amina despite my research restraints. Furthermore, as I'll come to argue, the way our gendered bodies were granted mobility/lack thereof in these sites aligns with the contradictory collisions of appearances versus actualities within contemporary five-star hotel *raqs sharqi* sites.

Case Study: Amina at the Marriott Hotel's Empress Nightclub

"Hey! Hope you haven't been waiting long, I got stuck in a bunch of traffic." I was stirred from my ponderings on the lounge couch just outside of the Marriott's Empress nightclub as Krystal plopped down beside me. Krystal was one of many foreign professional belly dancers currently working within Cairo, and she had previously connected me with the manager Yasser, who organized the singers and dancers at the Marriott during this time. Krystal, originally from the United States like myself, had worked a number of five-star hotel contracts in the Gulf area before trying her luck in Cairo.[19] She felt the dance scene might be recovering from the revolution enough for her to make her name here before eventually moving on to the international festival teaching circuit. The normal minimum charge for the nightclub at this time was just under 100 U.S. dollars, so the only way I was gaining access to this location was through connections. We were waiting for the manager to arrive and physically seat us in the venue in order to bypass the minimum charge.

While we waited for Yasser to arrive, Krystal gave me the scoop on the evening's entertainment. "In five-star hotels, especially ones with a history of reputable dancers like this, you must make a big show. It needs to be dynamic and artistic. You need to hire a big band and hold the audience's attention for at least forty-five minutes. You can expect to see three costume changes and a well-rounded range of dance genre styles and music." She paused and then rebutted, "Well, I mean, that's how it's supposed to be. The dancer here currently is Amina from Alexandria. She's actually from the cabarets. The thing is, now all the nice venues are just trying to get back on their feet and lots of licenses for entertainment have lapsed and things, so it's just easier for venues to hire Egyptian dancers instead of foreign because they don't require the expensive paperwork and contracts that we're required to have."[20] Before I could press Krystal further on her nationalist and classist conflation between Egyptian dancers and cabarets and foreign dancers and "nice" five-star venues, Yasser arrived.

Yasser was a stout Egyptian man in his forties, and he managed the entertainment, including singers and dancers, in a few venues throughout Cairo. He beamed brightly as he approached Krystal. He leaned over and kissed her upon both cheeks, making sure to linger a bit longer with each kiss than would be expected, then eventually turned and offered me a light handshake. Rather than take the wide-open end of the couch, he gestured for us to split so he could sit between us in the middle, thus flanking himself with the prestige of two white-skinned foreign women on either side of him. He made a flirty joke about me in Arabic to Krystal, grabbing my hand and holding it against his chest. I awkwardly pulled away and wondered if he was aware that I could understand him. Either way, I pretended not to.

He then pulled out his cell phone and twisted toward Krystal as he showed her photos of the working Cairo dancers, foreign and Egyptian, alongside detailed commentary that did not focus on their dancing abilities, but rather on their makeup, bodily attractiveness, and costuming. He came across a photo of Krystal wearing a thousand U.S.-dollar designer costume, zoomed in on her well-endowed chest, and stated how beautiful "they" were, and that audiences thought they were natural. Krystal giggled and pumped her fist victoriously in the air, "That's what happens when you get 'em done in the USA!" she cheered. Yasser nodded in approval, and he scrolled to a picture of Amina. Krystal suggested that her large round butt must be surgically enhanced in some way, that it couldn't be real. Yasser wasn't sure but was definitely intrigued at the suggestion.

As if by clockwork, we looked up to the sound of the rolling wheels of a dancer's gig suitcase as the technical assistant Abdu, working under Yasser, arrived escorting Amina. Amina was wearing a blouse and a very tight-fitting pencil skirt. I think all three of us were immediately drawn to her extremely full butt; I even found myself siding with Krystal that it was likely enhanced somehow. As mentioned, bodily enhancements, surgical or otherwise, were almost a work requirement to be a professional belly dancer, particularly in cities such as Cairo where *raqs sharqi* is taken as such a serious professional industry. Yasser rose to greet Amina and explained that I was writing a book on dance and that we should do an interview together after her show sometime. She politely nodded in response as they both turned to enter the nightclub.

Yasser leaned in, and as they walked and exchanged a few whispers, suddenly Krystal and I saw him reach down and intensely squeeze a large handful of Amina's butt cheek. She spun around to us, eyes wide in shock. I think I must have returned the same wide-eyed expression back to her. She paused, just for the briefest moment, then threw her head back and burst into laughter. She then quickly grabbed her suitcase and skirted into the club. Yasser turned to us as well. "What? I asked her if it was real, and she was joking with me asking if I wanted to try it, so I tried!" He violated her during what was supposed to be a joke. Still, Amina's conclusive cackle showed her negotiation of uneven power dynamics in the encounter, and in a way that let her move as quickly as possible into the space where she could continue with her prerogative for the night, her lucrative paid work.

Suddenly, Yasser puffed up his chest, lifted his chin slightly, and offered his arm to Krystal. It appeared that he was transforming his performance into that of the "gentleman" to walk her white upper-class foreign body into the site. As for me, I sluggishly trailed behind them with my head down, while Amina was skilled in thinking on her feet to deal with the situation in a manner that let her efficiently attend to her own objectives within the site; I as *agnabiyya*-ethnographer was not so clever. *Abyud* (white) . . . *ashta* (cream) . . . as I step into the nightclub, all the incessant yet unsolicited compliments men in the streets would call out to my "beautiful" white-skinned body seemed to weigh down my steps with a heavy and sticky molasses-like consistency. This muck slowed my dragging pace even further. Despite the feeling of wading through a thick muck, it was this exact racially gendered component that was paving the way for my body to enter the site with such ease despite my lack of financial resources.

After Yasser sexually harassed Amina, both Amina and Yasser immediately turned, not to one another, but to the two white U.S. spectating bodies in the lobby, highlighting how the interaction was an exercise in power that our two white U.S. bodies were not only complicit in but aided in creating the conditions of possibility for. Our U.S. whiteness, and all the historical and contemporary muck it carried into the encounter, placed limits on the wiggle room Amina had in humorously attempting to deflate and avoid bodily violation while still capitalizing upon her sexual appeal in a male-dominated industry. At the same time, our spectating bodies granted more entitlement and a sense of virile masculinity to Yasser. Altogether, our choreographic entrances into the site highlighted just how heavy and deeply the quagmire of mobility, access, and corporeality was tied to gender, race, class, nationalist, and sexuality politics.

Crossing into the interior of the Marriott's Empress nightclub, I was taken aback by the emptiness of the space. The large room had a dance floor and stage as its primary highlight, placed directly in the middle of the room as the focal point of the venue. Circling up and around the dance floor was tiered raised seating. Often this seating style was even further class-divided like a concert, with front-row seats costing more than those way up in the back. White floral-clothed tables set to seat four or more people were organized throughout the room while mini chandeliers dripping with glistening lights spread across the high ceiling. Multiple waiters in suits and bow ties stood about idly, the decadent space contrasting with the mere scattering of bodies that tried to take up space within it. Only a scant handful of tables spread throughout the nightclub had patrons, mostly wealthy men from the Arabian Gulf, Levant, and Egypt, with elaborate food dishes and expensive alcohol piled high in front of them.

The negligible number of bodies within the extravagant space gestured toward the post-revolution state of economic decline within these sites as well as the haunting of their once robust glamorous past. Amusingly, a white European couple squabbled for their bill and the rest of their meal to go; apparently, they had an early morning awaiting them to view some of Egypt's famous Pharaonic sites, or perhaps it was the pyramids. Regardless, they complained loudly about the high bill and the entertainment not getting started until after midnight as they took their leave. They missed the entire show, as their focus was elsewhere, including a unique lens on Cairo. The manager dismissed them apathetically; the show wasn't centered around them anyway. A male and female singer each switched places throughout the night. When we arrived, Gigi was belting out tunes from across the MENA with a strong focus on Egypt, the Levant, and Arabian Gulf. After a few more tunes, Gigi took her leave, and the dancer's band started setting up their instruments behind the curtain on the raised stage just past the large circular dance floor.

Suddenly the curtains drew open, and we were greeted with a band with about a dozen musicians playing, including two keyboard players, an accordionist, violinist, and several drummers. They began playing the dramatic opening notes of a classical *mejance* for Amina to make her entrance. Four youthful *funun al sha3biyya* came out in shiny suits with sparkling gold vests and bow ties. Though the music was a pulsating *malfuf* rhythm with dramatic flair, the men appeared to perform pivot spins only half-heartedly alongside large sweeping arm flourishes. Their lack of enthusiasm and energy worked to chisel away from the otherwise building energy of the musicians laboring behind them. Unfortunately, this flattened atmosphere is what Amina found herself making her grand entrance into. She came out in a bright yellow bra and skirt costume, the hips and bra cups adorned in three-dimensional flowers, with her yellow booty shorts showing beneath her transparent yellow chiffon skirt. She had a beautifully soft and curvy body with olive skin and long thick black hair. Her bodily charms added a lot to her physical appeal despite the cheaper quality of her costuming. There were no crystals, elaborate beading, or stones to catch and sparkle in the dazzling stage lights, all attributes that would raise the cost of the costume.

She held up large golden lamé wings of Isis, with which she then spun onto the stage. The wings length and golden sheen add to a dancer's sense of stage presence for their initial *mejance*. The *funun al sha3biyya* framed the four corners of the circular stage as Amina spun, sashayed, and performed hip drops center-stage. The golden wings extend the dancer's natural arm and body lines, but due to the framing of the *funun al sha3biyya*, rather than grant her a "larger than life" presence, they served to shrink her on stage. Several times I noticed Amina pull her arms inwards to a chicken-wing-like position to avoid whacking the men as she spun and maneuvered about the stage. Likewise, the *funun al sha3biyya* performed uncomfortably around the winged dancer, often hesitating between step-together-steps and arm flourishes to make sure an extended wing wouldn't whack them. The hesitations, power posture shrinking, and lack of synchronicity between the male dancers and Amina highlighted the scant economic and resource realities within contemporary Cairo. Unlike Farah Nasri and her *funun al sha3biyya* discussed in Chapter 1, there was not a steady and reliable enough flow of work for Amina and the *funun al sha3biyya* to be able to afford investing in rehearsals together. Likewise, due to the absence of beaming smiles full of pride and joy found on Farah's *funun al sha3biyya*, it was likely that these male dancers were there primarily to pick up extra cash for night work, rather than because of a more invested dedication to creating art with a *raqs sharqi* dancer.

Here, the *funun al sha3biyya* were contracted not by the dancer herself, making her their employer, but rather through the venue. Therefore, Amina lacked the purchasing power to claim greater authority and respect from the men on stage. Instead, uneven gender and sexuality power struggles became center-staged in their professional relationships. As an example, though all of the dancers were stigmatized for taking up dance as a profession, particularly in a nightclub, the golden bow-tied suits of the men versus the revealing golden booty shorts of Amina highlighted a greater suspect stigma through sexualization of Amina's female body.

This uneven stigmatization led the *funun al sha3biyya* to challenge Amina's occupation of the space as the dominant authority figure during the show. This challenging was made evident again when Amina tossed the wings aside and began to circle the perimeter of her stage with a series of quick pivot spins. One *funun al sha3biyya* was in her directional path, and she had to gesturally wave him out of the way before crashing into him. He obliged, but not without hesitation and a dirty sneer. *Funun al sha3biyya* were originally incorporated into large five-star hotel *raqs sharqi* productions to create a grand spectacle and supposedly more "dignified" and de-sexualized context for the solo dancer. However, in this case, the lack of a sustainable and sound economic foundation with the female dancer at the helm resulted in greater power hurdles and labor for the solo female dancer to negotiate.

Upon Amina's cue, the *funun al sha3biyya* took their exit. They stood with erect posture, lifted and posed toward Amina with strong L-shaped arms, and then quickly turned and exited the stage to allow her to finish her *mejance* solo while they changed into their next costumes for her folkloric tableau. I was relieved to see the male dancers take their leave. Their presence, though ideally meant to enhance Amina's stage presence, had the opposite effect of diluting her stage power. I was frustrated with the male dancers, and how they knew they could get away with giving such a lackluster performance because it was ultimately Amina's show. In the end, Amina would bear the weight of having to crank up her own charisma, technique, and power to make up for their watered-down dancing. Although the show was created by a dozen bodies, from Amina to the *funun al sha3biyya*, manager, technician, and musicians, it was Amina's responsibility to carry the show. The *funun al sha3biyya* were getting paid poorly but knew they would get paid despite their bare minimum quality and effort, in doing so inadvertently dumping excess labor, expectation, and responsibility on Amina, who did not have as secure a job position within the nightclub.

The professional *raqs sharqi* industry is set up to centralize the dancer; this can hold great power and potential for her. On the other hand, it can vilify her and hold her accountable for any number of scenarios that are largely out of her hands. Furthermore, from displeased sneers to the ways the male dancers didn't allow Amina to take up her stage space fully, the framing men not only placed undue labor burdens on Amina, but they also reinforced their own sense of heteronormative masculine power. They did this through micro-level corporeal aggressions aimed at challenging the established status quo of gendered bodies on stage. For whatever minuscule and momentary sense of entitlement this offered the *funun al sha3biyya*, on a larger scale of revamping the Empress's nightclub shows in the long run, this wasn't a sustainable form of cultivating gendered relationships.

After the men left, Amina seemed to relax more into her signature technique and style. She performed most of her technique with a wide-legged stance, additionally apparent due to the transparency of her chiffon skirt.

She performed most movements flat-footed, only occasionally going up onto relevé for a few spins from her introductory *mejance*. She performed juicy hip swivels center-stage while her hands gently slid down and caressed the sides of her body. Then she began to walk toward the all-male audience seated around the stage's perimeter. She walked just past the edge of the wooden flooring demarcating the stage, stopping to perform full-body undulations, hip figure-eights, and hip drops while intimately standing just a few feet away from the seated patrons. The men would wave their hands to the music or offer words of beauty to Amina as she directly engaged with them. It seemed Krystal was also able to focus more on Amina's show after the distracting *funun al sha3biyya* had left. She leaned over toward me to offer a critique of Amina's costuming and technique. "I just don't understand why she always wears these see-through skirt costumes; it makes her cabaret stance all the more obvious when she could at least hide it. She should wear skirts that aren't see-through and don't have slits."

A wider-legged stance is one of the first "mistakes" belly dancers worldwide are corrected upon in class and workshop settings, instead being told to keep their feet and legs close together. Globally, this is taught to add the esteemed mark of a "trained" and "correct" technique to practitioners. Teachers often state that a wide-legged stance doesn't look as modest, or simply looks more vulgar, or "not classy." In contemporary Cairo contexts of professional *raqs sharqi*, as noted here, this wider-legged stance signifies a working-class cabaret dancer. Here, too, it signifies being "untrained" in reference to having gone professional directly from a social *baladi* foundation, without training either by a *raqs sharqi* choreographer, one of the folkloric troupes, or through other techniques such as ballet. However, all of these critiques of wide-stance technique have roots derived from when *raqs sharqi* split into a staged professional performance form from the popular *awalim* dancing. One of the hallmarks setting apart this split in professionals was if the dancer's legs were close together (*raqs sharqi*) or wider (*awalim*).

Thus, the distance between a dancer's legs came to embody classist connotations that also became conflated with sexual modesty or impropriety, wherein the wider the stance the lesser the sexual modesty and "class."[21] Krystal's comment that Amina could easily hide this "cabaret stance" further elucidates how certain bodies are policed and marginalized according to economic class within sites of *raqs sharqi*, particularly five-star hotels. Her words also highlight how these borders are not fine lines that have been, and especially during hard economic times continue to be blurred by the bodies that cunningly and courageously cross them.

Amina continued, performing hip drops and large loose hip shimmies. However, within moments it became clear that her signature 'go-to' moves included the wide variety of robust chest articulations, from rapid vertically oriented chest circles, loose shimmies (with lots of jiggly cleavage reverberation), and chest pops and bounces. Her execution of chest movement vocabulary was particularly impressive, as she confidently wielded a wide range of motion in her chest and sharply caught the percussive accents in the music with powerful punctuation. At the same time, her emphasis of this chest movement vocabulary was more reminiscent of the popular MTV-style *sha3bi* music video clips proliferating across YouTube and television screens across Cairo, more so than the technical aficionados of *raqs sharqi* expect in a five-star hotel show. In an interview, Yasmina, a seasoned professional dancer who is now retired and running a bed and breakfast in Cairo, elaborated: "people are telling me that the dancers getting hired now are the more 'out in your face' type dancers. They are not hiring the gentle relaxed Egyptian dance style from before, it's highly sexualized nowadays, and that seems to me to be partly a result of also the video clips, it's not about dancing as much as just eye candy."[22]

Certainly, Amina's performance was very robust and directly "in your face" sexy. There was no subtle, delicate, or playfully shy *dalla3* in her show. In MENA contexts of *raqs sharqi*, the mutually exchanged performer-audience corporeal interaction is a key circulation that creates the atmosphere of *ihsas* (feeling) and togetherness. However, it was notable how much of this exchange Amina elicited through such immediate and direct personalized attention to the male spectators at the borders of her stage, as opposed to commanding this from center stage through more subtle movement and interaction.

However, Amina's signature move, and one I mostly saw performed in cabarets and disco-clubs elsewhere, was to stand with her feet wider than hip-width apart, backside directly facing her audience, then to fully bend over and vivaciously shake her well-endowed derrière. The extensive emphasis Amina put on this technique registered a specific set of connotations across audiences. Matching her costuming, Amina's dancing was transparent. She was sexy, directly engaging, and not partial to hiding the roots of where she came from to make her taking up of this elite space more palatable to traditional upper-class sensibilities and "golden era" nostalgia. The scattering of alcohol-drinking male patrons from throughout the MENA enjoying her show with attentive eyes didn't seem to mind, either.

Though historically, tipping within five-star hotels was strictly forbidden, in order to differentiate these sites as hierarchically "better" than cabarets, during the time of my fieldwork it was quite rampant, though still stigmatized. An older man from Saudi Arabia, sitting with three other colleagues, took a few hundred-pound notes out from his wallet and extended them out toward the stage, gently waving the bills to the melody of the music. The male singer who was accompanying Amina lifted his eyebrows toward the client and began to stroll over to him to accept the tip. The Gulf man shook his head as the male Egyptian singer approached, instead tilting his head toward the dancer. The singer looked disgruntled for a moment then turned to face the other patrons as Amina caught the eye of the client and began to slowly walk over to him, gently swaying her hips in a figure-eight pattern. She held his gaze as she took her time to cross the stage. Her slow pace, matched with the continued eye contact, worked in her favor; she'd only crossed halfway when the man began to dig back into his wallet to take out another hundred-pound note.

Notably, a similar sneer to the one I'd observed earlier from one of the *funun al sha3biyya* crossed the singer's face as he side-eyed Amina's interaction with the tipping client. Amina's ability to solicit increased economic capital from the client under these conditions is impressive. Typically, the singer would wave the dancer over, and they both would work together to give personalized attention to the tipping client to make him more willing to dig deeper into his wallet. However, in this case, the singer literally turned his back on the opportunity. This negligence created an even more difficult environment for Amina to be lucratively successful within, a feat she was able to surmount independently even from across the stage.

Amina approached the table of Gulf men. Standing barely a foot in front of the man holding out the notes, she gently took the bills from his hand with her own. She then continued to hold his gaze as she lightly half-tucked the tip into her left bra cup. She shimmied her chest loosely, the exposed half of the notes flapping in a catered display of personalized attention to the tipper. His table chuckled and clapped in approval. Then Amina removed the notes from her bra and walked over to Abdu, the technical assistant standing at the perimeter of the stage. She handed him the notes, and he eagerly accepted them, then jogged over to our table to graciously hand them over to their manager Yasser with a huge grin. Yasser stoically took the tip and then counted it, twice, before pocketing it.

Yasser didn't seem disturbed or worried by the blatant accepting of tips in a five-star hotel setting. From my observations, this was quite a common occurrence at this particular time, but I couldn't put my finger on his indifferent body language. Amina continued to dance around the perimeter of the stage, giving very intimate eye contact and robust chest articulation to the men flanking the stage's border. Yasser shifted toward me, "They are supposed to give me all the tipping when they work, but I never see her make this much tipping when I'm not around. What this tells me is that she's sneaky, she keeps the tips for herself and maybe gives Abdu a share to stay quiet if I'm not here to supervise. For sure, I know they do this."[23] I was stunned by his calculation. That he distrusted Abdu and Amina in their work for one, but more so for how the blame and responsibility were, once again, dumped onto Amina's laboring body with such disapproval and disdain.

As a practitioner, I was well aware of the plethora of tactics possible to hide the full amount of tips from a singer, DJ, or venue owner that may want to share in the spoils. For example, Amina could have plunged one or two of those notes deep inside her bra cup where it would solely be hers, rather than spread and dangle them out for all to plainly see. However, I also wouldn't be surprised, or condemnatory, if she, or she and Abdu, did engage in this practice, considering the tips are only exchanged and circulated due to her singular labor. Further, as the rejection of the singer showed, this tipping was solely meant for the dancer. Despite which bodies engage in the most physical and demanding labor, it is predominantly male managers who take the biggest cuts of the total income from the dancer. Many dancers I interviewed weren't aware of what the total price was for the jobs they were working.

I was taken aback by how, despite the dancer's clever performance in sultrily accumulating capital within an environment of scarcity while simultaneously performing propriety under suspect surveillance, she was still ultimately disparaged, by both singer and manager. In other words, Amina was incredibly honest and straightforward in the tipping interaction. She could have plunged the bills into the hidden depths of her costuming or kept them clumped in her hand, but instead, she chose to fully spread out and display the full amount for all to see. This display worked both to increase the sexually stimulated pleasure of the tipping client and give him an inflated sense of importance due to his capital, while at the same time also gave an open and public display of the transaction under multiple policing gazes. From where I sat, she seemed to be doing everything strikingly right in an incredibly improvisational moment. However, the male singer's sneer highlighted his disapproval of her gendered and sexualized performance taking the spotlight over his own singing labor, despite the fact that the dancer is the draw for this type of shows, and singers are more replaceable (outside of celebrity singers.)

In the end, Amina's overt five-star hotel performance of a straightforwardly sexy and desirable dancing body, coupled with her successful tipping exchange, still fell short of overriding her stigmatized and suspect position as a working-class Egyptian cabaret dancer. The combination of her class, nationality, and cabaret work origins worked to overshadow the actuality of her laboring body in an air of suspicion, greed, and distrust. It was a notable contradiction that, despite working in a five-star hotel, her body remained marked as "working class" and "cabaret." Furthermore, that her working-class "cabaret" body was more heavily policed within the elite space, despite the fact that her class-border crossing was the principal reason that capital was being exchanged and accumulated within the Empress.

Thoughts whirled within my head. How would Amina's career, this five-star hotel nightclub, and *raqs sharqi* within five-star hotels end up? I was withdrawing into my own thoughts when I abruptly snapped back into the performance. Amina had finished her *meleya luff eskandarani* (Alexandrian character dance) tableau number with her *funun al sha3biyya*, in which she had been monotonously teasingly shimmying and undulating in front of one backup male dancer after another. Again: a repeated and blatant outward display of heterosexual sexual appeal between her body and the male dancers.[24] In the 1960s the Reda Troupe used the *melaya*, a long black sheet-like outdoor modesty cloth for women, as a prop to accentuate the character of the flirtacious and teasing Alexandrian woman. Typically, she starts the dance more fully covered and then teasingly and playfully unwraps the *melaya* as the dance commences, eventually tying it around her hips as a dancing scarf. While this tableau is extremely popular for *raqs sharqi* dancers throughout Cairo, it could also be used to highlight Amina's own roots and regional background from Alexandria, as I observed she always utilized this number in her show.

Amina then surprised me by hopping up and sitting upon the edge of the musicians' raised stage at the back of the central dance floor. She crossed her ankles and took a *mandeel* (tissue) packet from one of the drummers and used it to take her time dabbing away at her sweaty brow, cheeks, and chest.

She fiddled with her hair a bit and gently rocked her legs forward and back, leaning back onto one arm in a relaxed posture.

Amina was taking an on-stage break, the length of which created a sense of suspense and curiosity. What would happen next? It reminded me of those moments in high school when the class would start to get out of hand, becoming a bit too unruly and rambunctious. Rather than yell and demand her authority, our teacher would simply sit back in an unpredictable and gripping silence. Amina chatted casually with the singer and a few of the musicians, and after another moment, slowly rose, shook out her hair, and then casually walked to the center of the stage. Still holding the *mandeel* in her left hand, Amina pliéd as she simultaneously rolled her left hip down, then slowly circled her left hip up. She likewise raised her arms powerfully above her head as the deep reedy bellow of the accordion filled the room. She and the accordion breathed in unison. As Amina inhaled deeply, lifting her arms, and her gaze, overhead toward the ceiling, the accordion's bellows expanded with her.

At the apex of the movement, they both paused. Amina closed her eyes with her sweat-stained *mandeel* still held high, and after a moment of lingering stillness, they (Amina and the accordionist) exhaled in harmony. Amina exhaled while slowly and purposefully bringing her arms down as her head gently fell back, and her belly relaxed, as she again pliéd and sunk her full body weight deep into her hips and straight down through her legs into the ground.

I felt chills on my arms. The entire atmosphere was somehow caught up within the stillness of the performers. As both Amina and the accordion's collapsing bellows exhaled and sank deep down into their cores, the audience, including myself, were completely drawn in. The men put down their glasses and forks, abandoning their hot entrees. Their only motion was taking long draws from their cigarettes as their eyes remained fixated on Amina. Amina was closing out her show with a *baladi* progression, a structured form of musical improvisation often between a *tabla* (drum) player, accordionist, and dancer, which highlights the deep *baladi*-rooted power, pride, and femininity of the dancer.

A *baladi* progression is also known as a *taqseem baladi*, and there are specific versions gendered male (*tet*) and female (*awadi*), both of which consist of a number of distinct sections following a traditional yet loose improvised structure based on the dancer and musicians' feelings and skills. Amina always closed her shows out with *baladi awadi*. *Baladi* means "of the country,"

Figure 2.4 Accordion player in a Cairo *raqs sharqi* band. Credit: Tracey Gibbs www.traceygibbs.co.uk

and connotates things "*aseel*," authentic, and honorably country-rooted and non-tainted by Western *afrangi* influence. It denotes those *ibn* and *binat al balad*, sons and daughters of the country, the "real Egyptians," with positive connotations of being good, honest, clever, street-knowledgeable and of high integrity. While *baladi* progressions developed in the countryside areas outside of urban Cairo, the tradition moved into the urban center with working and lower middle-class *baladi* families that migrated to Cairo for better work opportunities while still maintaining pride and traditions from their countryside roots.[25] Amina and several other Egyptian dancers related to me how much they cherish *baladi* progressions; they feel they have the greatest freedom during this part of their shows.

Amina began moving, the accordionist following her lead, with buttery smoothness. Her feet were planted deep into the earth, and she dug deep into the ground through the balls of her feet to then slowly transfer that power to swivel her hips like syrup, one after the other, in rich circles and loops, moving throughout with the consistency of honey. She held her hair up above her head with both hands as she looked down toward her heavy hip work, her ribcage gently rising and falling. She was taking her time to breathe and relax as her hips slowly melted into downward figure-eights. Amina's hip work was like the trickling of honey, slow and thick, with the subtlest dribble adding the perfect taste of lingering sweetness to any cocktail. The lead drummer began kicking in with the call and response percussion accents. Amina embodied and drove the percussion with spot-on punctuated hip and lower belly accents. She used the accordion's melody to accumulate her energy, such as pulling her left hip up into her rib cage, then holding, pausing with engaged muscles as she held the worked-up energy, before relaxedly plopping the hip down to catch the drummer's accent.

It was this sustained stillness before the powerful accents that created a palpable sense of stage presence and power. The men at the perimeters of the stage responded with encouraging utterances of "*aiwa*" and "aaah!" No longer were they using their physical gestures and verbal cues to beckon the dancer over to them and their wallets. Rather, they were now thoroughly pulled into her hurricane of power. The accumulation of authoritative presence Amina was circulating throughout the space, with the collaborative aid of the musicians behind her, overrode any other directional flows. The centralized power of the dancer was further enforced by her centrally planted, unwavering, and spotlighted position on stage. The *baladi* progression calls for a more stationary performance. Amina's choice to perform a *baladi* as the finale to her show created a powerful spiraling effect. She started her show circling the peripheries of the stage, giving and receiving attention through explicit interaction that crossed over the circular stage border. Now, to conclude her show and make her final statement, she stood as the eye of the storm, the stillness strengthened by the whirlwind of struggle previously all around her.

The male musicians behind her were also given greater spotlight during this more intimate, improvisational, and personalized *baladi* progression. The accordionist and drummers became more animated, smiling, joyful, and energized as they all creatively and collaboratively work together in a synchronized and mutually respectful performance flow that created space to honor each artist's talents. Though directed by the dancer, this collaborative flow was founded in a musical tradition of honoring *baladi* roots. Honoring where you came from, where you currently stand, and pulling on the deep linkages between these potentially two distinct foundations generated abundant power, pride, and surety of Self.

The gender and class relationships between bodies on and immediately surrounding the stage were now done differently. The relationships between the working-class male musicians and Amina were highlighted, their mutually creative and collaborative solidarity cultivating an atmosphere where once marginalized bodies were given greater emphasis and exchange value. Meanwhile, any subtle but fully committed to movement or pause from Amina elicited both positive verbal and kinesthetic responses from the male audience. They clapped, waved their hands, sat up in their seats, all the while with their eyes fixated on Amina's hips as their dinners grew cold. Gone were the sly smirks and teasing jokes of privileged patriarchal masculinity. At this point, Amina had taken her audience on a journey where the end destination was not what her audience had come to expect. Amina simply waited, building up to her finale (and in the meantime thinning the spectator's wallets), but now she fully committed to claiming her singular spotlighted position center-stage.

The drum solo section of the *baladi* progression was underway. Now Amina and the lead drummer showed off their precise technique and creative accents together as the pulsating beats further amplified the energetic atmosphere. To wrap up the drum solo, and her forty-five-minute performance in total, Amina started a large smooth hip circle, but paused halfway through and transitioned to her signature move, the fully bent-over vigorous butt shimmy. She bent fully over so her backside was entirely the focal point of the finale, and placed her hands lightly on the ground in front of her feet as her head hung loose and her long locks gently caressed the floor. Completely folded over, Amina shimmied and shook her butt vigorously, the drummers heightening the movement with *rishes* from their instruments. Amina kept the movement going. Sustaining this volume and intensity of a shimmy from this body position is particularly difficult. For many dancers, it is hard to sustain this type of movement when you bend forward at all, but it seemed Amina could continue throughout the night. The fervor with which Amina shook and the drummers' fingers played the drums amplified. Amina embellished her sustained shimmy by adding heavy heel drops to catch the bass drum accents, adding a percussive element that showed off her difficult technique, but also continued to pointedly draw her audience intensely and exclusively to her booty work.

However, although this technique was previously largely read by a specifically moneyed male audience as sexually enticing, after the accumulation of her total show, and within the specific musical context of the *baladi* progression, its significance shifted. The difficult labor it took to sustain this technique, and the heightened excitement driven by the handful of drummers mirroring her shimmy-action through drum *rishes*, constructed a sense of earned and unabashed pride and honor to Amina. An often-demonized movement, and a stigmatized body, so denigrated by the dance industry as well as general MENA population, was instead honoring and celebrating her roots.[26] Additionally, she honored the specific aspects of her artistic technique that marked her body as otherwise not belonging within the elite space. The sustained and spectacular shaking of her backside shook up the spectators' sense of superiority and sure-footedness within the elite space. It shook open stereotypically stigmatized and unidirectional top-down readings of her performance and her interpolated dancing body, gesturing that the actualities are always more complex and richer than the surface-level appearances.

Next, during a particularly sharp drum hit, Amina flipped her hair overhead as she rose and spun to a fully standing position facing her audience. She stood with both hands placed firmly on her hips in fists, and with her chin tilted slightly down, taking her time to scan her audience with a smoldering glance. She held this power pose. Her chest heaved slightly from the show's extended physical exhaustion, but otherwise, she stood unwavering, her hands still boldly placed upon her hips.

She continued to eye the room, one body to the next. I felt she was daring any spectator to misread her dancing body as weak or passively consumable to the whims of larger sexually charged economic and patriarchal flows. I interpreted her eyes and stance to be daring anyone to challenge her earned spot, center-staged, lucratively paid, and spotlighted in the five-star hotel. After a powerful pause, the audience erupted in applause and verbal approval. Amina grinned with joy but held her pose a moment longer. I felt my heart swell as I flashed back to one of mine and Amina's many dressing room quips encapsulating her same verve. Yasser had just scolded Amina that she'd gained an unattractive two kilos of belly fat and to lose it. Amina took a slow sip from her mango juice while turning to me. Disregarding his condescension she retorted with verve, "Write about me now, for I'll be a star soon."

Throughout her finale and end pose, Amina's *mandeel* never left her hand. Just as dance scholar Priya Srinivasan's focus on the sweat-stained Sari of the Indian dancing body argues for the making visible of otherwise erased forms of transnational labor, Amina's sweaty-tissue likewise demanded recognition for her marginalized, yet successfully lucrative labor in the face of larger global patriarchal and economic disparities.[27] The border crossing of her working-class cabaret body into the elite and lucrative space was not hidden or covered up in opaque skirts, sweet *dalla3* interaction, or swiftly wiped-away sweat. Instead, she expanded upon Srinivasan's analysis, as she chose to bear these denigrated bodily markings in the palm of her hand for all to bear witness. She held the power to shake up limiting preconceptions, prejudices, and peripheralizations. Furthermore, she wasn't ashamed to show the grueling and unforgiving labor that such work pragmatically required in post-revolutionary Cairo.

Checking Out: A Conclusion with/out Closure

I remember my heart racing as I sped down the grand staircase to catch Yasser and Amina as they made their weekly entrance into the Empress. I had been observing Amina's shows for a couple of months now, always spellbound by her *baladi* progression finales, and tonight I was sure to secure the much sought-after interview. I had a translator waiting in the lounge lobby, the money to pay for his entrance fee if necessary, and a third back-up plan ready in case of any other haphazard, last-minute obstacle. I thought I had all my bases covered. I beamed excitedly as I approached Yasser, he was speaking on his cell phone in the lobby. After he hung up, I asked him when Amina would arrive; he looked at me sardonically. "She's not coming," he retorted abruptly as he began to walk into the nightclub.

I was confused, and Yasser didn't seem to be offering any additional explanation or clarifying details. I inquired about why Amina wasn't coming, and when she'd be back. "She stopped," he responded curtly. I pleaded with him about her whereabouts, where I could contact her, and that I could pay her for an interview at her home or any other location. "She stopped, she is pregnant, *khalas*." Yasser looked at me like I was an idiot. "She's pregnant," was all he answered to my continued beseeching. He turned his back on me and entered the venue. He was done talking to me and was clearly not going to aid me in contacting Amina. I felt crushed. I wondered about Amina. Was the pregnancy planned and had she saved up enough income from dancing to resign from her work comfortably to motherhood; was motherhood her ultimate aim? Would she miss the spotlight of the stage, and eventually return to dancing after her child's birth, or was her performance career just a quick and lucrative means to a preferential end of marriage and motherhood? Particularly for many non-elite Egyptian dancers, this was certainly a common and desirable trajectory.

Surprisingly, as these thoughts continued to brew within my head, I began to feel comfortable with the uncertainty of how Amina ultimately took her final exit from the stage. The plethora of possibilities served as a reminder of how many hard-earned opportunities Amina accrued for herself, as well as a reminder that there were multiple modes of being female, all of which embodied a range of desirable power positions. These modes stretched across the range of identities that were socially centered and peripheralized, from respected domestic motherhood to stage-commanding yet stigmatized *ra2asa* (dancer). Ultimately, Amina's Empress check-out without closure left me impressed with the colorful array of potentialities available to her that she garnered despite the multi-layered hardships she endured. She left me with hope for a rich and fruitful future, and the reminder to seek out abundance in the fissures and opportunities of what is dominantly read as becoming scarce.

Observing Amina's Empress performances week after week, from the initial multi-directional male-dominated power plays to her finale, where she claimed and commanded the center stage with her earthy *baladi* progressions, was moving. Amina left her audience assured that the closure of the show would be on her terms, strongly, honestly, and deeply rooted in her own *aseel* journey and Self. Furthermore, Amina animatedly shakes up the understanding of *aseel*, which typically means "authentic" in a *baladi* Egyptian sense, often dualistically contrasted with things and traits considered *afrangi*, or Western-foreign.[28] Amina's performance takes audiences deeper into a more complex and richly entangled understanding of *aseel*.

Here Amina highlights a transparent recognition of Self as engaged in interlocking class, nationality, race, gender, and sexuality interpolations and constructions that attend to both the drawbacks and catalytic potentialities of the present moment and place where one must stand one's ground. The sense of a particularly local Egyptian honor and pride remains in Amina's performed understanding of *aseel*, but matching the honey-like consistency with which she swerves her hips in the *baladi* progression, her understanding of *aseel* is sweetened and enhanced with a richer, thicker, and more nuanced density. This nuanced focus on heavily grounded and interwoven dynamics of race, class, gender, sexuality, and nationality is of paramount importance to how larger audiences, inside and outside of Egypt, situate and contextualize what is happening not only within five-star hotel *raqs sharqi* shows and their unknown futures, but also in regard to the country's economic and political romanticism and realities at large.

Popular discourse inside the Cairo and international dance community may posit that *raqs sharqi* is "dying" in Egypt because of the decline in elite and extravagant five-star hotel shows and the ever-increasing popularity of cabaret work and MTV-style *sha3bi* music video clips. However, this dismisses the necessary work of looking at how *raqs sharqi* within hotel sites has changed and what these changes are saying about dance, economics, and politics at large. Furthermore, in reductively dismissing the changes in five-star hotel *raqs sharqi* as declining into non-existence or depravity, practitioners and members of the dance industry at large are placing themselves in the limiting pitfalls that Amina so directly disrupts: of unidirectional understandings that reinforce dominant hierarchies of power. Instead, Amina's performances inspired me to listen across senses and peripheralized perspectives to dwell in the depths of lived actualities and possibilities beyond dominant appearances. From this foundation of listening, my interpretation of Amina's choreography argues for seeing across senses with polyvalent significations that may slightly but meaningfully shake up normalized hegemonic discourse. In so doing, she shatters fears of scarcity in favor of standing one's ground and seeking peripheralized yet ever-present abundance.

Taxi Transition: Checkpoint

One of my favorite things about when my friends and I would take one of their private cars to get around the city, instead of public transportation or taxis, was that it allowed us the liberty to have all-out vehicular dance parties. Driving around Cairo late at night when the traffic had mostly dissipated was relaxing. Karim, Wael, and I enjoyed this ride home by blasting music and dancing. We wildly used our arms, hands, and upper bodies to swerve and percussively accent the song's beats while laughing and feeding off each other's frenzied creativity. Frequently, these car jams culminated in each of us trying to outdo one another, seeing who could dance the weirdest by garnering the most laughs.

The singers Oka and Ortega of the hit *mahragan* song "El3ab Yalla" boomed out through the speakers as we cruised down the sparsely occupied streets. This was one of the hit songs, particularly among younger generations, during the latter end of my fieldwork in Cairo. The lyrics sang of a man who was trying to stay on the good and straight path, but whenever he tried, the devil would come up to his ear and tell him to play, drink, and do other things that would, once again, lead him astray. Karim usually chose this song to start our dance parties and then repeated it multiple times throughout the drive. The pulsing energy of the song was contagious, and the lyrics resonated with my friends.

That night, when we were in full dance mode, Karim abruptly cut the music. I saw him and Wael exchange glances then quickly put on their seatbelts. I leaned over from my position in the backseat to peer out the front window. I saw that we were coming up to one of the many random police checkpoints scattered throughout the city. Any vehicle could be stopped and searched for whatever reason. This wasn't, in itself, that unusual, and it was common to at least pass by a checkpoint when driving around the city. As Middle Eastern ethnologist Farha Ghannam elaborates, random and prolific police presence, checkpoints, and corruption in Cairo are one way that Egyptian male youth are interpolated with suspect criminalization.[29] Young men may be questioned, or taken off the street, for simply being out and about in their own city. Just as Oka and Ortega's hit lyrics could be heard blasting sporadically throughout the city streets from vehicles, so too, and perhaps with subtle synchronicity, were these checkpoints sporadically encountered.

Surely enough, our vehicle was stopped, and two armed policemen told my friends to hand over their identifications. I started to unzip my bag to hand over my U.S. passport; it usually worked as a "golden ticket" in these instances to quickly be "green-lighted" to pass through without any delay. Karim winked at me as he gestured for me to wait, and I saw him and Wael exchange furtive smirks. I didn't understand. The police then asked my friends to step out of the vehicle; only as he was exiting did Karim quickly whisper to me to hand him my passport. He grabbed it discreetly and put it into his pocket as he reassured me everything was all right. I waited, nervously watching from the backseat window as they spoke with the two police and a third officer a few feet away. Wael waved his arm toward me and the group turned, then Karim swiftly pulled my passport out from his pocket and presented it to the officer as if it were a winning lottery ticket ready to be cashed in. The officer grabbed the passport and flipped it open. He looked up and marched over to me. "You are American?" he asked. I nodded. "Welcome to Egypt," he responded as he handed me back my passport through the rolled-down front window and my friends came back to the car.

My friends quickly buckled up as we drove past the checkpoint. As soon as we passed, they burst into roaring laughter and triumphantly clapped their hands together. They animatedly joked back and forth as their laughter continued to bellow. I was still stumped, obviously missing what was so enthralling about what I found to be a nerve-wracking confrontation that they unnecessarily extended. Wael turned to me, "Sorry, we just wanted to see the look on their face when they realized you were American," Karim agreed, "His eyes stuck out like a bug! Then did you hear the officer scold them, calling them idiots!?" "So great!" Wael shouted as he grinned from ear to ear. I must've still looked perplexed. "Look, it's just . . . *ya3ny* . . . a tiny 'fuck you' . . . because these guys think they can do anything." They carried on their enthused banter from the encounter as we drove on.

My comrades didn't need to disrupt their travel and seating arrangements, they could have flashed my passport from the moment they rolled down their window. However, they chose to purposefully extend and linger within the confrontation before revealing my identification. Personally, I was a bit uneasy that their sense of rebellious success was only possible because it centered around my little blue U.S. passport and my white *agnabiyya* body that it identified. I was reminded of Middle Eastern feminist scholar Lila Abu-Lughod's caution against romanticizing small acts of resistance. Abu-Lughod ruminates on how these acts lead to tropes of liberation that don't do justice to the complexity of marginalized people's lives, while still acknowledging the importance of calling attention to these acts as tactics people use to negotiate larger dominating systems.[30] As a transient outsider and non-citizen, the fact that I had the "golden ticket" of privilege, that my friends, as rightful citizens did not, felt terribly unjust. I wondered how significant their fleeting moment of resistive pleasure could be, particularly when it was enabled due to the political weight my U.S. passport carried?

Yet, as a dance scholar, I was still drawn to how Karim and Wael choreographed the passport performance. They purposefully extended the time of the unidirectional top-down corrupt police power, and only after this lingering, where the sense of authority and power was able to accumulate, did they decide to shatter it. Thus, not only did my material little blue book carry a heavy political weight, but likewise, so too did the quick-thinking creativity and guts of how Karim and Wael choreographed the show. By keenly playing with the time, material resources, choreography, and bodies within the shared space, they imbued their fleeting moment of resistance with more grit and, quite apparently, personally meaningful satisfaction.

3
Discos

Risqué Moves and the Exposure of Policing Politics

Exhausted, I flung my purse down onto the kitchen counter and flicked on the switch of the tea kettle. I was boiling water for the Nescafé that would get me through an additional waking hour or two of fieldnote writing after a hectic night out. I had a small research grant to spend the month clubbing in Cairo's prolific discos to finalize this chapter's research, and my insightful dancer-friend Zara was the perfect "club buddy" who regularly took me out to the trendiest nightlife spots with her group of well-off friends. My clubbing grant was admittingly to their great amusement. While waiting for the necessary Nescafé, I flipped on the TV to my usual music-video channel. I needed pulsating music in the background to keep me going. I smiled as I saw my other friend and collaborator Farah Nasri hip dropping in the *sha3bi* music video, glad to see that she was still thriving. These music video clips often featuring dancers were intimately entwined with the discos I had just returned from.[1]

Sha3bi, mahraganat, and pop were the main Egyptian genres heard and performed to in discos, mixed in with Western commercial tunes played by popular DJs when there was no performer on stage. It was during Mubarak's presidency (that is, pre-revolution) that technology and globalization shifts (satellite TV and platforms such as YouTube, etc.) rushed in a series of music videos that became popular throughout Cairo and became the main medium of dissemination for *raqs sharqi* throughout the MENAT. Notably, these videos with dancers were often critiqued as "risqué" and detrimental to societal and family values due to either their lyrics, dancing, or often both.[2] It was also during this time that DJs began replacing full orchestras as fashion, musical, and economic shifts led to their popularity at weddings, and parties.

During this time, songs and artists that couldn't get official state-regulated air time could now resort to YouTube as a less censored and regulated avenue of dissemination. Starting around the beginning of Sisi's presidency and continuing with increasing fervor up until the time of this writing, foreign dancers, particularly from the United States, Eastern Europe, Russia, and South America have begun dipping their toes back into the Cairo work scene. One Armenian dancer in particular, Sofinar (also known as Sofinaz), became wildly popular throughout Cairo as a *raqs sharqi* dancer after her role in the film *The Sweeper* (*Al quashash*) and a series of both homemade YouTube performances and professional music video clips since 2013. A non-MENA foreigner has never achieved such popularity in Cairo in such a short time, which was largely helped by *sha3bi* music and film media presence and dissemination. Sofinar is credited with popularizing the percussive chest "pops" now common in disco performances and was controversial amongst other dancers for her dancing's perceived vulgarity and unabashed *sha3bi* aesthetics.

During the early 2000s, *mahragan* (festival) music, a blending of electro-*sha3bi* with EDM, hiphop, and *mulid* elements began in the lower socioeconomic areas of Cairo. It was a musical genre that boomed in popularity across classes just prior to, and post, 2011 revolution.[3] It also extolled a range of working-class political, economic, and everyday life sentiments. In other words, this genre is akin to "the digital age descendent of 1970's *sha3bi*."[4] For Cairo's youth, over half of whom are reported to live in poverty with high unemployment rates, the street-savvy lyrics are particularly appealing.[5] This group's experiences and woes were often silenced by the state prior to the 2011 revolution, and *mahraganat* was one way they found a voice, with a far-reaching and continuing audience.[6] *Mahraganat* did not start due to the revolution, a common misperception, but began before the 2011 revolution, and touches on a heterogeneous level of topics. (For Egyptians of the upper classes and the global belly dance industry *mahraganat* was popularized post-revolution.)

Immediately post-revolution, when the state was still in upheaval, these music video channels and clips fell into a pattern of loosened censorship alongside the accessibility of now flourishing autonomous media technologies and platforms. For example, one television channel, "El Tet," which came out during this instability, exclusively played music videos and ripped YouTube belly dancer clips 24/7, with advertisements running across the screen, sometimes for adult entertainment products and services such as Viagra.[7] These prolific clips not only became the main dissemination of screened *raqs sharqi* throughout Cairo, setting a new aesthetic and musical tone, but they also aided in ushering in a resurgence of having dancers "in the flesh" for the upper classes at weddings, parties, and within recently popularized commercial disco sites.

As I listened to the pulsating song I wondered, was my desire to play this now during my fieldnote ritual due to the desire to ethnographically embody the club "vibe," or was it simply to keep myself awake? From this page onward, the excursions, analysis, writing, and the ethnography at large, became heavier. Not to say that keeping your company thus far along the ethnographic ride has not been valuably exhilarating, but at this point in the book, the final two chapters centralize the commercial sites of *raqs sharqi* most stigmatized, shamed, and policed. While I should have been writing, I likewise found myself opening Instagram.

My feed was bombarded with clips of the very site I flew all the way back to Cairo to research, the discos—although from quite different perspectives. Primarily foreign dancers are featured in these clips, often looming larger-than-life in the close-up clips filmed from an agent or guest standing merely inches from the small, raised stage or bar the dancer performed above. If you recall, the opening dance vignette of this ethnography was also from one such disco, fitting to appear on both pages, there and deep down here, as these snippets of thirty-second to one-minute clips are the primary, and often sole, access point for outsider foreign dance audiences to the current happenings of Cairo *raqs sharqi*. I gently shook my head at the thought, and unfortunate reality, that for most foreign practitioners, and everyday Egyptians, such trimmed, partial, and decontextualized clips were how they understood and related to the historic and ongoingly vibrant global hub of *raqs sharqi*.

The clip began zooming in on the dancer's vivaciously shaking butt from a bent-over position. The white-skinned dancer then spun around as she arose; as she turned the bright name of the disco shone behind her on the video, easy free marketing. A bright smile lit across the dancer's face before she suddenly transitioned into furious head spins that sent her long brown locks hurricaning around her to the crowd's wild cheers. I couldn't see much of the crowd from the clip's frame; the lights of a dozen or so camera phones blinded most of the audience's expressions. The dancer threw her head back and laughed, although the lyrics of the song were extolling heartbreak; did she not understand Arabic? I recalled attending gatherings of foreign dancers in Cairo where "newbies" to the scene would almost haughtily joke that they didn't know a lick of Arabic but were already working the club circuit, sometimes with faces still freshly bruised from aesthetic work—perhaps, the sexy "look" was what they felt was worth more investment in? (I also recall their disappearance from the market often within months, gesturing to the ephemerality of such a strategy.)

Discos were sites dominated by foreign dancers, particularly when it came to social media exposure. At the time of my fieldwork, there was only a handful of Egyptian dancers popular in disco sites and openly sharing social media clips from the stages, although more Egyptians occasionally worked there without social media exposure. By the time of my writing, more Egyptians were performing in discos and using social media for marketing, although light-skinned foreigners still dominated. Multiple theories and attitudes circulated regarding what was often termed the "foreign invasion" by those in the industry. One echoed numerous Egyptian dancers, saying to me, "It's not a problem. They're like cheap Chinese products. They are popular but break after a short time and get thrown out, just wait and see, then another comes to replace her."[8]

This Chinese-product metaphor was shared with me so often throughout the years of my fieldwork by Egyptian dancers that I imagined it had to be a common saying amongst them. Likewise, the capitalist comparison to Chinese products highlights the primacy of globally uneven capitalist dynamics as entwined with nationalist and ethnic access to resources. Further, the "getting thrown out" tagline gestures simultaneously to the objectification of female dancing bodies but also to other use-values within disco dancing not tied to purchasable products and privileges, but rather something else more sustainable and locally derived.

My friend Zara also referred to this dynamic as "the rigged competition the Egyptian dancer just can't win," highlighting that so many Egyptians cannot even step on these disco stages to prove themselves without two major setbacks. The first is culturally suffering lived repercussions of so publicly becoming exposed as a stigmatized dancer, and the second is having economic access to the now near-requirement to have affluent cosmetic work done to fit the Westernized upper-class "image."[9] In other words, the "instagrammable" look. Meanwhile, many foreign dancers I spoke with simply brushed the "foreign invasion" aside with a hand wave, with privileged statements such as, "you gotta spend money to make money," or, "it's simply supply and demand, they want us, not them, so here we are." These statements further brush aside the ways capitalism

Figure 3.1 Zara Dance performing at a disco. Credit: Zara Dance

functions unevenly and inequitably throughout the globe, necessitating entwinement with racism, classism, patriarchy, and imperialism to maintain churning profitability.

My focus returned to the clip. Perhaps the laugh was simply due to someone or something catching her eye out of the camera view? Too much is left unknown. The youthful fair-skinned dancer—I'd assume Eastern European—then pulled her long sweaty hair back behind her as she winked directly at whoever held the camera. She then preceded to take a wide stance and slowly milk her way down to the floor in a sultry sinking front split. With her final accented "thump" onto the ground with her now well-exposed bright pink booty shorts underneath her skimpy costuming, the crowd cheered—clip over.

While my aim was to close Instagram to get to writing, I found myself having simply closed one social media application to be sucked into another, Facebook. *Oh, here we go again.* Just reading the post at the top of my feed, I felt a fiery heat stir up into my chest, further fuel to get to my field notes to get this ethnography out there. My feed greeted me with a popular post by a well-renowned U.S. instructor, spreading discourse typical of the industry outside Cairo at this time:

> I hope that this is the year we get all the porn stars, prostitutes, and trashy dancers out from this art form of ours. My hope is that they all get arrested or deported. There is no art left, just women doing raunchy dancing, women jumping down slowly into splits like they're having sex, acrobatics and street moves rather than sensuality; these women must be reported, arrested, and if foreign, deported. Our art has been hijacked. The latest example in the stream of depravity.

The Facebook post concluded with a linked online news article of a foreign dancer sentenced to one year in jail over provocative dancing.[10] The article was a one-year follow-up from an incident when the dancer Joharah was in trouble for making viral videos wearing a white belly dance costume and was perceived from video footage not to be wearing proper shorts underneath, and "inciting debauchery." While legal repercussions began and were feared for Joharah, ultimately as a foreigner the incident and media exposure only led to her heightened popularity and increased capital, with her deemed the "white lace" or "white dress" dancer.

This discourse was a perfect example of my ethnographic exhaustion, and relationalities cultivated without heart. My heart sank at the burden these working dancers had to endure, on top of their already grueling work schedules and demands. Most of the sustainably successful dancers I interviewed, foreign or Egyptian, told not only of the hardships of working through their own internalized shame and policing about working in these sites at first (feeling they were breaking the rules and expectations of what "art" and Cairo *raqs sharqi* was), but also of the societal shaming and ever-present risk of governmental arrest or deportation and the consequent demeaning media exposure. Dancers are regularly arrested, deported, and scandalized in the media for their work, and here they had an applauding and encouraging international audience.

Is this how you're entering into engagement with Cairo *raqs sharqi*? Mere glimpses of a particular style of dance in a specific niche site from incredibly pinpointed yet unknown filmed perspectives? What about the literal insight of the tangible in-site? In other words, the knowledge of the meaty material on the ground, in still partial albeit more fleshed-out perspectives from differently mediated bodily realities. Furthermore, I must be direct: the grandiosity with which one must view their own role to demand the criminalization of dancers is patriarchal imperialist orientalism; it defines more of one's own neocolonialist character than the MENAT corporealities one claims to have knowledge of.

Entwining with the discussion above, another shift during my years of fieldwork went from foreigners lamenting the "deserted" Cairo scene to now flooding the market; any commercially viable dancer within her own community will hop on a plane to dance for free or peanuts in Cairo to "make her name." Dancers seldom take time to consider the damage their imperialist behavior is wreaking on the local professional economy and dancers' livelihoods.[11]

During my fieldwork the reach and access of social media is greatly enabling this toxic behavior. The dynamic is similar yet intensified from how larger economic and cultural dynamics destabilized the long-held monopoly of Mohamed Ali Street entertainers in Sadat's time. With less esteemed disco sites in particular, many former musicians, technicians (men that carry the dancer's gig bag), and folklore or *tanoura* workers are suddenly deciding to become dancer agents and ripping off foreigner dancers while further decimating the local Egyptian market. Many of these foreign dancers are putting themselves, and by consequence local Egyptians, into gravely exploitive and often dangerous positions. Consequently, if your immediate reaction to a social media clip that doesn't meet your fantasy orientalist expectations of what *raqs sharqi* is is to have someone criminalized, or if your first intention is to come to Cairo to catch your own spotlight rather than to learn, I invite you to have a seat and come along for this ride so that we can listen deeply and lovingly with more open arms and heart.

If this chapter is feeling more in-your-face and personal, good. That is what I want. This chapter's tone reflects the up-close and in-your-face nature of the disco performances. What I mean is, that the professional dancing in this site is often critiqued (albeit not inaccurately if you remove the condescending tone), as being "in your face," due to the proximity of the audience partying right up against the intimate bars or small stages. This proximity alongside the embodiment of hard-hitting *mahraganat* musicality and aesthetics generates corresponding dance techniques and postures deemed in your face (obviously unavoidably so when witnessed from such proximities)! Additionally, discos are the site where audiences are the most kinesthetically active and involved in the show. I couldn't just sit in the disco and observe; I was pulled up to dance socially, bopping along with the groove, and invited to get up and get "hype" when a hit *mahraganat* song came on with my club buddies. What distinguishes this site the most from other chapter sites is that in discos you go to dance yourself, not just sit passively and watch a dancer's performance. My approach also fits this chapter's choreographic writing structure because of how foreign audiences have the most partial access, and consequently some of the most misconceptions and assumptions about this site. As an ethnographer, I feel I must pull you into the grooving "vibe" of the club as well to get you to shake off some of those preconceptions and misunderstandings before we can open our hearts to alternative knowledge. It's on you to get with the vibe of the disco.

Taken in tandem, the social media stigmatizing, state policing, and scandalous headline news exposure contributed to a shift throughout my years of fieldwork, from the "myth" debunked in the previous chapter that *raqs sharqi* was dying or dead to the now prevalent myth that *raqs sharqi* was, for sure, still around, but experiencing a decay, particularly a scandalous, risqué decay as the above commentary demonstrates. These social media allegations of decay through perceived "vulgar" modern sexy costuming, more percussive and overt *sha3bi* and *mahraganat* musicality, technique, and aesthetics confronted the global belly dance industry whenever we logged into social media. Likewise, particularly during the latter years of my fieldwork, news articles decrying the scandals, arrests, and deportations of dancers were abundant.[12] While this risk of policing exposure could operate as increased social capital particularly for foreign dancers (for example, in the above example, foreign dancer Joharah only gained greater fame and popularity) the risk is always graver for arrested and publicly exposed Egyptians—potentially career, family, and social life-ending.

As a dancer, my gut tied up with that all too familiar feeling of having my own expression of my multiplicitous identity disciplined and policed into a lesser way of being in the world. Likewise, my chest aches when witnessing the physical manifestations of this same disciplinary policing among my dance students. I see it in my students learning to shimmy their shoulders but with chests so tight and bound from shame, and in my dancers who labored years to gain the self-worth to take up space on the stage. How many teachers hypocritically preach empowerment in their classes but police such expression through finger-wagging and refusing to value the spectrum of expressive movements and aesthetics available to our bodies, perhaps best currently revealed through the refusal of many teachers to even allow popular *mahraganat* music and techniques to enter their studios.

As mentioned previously, policing of dancing bodies was nothing new, despite the claims of many contemporary practitioners and audiences nostalgically extolling the supposed virtues and moral decency of dancers of the past.[13] Dance historian Heather Ward theorizes this as "deviation discourse" and argues that it operates to reconstruct history for contemporary political purposes as well as enables contemporary policing.[14] However, this contemporary renewed surge of policing across self, societal, and state levels interests me as it interweaves with how the "myth" of *raqs sharqi* has shifted over time, as well as with the goals of Sisi's state legitimization. Further, the particular ways *raqs sharqi* is policed at this moment in Cairo in comparison to other forms of arts and entertainment warrant heightened attention. Just as *mahraganat* and *raqs sharqi* mix together to great criticism within discos and music videos, both forms have also shared corresponding waves of heightened policing, as well as loosened censorship and control, pre- and post-revolution.

Turning toward other dance genres, dance scholar Rosemary Martin has likewise researched the contemporary effects of government censorship on theater and contemporary concert dancers in Cairo and throughout the southern Mediterranean. Martin's research contends that policing, primarily in the form of censorship in her dance genre, works as a tool across self, societal, and state levels, to control and curb free and alternative thoughts and movements that challenge the dominant power structures and systems of the government.[15] She argues that this policing is most dangerous when it operates cohesively across all three levels, self, society, and state, to create a totalitarian ideology.[16]

She, and the other dance theorists within the edited book her research appears within, conclude that with policing rampant, governments are increasingly not serving their own citizens, and if there is any hope to overcome the inequitable strife in the southern Mediterranean and the world, that hope will come in the embodied form of choreography.[17] What form will this choreographic "hope" take? Perhaps *raqs sharqi*, far more viscerally and profusely policed, can offer such insight? In particular, this may come because *raqs sharqi* policing is especially corporeal, pinpointed on the sexually scandalous, the "risqué decay." As a feminist emancipatory practitioner-ethnographer, this policing raises a red flag to me. I recall how the Supreme Council of the Armed Force's military rule similarly worked to police female revolutionaries using corporeal morality in Tahrir square in the months following Mubarak's resignation post-revolution.

Not only were women revolutionaries marginalized in the political realm, but in the public space of Tahrir Square their bodies increasingly became violently unwelcome under SCAF's rule. Reports of sexual harassment against women in Tahrir Square started to rise during the continued protests after SCAF's taking over, and women were excluded from the committee on constitutional reform, as well as the constitutional changes that were then put in place.[18] Women protestors were subject not only to sexual harassment and violence but arrested and forced to undergo invasive virginity tests.[19] In order to productively and safely protest in Cairo , women actively pursued a range of corporeal tactics that aligned with values and norms of nationalist loyalty, patriarchal protection, and religious honor. For example, many women came to Tahrir with their children or husbands, identifying as mothers of the family and nation, while others adorned their bodies with flags and symbolism of patriotism to Egypt as a nation, and others engaged in pious activities such as praying.[20] Yet the military regime tried to justify and normalize their militarized masculine violence with claims such as, "These girls are not like daughters of yours or mine," constructing protesting female bodies as marginalized "others."[21] My aching chest urged me to lean deeper into policing politics through *raqs sharqi* dancers' choreographies and corporealities. What's the connection?

Sliding down into Martin's argument with more scandalous fleshy excess, how is disco *raqs sharqi* expanding upon her arguments? Just as costumes with excessive mesh cut-outs and movements which flash bright-colored booty shorts garnering peeks of gyrating butt cheek slipping beneath, what is *raqs sharqi* exposing? This chapter takes the overall book research question and bends deeper into its disco contextualization; what revolutionary possibilities does *raqs sharqi* move us toward when such moves are deemed risqué? In other words, what's the role of the risqué in the revolutionary aftermath? What bodies and forces does it mobilize, scandalize, threaten, and police? Let's listen and slide deeper by stepping into the disco.

Bodily Insight of the In Site

My Uber driver dropped me off outside the large docked multi-level boat that housed one of the trending discos during the latter time of my fieldwork, Clubhouse. The boat housed several elite restaurants, clubs, and newer cabarets. Walking up the main stairway I noticed lots of well-dressed men and women around me. I glanced down at my outfit and felt underdressed. I should have packed clothes that were comparable to the fancier dresses and heels I'd put on after my own U.S. *raqs sharqi* shows at nice nightclubs, but that always felt "weird" when explaining my role as a Ph.D. scholar. Why is embodying the multiplicity of our identities such a struggle? I shrugged it off, I was all right, I was going for the sophisticated chic look to balance out the two roles. Due to my fretting, I didn't even notice when I had reached the main stairway and elevator. I went up the steps toward the Clubhouse entrance and felt all eyes on me, scanning me up and down. Unlike my entrance into the hotel site, these felt more like calculating stares, seeing if I measured up to the elite standards and codes of high society.

I caught myself oddly kicking my right heel back, turning my walk into more of a strange waddle; what an awkward way to try to discreetly cover up the fact that I was self-consciously checking my black tights for holes. I only brought two pairs, which the zipper on my knee-high boots had already decimated. Geez, of all the places I've "written in" myself as an ethnographer this seemed the most . . . irrelevantly vain. At the same time, my own site-entrance insecurities and foci lay bare the class and image consciousness that's prevalent in these sites. I tried to shake it off, telling myself that I already didn't fit in. Even if I looked the part, I was, as my comrades from the disco group endearingly dubbed me, "the belly dancing journalist." At the same time, my identity as a white American dressed me in social capital. Ironically, my U.S. nationality here outshone and blanketed my localized class-positionality "back home;" including the broken-down backyard trailer I wrote these words from.

Speaking of my comrades, as I approached the main entrance desk of the disco I spoke the magic word that made this entire chapter possible, "Ahmed Ali." Ahmed, I guess you could say, was the "ringleader" of our clubbing group, meaning he usually organized and footed the bill for club nights. I would say his name at the entrance and a suited man working the door would nod and briskly escort me to Ahmed's table.[22] If you're wondering about that amusing "clubbing" grant money, well, it wasn't even enough to reimburse my plane ticket. (My university also chose to "blanket" the now thinly dispersed research funding across lecturer faculty, without localized awareness of the impracticality of such seemingly grandiose generosity in lived contingent faculty reality.) I never went to a disco on my own bill after my first trip, my shoulders sank at a minimum spending equivalent to US$100. While I know minimum fees can vary depending on who you are (or who you're perceived to be), these were definitely sites for the upper classes.[23] As usual, my main access to all my research sites materialized out of relationships, those imbued with both generosities but also *wasta*. (*Wasta* is an Arabic word meaning political connections or those of unofficial influence channels. The meaning varies depending on the context.)

Ahmed Ali was introduced to me by Zara as a self-proclaimed "belly dancer aficionado." His father worked in some sort of financial company dealing with corporations outside of Egypt, basically circulating dollars or anything more esteemed than Egyptian *ginneh*. In essence, he was one of what they call the "A class" in Egyptian society. While I do believe Ahmed's a generous person, I can't deny that my presence also granted him social capital as a young single American woman. Additionally, these discos did not allow entry to single men; you had to be 21+, in co-ed groupings, women, or a in a couple—single men or groups of men were denied entry to avoid "problems." I'd also failed to notice *hijabi* women in these discos, I'm sure I missed some but did also hear that covered women were often denied entry. For example, one article cites an incident where a *hijab*-wearing woman was denied entry due to a supposed "no hats" policy.[24] I'd asked doormen about this, and the few who would actually speak to me about it all responded with a similar sentiment: "It's not the right environment, *for them*." The doormen's phrasing often made it seem like these literal male gatekeepers were doing a favor that was "best" for the women themselves, despite the women's wants. This gatekeeping gestures toward the upper-class notions of identity and image as well as narratives of modernity being performed and policed in discos. Simultaneously, this gatekeeping of identity and mobility intersect with capitalist dynamics within commercial sites centered around producing a profit by cultivating a certain image and experience.[25]

Figure 3.2 Farah Nasri Dancing at Clubhouse Disco. Credit: Farah Nasri, Clubhouse

As I was escorted to my table, I often felt like I could have been back home. The environment seemed similar to any club, albeit with less sexually suggestive couples dancing. Guests tended to be more youthful, in their 20s–40s, the age majority often depending on the disco and the night; and again, similar to back home, women dressed in ways less conservative and more glammed-up than what you'd see in the everyday. What did catch my eye was the plethora of green and blue contact-lensed female eyes, still able to penetrate my own amidst the density of cigarette and shisha smoke. Flashing party lights and pulsating commercial music enveloped the space, with English commercial music often warming up the night before Egyptian *sha3bi, mahraganat,* and pop took over. As for the guests inside, Farah Nasri succinctly put it, "You see it: play English music, they drink; play Egyptian, they dance."[26] The stage was raised but narrow and winding throughout the main room. I remember glancing at it thinking it would seem nerve-wracking to dance full-out on such a small stage. To claim that precarious stage with such class-conscious youth partying just inches in front of you had to demand a highly confident dancer. Other discos did away with the stage altogether, just hoisting the dancer up onto a bar to dance. I was told in multiple interviews by early disco popularizers that in addition to being "innovatively trendy" this small or non-existent bar "staging" had to do with economizing on licensing required for these commercial venues as well as fitting in more paying customers to spend more money.

Of all my research sites, discos were the newest, ironically becoming popular during the tail end of Morsi's ultra-conservative Muslim Brotherhood rule and remaining so until the time of this writing.[27] Morsi's time was consolidated around power-grabbing and Islamicizing more so than that of any other president, rather than concentrating on the lived reality and concerns of citizens on the ground. After the revolution against Mubarak and a period of rule by the SCAF, a series of popular elections resulted in the Muslim Brotherhood taking power in Egypt. They accomplished this with the election of Islamist President Mohamed Morsi in June 2012 along with winning more than half of the parliamentary seats.

However, Morsi's Muslim Brotherhood rule encountered fierce opposition after his attempt to pass a constitution that followed extreme Islamist views and after attempts to abruptly change laws in ways that would grant himself unparalleled powers, more so than any other president in Egyptian history. (This says a lot considering the history of autocratic rule in Egypt since the monarchy era.) Morsi attempted to implement laws that would place his presidential edicts above judicial scrutiny. This move among others would also alienate the military's historic grasp on power which also pitted the military regime against Morsi. His proposed constitution sparked general outrage from secularists, Christian minorities, women's groups, and members of the military, and was followed by mass protests as political unrest and instability continued. Morsi's focus was further critiqued as it sidelined prioritizing the distressing economic situation. Political and security instabilities only continued to impact the economic realm negatively. Inflation and unemployment rose during Morsi's presidency, while foreign investments and tourism continued to fall.[28]

Additionally, Muslim Brotherhood gender ideology from key organization figures focuses on natural discourses of the female body as necessarily reproductive and subordinate to men, constructed in distinction to Western discourses which are discerned to disregard gender norms. Women and men are constructed as different but complementary with women belonging to the domestic world as mothers and teachers of men who are prepositioned to the public sphere.[29] Conservative Islamist dress and veiling for women became more common again, as women had heightened pressure to negotiate their bodies in public masculinized spaces during Morsi's rule.[30] In the numerous protests that occurred during Morsi's presidency, sexual attacks and harassment were particularly vehement against women, but cross-gender alliances were formed in retaliation, creating groups of anti-harassment task forces and resources.[31]

During Morsi's short rule anyone from a marginalized identity as well as performers of all genres were walking on eggshells, worried about repression. Winter of 2012 is when I first visited Cairo for a little over a month, and I recall all my friends glued to the news, constantly worried about repression and even direr economic conditions. A dense air of uncertainty permeated the streets, though dancing started trickling back since the initial pause of the 2011 revolution. The sense of power some Brotherhood-allied men felt via exertion of that power in punishing ways over marginalized bodies was a palpable anxiety during my initial visit to Cairo as well as in interviews from men and women in the dance industry. This anxiety was not just affectual, it was material. During Morsi's regime, harassment, attacks, and legal crackdowns against non-dominant groups such as dancers, women, Christians, and non-heterosexual men were on the rise.[32] Concerns over power and repression were felt throughout Cairo by the military and marginalized groups, and on July 3, 2013, just past a year since his election, Morsi was deposed by a military group led by the minister of defense, and now President up until the time of this writing, General Abdel Fattah El-Sisi.

While a breakdown in the usual government censorship of arts and entertiainment ruptured post-revolution, this sealed up with Morsi. For instance, the 24-hr dancing tv satellite shows were canceled with the Brotherhood endorsement of protecting "family values."[33] Ahmed Widan, the founder of one of the first popular discos in post-revolution Cairo, an already successful businessman, was questioned about why he would choose to open a disco during such a precarious time. He responded, "it's a good business, and also a type of unity."[34] These clubs had DJs as opposed to live bands, and often had the dancer work on a bar, very small stage, or no stage at all, economizing on the elaborate extravagances of commercial venues for elite audiences of the past, while desiring dancers to perform in a style similar to what was disseminated on the satellite and YouTube music video clips. As an Egyptian dancer who helped popularize Tabla disco (but now prefers to remain anonymous as she's disassociated from the disco circuit), told me in an interview,

> These clubs started right after the revolution, they were trying to have any kind of entertainment, at the time it was very difficult because there was curfew, sometimes clubs were open all night so they'd open right when curfew started and close in the morning when it ended, the curfew was changing all the time, at the time when the Muslim Brotherhood was on the bridges shooting. They started, of course, all the belly dancing was canceled from hotels because there was no tourism, so these clubs became the only place to go out, and they started as a way to economize and not have to pay a lot of money, but they'd charge a lot of money because all the A-class rich people want to go out, so they started hiring dancers too. For the 'show,' they'd tell me to stop dancing so much! They said just be sexy and give a wink here and there, twiddle my hair, and stop trying to be so classic. There wasn't even a stage or space for me to move! It was something new and my look and style was totally different but I'm also Egyptian, so there was this curiosity about me as it was previously all about Sofinar at that time. This was how my work was in the beginning.[35]

In terms of actual show structure, here dancers would often perform one or two mini-sets of about four songs each, with a costume change in between if two. On busy nights the main highlight of the evening was often a celebrity singer's performance. Predominantly, these were now celebrity-status *sha3bi*, pop, or *mahraganat* male singers. The dancer's set had no "show structure" like in hotels and boats; here it was dominantly popular Egyptian pop, *sha3bi*, and *mahraganat*.[36] Maya, a half-Egyptian half-Moroccan dancer was also an early pioneer in popularizing these discos as well:

> When I came to Cairo the dance wasn't fashionable with people anymore, the old rich people that like dancers search only maybe for Dina in their weddings, but younger people were searching for music only, *sha3bi*, *mahraganat*, and DJs. There was a generational difference. So, I made a different thing, I brought classic dancing and started to popularize this in Sahel parties, wedding parties, and clubs. I'm the one who created and popularized this idea for having dancers in clubs on DJ music and in wedding parties again for the newer generation coming up. I worked with owners and management to make the dance modern and also modernized my costuming, so modernized everything but in a classic way. The clubs would bring me as a superstar, it was my name bringing the guests, but then of course everyone took this as a good business opportunity, and it became too open. I stopped dancing in clubs four years ago because it changed so much. The problem is when everyone saw it as a money grab, owners and dancers, rather than seeing the dance as saying something bigger. If you only dance for work for money, rather than to make a statement, you lose a lot. Our cultural traditions in Egypt are so against this dancing, so especially for us (Egyptian) dancers, it became too hard to deal with it all.[37]

I reflected upon this history as I headed straight for the bathroom to apply lipstick. I opened the door and jolted back at the intense commotion I happened upon. Two bathroom attendants furiously flocked about attending to women's needs throughout the large bathroom. Every inch of mirror space was taken up with women changing their clothes into something more "clubwear"-appropriate and applying full faces of makeup. Skirts were hiked up a couple of inches shorter, breasts pushed up a cup size or two bigger, and eyes more darkly lined. A transformation in the codes of femininity was transpiring here. However, as usual, particularly in Cairo, the bathroom offered no respite, not for a shy "belly dance journalist" nor from the policing Martin theorized.

I recalled another disco night with my wealthy friend Hameed and the six women my age from his area he footed the bill for to enjoy the night with us. They were intrigued by me, Hameed's American female friend when he spoke no English, but I was more so intrigued by how my sweet friend Hameed pulled up to my apartment in his Mercedes full of six beautifully dolled-up ladies! When I went to the bathroom with them, the necessary female social ritual upon disco entrance, Leila, one of Hameed's recently divorced friends, was debating on how much cleavage to show for the night. Leila's little cousin chastised her over her unbuttoned blouse with a stern headshaking and aggressive buttoning back up of her shirt. Her other cousin preceded to unbutton not only the first two buttons but also a third with a wink, joking with her that this is how all the divorced "go about." The first cousin swatted her away and covered her back up. Finally, Leila shooed them both away, completely rebuttoning as she policed herself back into covering up with a self-conscious giggle.

Local gendered norms still permeated the space, even if more loosely undone. I remembered speaking with Reda troupe principal lead, Farida Fahmy on upper-class women and dancing. She was happy that she noticed more and more upper-class women publicly socially dancing and with more abandon since she was in her youth; she noted this change as a sign of elite women's societal progress.[38] Fahmy's observation and analysis align with dominant state narratives of modernity and parallel the policing of *hijab* at the entrance to these sites as well. Within nationalist state projects women become burdened as bearers of both national cultural identity as well as modernity, a particularly pressing labor as these identities often conflict within lived reality.[39]

Back at Ahmed's table, giant fancy cups full of various snacks and candies adorned tabletops alongside insanely overpriced shishas, red bulls, and hard liquor. Looking around, I noticed many men were also vaping; ah, now I understood why all my male companions that could never afford to party in discos had asked for me to bring them vapes from the United States—they were a status symbol. The DJ's stand shone bright with LED designs all around as he mixed commercial music, starting to sprinkle in some Egyptian pop. As more and more Egyptian hits began playing the energy in the disco shifted. There was an immediate visceral change in the environment when Egyptian music began blasting as opposed to the commercial English hits from before. It was time to start the first set. All in all, as expertly described by Zara, "discos are just how Egypt does clubbing. As the (professional) dancer, it is like you're a part of everyone's party. It is still all about that dynamic of connection. And I still feel empowered, I'm still a solo woman on stage, known by name, not an anonymous cage dancer, pulling the audience with me."[40] I turned with excitement as cheers from the crowd at the opposite end of the disco announced the dancer's arrival.

Set 1: Sahar

Sahar was escorted onto the stage by two muscled security men. Whereas at my previous sites security had focused on guests at entryways, here they focused on the singers and dancers, getting them on and off stage as well as flanking the small stage or bar's perimeter while they performed. This added to the celebrity "air" of each performer while also properly placing security to quell any disputes that arose during the performances, as crowds would often rush the stage, partying shoulder to shoulder with other guests. The choreography of the security made me wonder if and why proximity may warrant greater policing, and to what ends?

Complementary to her towering height, Sahar's powerhouse energy and instantly infectious charisma were already catching all the guests' attention even from our far end of the thin, winding stage. Rather than parade up and down the stage, making an "entrance" *mejance* typical of a full-length standard *raqs sharqi* performance, Sahar began by staying in place and interacting with the groups of guests standing immediately around her. She started off with a trending *mahraganat* song that had just come out earlier in the week. Unlike her foreign counterparts, Sahar already clearly had the lyrics memorized—of course, being Egyptian, she didn't need to dually translate the words while also memorizing. With her right foot planted, she hopped forward and back, with a heavy plié down into the ground with each hop of her left leg in a movement stylized from *mahraganat* street festivals. Meanwhile, her arms and hands imitated the gesture of cutting knives (*matwua*); a vernacular gesture within *mahraganat* referencing the ways predominantly men would wield butcher and small sharp knives in the original street festivals. Her mixing in of stylized street-style dance was fierce and sharp, the crowd encouraging her through verbal praise.

Social dancing performed predominantly by men to *mahraganat* during street parties, festivals, and weddings incorporates improvisational athletic and high-energy movements entwining aspects of social urban dance, hip hop, EDM, *sha3bi*, and break dance, and usually features *matwua* and machetes. It is distinctly urban Egyptian with a strong aesthetic of both hard-hitting percussive accents and powerful isolations as well as incredibly smooth flowing movements, particularly with the torso and arm work. The dance includes lots of floorwork such as squatting, kicking, and hopping movements. When performing it as part of their set, *raqs sharqi* dancers may incorporate a mix of *raqs baladi* movements, *matwua* dancing gestures (often with hands in a fist with just the thumb and/or pinky extended to represent the knives), and gestures and expressions that reflect the meaning of the lyrics with a more socially constructed "masculine" aesthetic compared to *raqs sharqi* technique and aesthetics.

Sahar then strutted over to our end of the stage and towered above us as she isolated her chest into wildly articulate and impressive circles. I was pulled in by her contrasting use of energies; she strutted over to us so slowly and self-assuredly before erupting into rapid-fire chest circles. She was constantly interacting with the guests, using the lyrics to joke and exchange with them through her facial expressions and vernacular gestures. Her interaction gave off the vibe that she was everyone's party buddy, there to hype up their celebrations, a factor further reinforced by the intimacy of proximity to the patrons the performance setting levied. There was a birthday party celebrating at the table beside ours. The women from the table all had their cell phones out as they sat on the edge of the stage filming themselves belting out the lyrics with Sahar just behind them.

Sahar was stunning. A renowned Canadian instructor and workshop host Melissa Gamal had dubbed her "Egypt's most innovative dancer," and this resonated with everything about Sahar. Sahar was truly a success story when it came to discos. She was *shatra* (clever) in knowing how to adapt her style, costuming, makeup, musicality, and movements in ways that perfectly blended the upper-class tastes of the disco audiences with her own natural charisma and strong Egyptian character. She was, like the popular songs she danced to, "trending," a key adjective of success in these sites. Her costume was a tight mermaid-fitted skirt with attached lacey waist straps that made it almost appear as if she had hiked-up a lacy thong from underneath. Her bra was cut out wide in the middle with cups emblazoned in pearls to really show off and highlight her enhanced and fit curvy body. Suddenly, Sahar grabbed the phone of the birthday girl and stood tall, undulating her body while giving a wink and laugh to what would end up as a live Instagram story. Sahar tilted her head down, holding the camera at arm's length, and winked again as she erupted into three robust chest pops while laughingly widening her eyes and beaming brightly into the blinding light from the phone's camera.

My friend and fellow dancer Roberto was visiting from the United States and had met up with Zara and I for clubbing that night. (He'd also graciously brought me a fresh restock of non-shredded tights.) He was dancing socially with Zara then stopped and snatched my arm while enthusiastically shouting in my ear, "Wow, can she command a room! Not just her literal height, but her interaction and how she just *grabbed* that phone with that LOOK!" I gestured that I could barely hear him over the blasting music, so he texted me the rest, shisha hose still in hand. *She is such a powerful dancer, and you know what? She is smart. It's like she's taking the technology used to promote herself, but on her own terms; owning it. Like, yeah look, this is me . . . now come catch my show next Saturday!* I glanced up from the text as a fit of laughter erupted from the birthday group beside us; the next song was a still popular *mahraganat* song with a slang line referring to a woman as a "scratchy cat." During this line, Sahar used her same smolderingly direct eye contact while bouncing her butt from a bent-over angled position and pointing and smirking at the enthused birthday girl. I smiled and nodded at Roberto's astute assessment. These *mahraganat* songs, necessary to dance on in this site, were full of *sha3bi* and double entendres that would often go right over the heads of non-native speakers but also often even those not from more *sha3bi* areas and backgrounds.[41]

The lyrics were calling a girl a "scratchy cat." Many Egyptians and foreigners might critique these as meaningless empty lyrics from a history of music that used to extoll honor and depth. But again, this represents not only a nostalgic reconstruction of history (akin to that of dancers) but also a misunderstanding. In a similar fashion to dance, the *mahraganat* musical genre, as well as preceding *sha3bi* and classical *tarab* musical genres, have all been critiqued at points in history as "less than," but as time changes aesthetics shift as well, and such critiques often embody reconstructed nostalgic histories embedded with classist and aesthetic politics.[42] I'd watched countless foreign dancers in discos also perform to this song and make adorable cat gestures, often ears or scratchy paws, to "show off" their understanding and create an exchange with the crowd. It worked; it was cute that they knew the song and had invested in learning the lyrics.

However, Sahar leans deeper into the potentiality available to her from her Egyptian background in this moment by vernacularly gesturing in a way that highlights the underlying meaning of the scratchy cat—that is, a woman who is clever and who you can't pull any tricks on. In pointing to the birthday girl with a smirk, she creates a subtle exchange that's connective in a mutually shared understanding of language and subversive powerplays of gendered culture. She doesn't have to use cliché exaggerated gestures to signal, "Hey, look at me, I know your language;" rather, she connects in ways that highlight solidarity and connection between shared experience of lived reality. In other words, scratchy as a tactic of gendered survival, albeit to varying degrees dependent on class background.

It was such a subtle swift exchange that I probably would have overlooked it if not for the timing of Roberto's comment. He could have easily just focused on her butt bounce, literally up close and personal due to the crowded space and raised stage, but his objective for returning to Cairo was, similar to my own ethnographic positionality, also to learn as a dedicated mentee. As belly dance scholar Sellers-Young argues, it's the relationship between audiences and performers that is crucial to the meanings at play around gender.[43] Again, as my aim is to not only have you take a seat and listen with me throughout this ride, at this site-specific chapter stop my hope is that you'll eventually get with the embodied environment the dancer is working to cultivate. This necessitates returning to the responsibility and agency we all hold within our interconnected weaved webs of relationality, on the part of audiences, participants, and performers. As the "scratchy cat" embodies, the more depth of understanding the more depth of connection.

Roberto and I both caught eyes, smiled, and began dancing all out with the crowd, foreheads dampened with sweat from the density of packed bodies. On nights like this, it was impossible to stay in clear "observation" mode due to getting caught up in the vibe of the disco. As I came to learn, this was essential to the possibility of disco-dancing knowledge. During the next *mahraganat* song Sahar made her way back down and up the winding S-shaped "stage" back toward our group. The birthday party beside us perked up and sprang out of their chairs to begin dancing right on the stage's perimeter with Sahar. The birthday girl caught Sahar's eye, and safely from the slight shielding the crowded dim disco enabled, saucily enacted one of Sahar's signature moves—the cross-armed, hand-driven breast side-side waggle. I was a bit taken aback that she initiated this, but Sahar burst out laughing and joined in on the movement, although Sahar was, of course, publicly exposed and visible from the raised stage and via the bedazzled push-up she wore. Although this move is popular and known as one of Sahar's signature moves, as the guest's imitation demonstrates it's important to call attention to the fact that most of the "risqué" moves popularized in disco dancing from the site's higher public visibility are commonplace in the more hidden sites of working-class dancers such as the cabaret circuit and *sha3bi* weddings. I've regularly seen moves from discos critiqued as the most "risqué" in working-class cabarets, and dance historian Heather Ward has likewise argued that such movements and aesthetics are commonplace in working-class *sha3bi* weddings by *sha3bi* dancers, they are just less visible.[44]

Both women laughed and then grasped hands together in solidarity, Sahar now extending her butt out to shimmy it intensely with the intensifying music. The birthday girl shook out her long curly hair and squealed in celebratory excitement; she was really letting loose! The birthday party cheered wildly as well, supportive of her letting go; well, at least for the moment within this time and place. Sahar spun briskly and then sultrily slowed down into sexy, wonderfully controlled syrupy body undulations before moving on to the other tables.

I was reminded of what my dancer friend Zara had stated about these sites and audiences in particular:

Oh yeah, they look forward to the belly dancer coming, you feel the change when she comes on, maybe it's a relief? Haha. Maybe all these folks would be way happier in a cabaret, but they'd never go there simply because it would be deemed low class haha, so they'd never allow themselves! Yet, they allow their barriers to come down and be more natural . . . not just when dancer comes on but also with *sha3bi*, they like Western music to feel chic, but it never touches us the same as our own music in our own language. They may have disassociated from *sha3bi*, but all these songs coming up are *sha3bi* singers, *sha3bi* lyrics, with *mawwal*, discussing personal and bigger problems, this is what pulls on your heart as an Egyptian, nothing touches you like that, it's like a relief from their superficiality, the dancers and *sha3bi*, it's our culture.[45]

I found myself nodding as I looked out across the crowd going wild to a hit Egyptian pop song, the music and dancer cultivating a looser environment than that of the image-conscious judgments I met outside the disco walls.

Zara insightfully touches on the seeming paradox of disco club *raqs sharqi* and working-class *sha3bi* and *mahraganat* at large: how the two can both be so denigrated in public discourse, yet so desired and popular amongst the upper classes in this site. The interrelation between the site itself, akin to Michel Foucault's concept of heterotopias, and Peter Stallybrass and Allon White's argument that "repugnance and fascination as the twin poles of the process in which a political imperative to reject and eliminate the debasing 'low' conflicts powerfully and unpredictably with a desire for this Other."[46] Foucault's heterotopias are spatial-temporal sites that exist in every society but are distinct sites historically contextualized in relation to other societal sites, existing as places where the norms and exclusions of dominant society may be transgressed and even celebrated.[47] Zara grounds his theory to centralize class elements negotiated by corporealities dancing in the disco through comparison to the working-class *sha3bi* cabaret.

Through putting the two distinctly classed sites, and the bodies working and dancing within them, into conversation she highlights the necessity of diving into a deeper dissection of the closed off disco's ephemeral liberating transgression of these class inequalities. This chapter likewise aims to step deeper into proximity with this critical intervention through exploring dancers' disco-situated embodied insight. The next song started and Sahar was gone, set over. Had it been fifteen minutes already? Disco sets fly by!

Scoot Over?

I started this chapter blasting disco-style music to "embody the environment" of the site to write fieldnotes; well, that was just an ethnographic warm-up. These dancers lived grueling lifestyles. Conducting my fieldwork I often felt exhausted from the all-nighters and constant commotion, but it also signaled to me that my fieldwork was embodying the dance frameworks. Tonight (this morning?) was no different. My friend Ayman and I had finished a long night of gig-hopping to follow Sahar, having discussed doing another round of interviewing between her shows—at some point. That point was now, after all her shows, sometime around 4am, pulled over in Ayman's car on the side of the highway a bit passed the venue where Sahar had just been performing. After a reshuffling of bodies, we all squeezed into Ayman's car, scarcely off to the side of the highway, to conduct the interview. At least it was quiet. Sahar and I caught up since our last round of interviews, and I congratulated her on her sustained success across elite performance venues.

She helped me understand her approach to discos and consequent success, one of the few Egyptians highly renowned in these sites.

> For discos I keep my eye on the trend, it's all about being trending. I know my people (Egyptians) very well, I know what they want to see, hear, and how. If they just want *mahraganat* and *sha3bi*, okay, *khalas*, I do it for the popularity and joy of the people around me, they are my guests. You always must dance according to the place and the people, any smart dancer knows this. Every place and audience has its own color, you need to be aware of this and implement it. Look, the problem with disco dancing is sometimes some foreigners, not all, come and do not understand the line between sexy and vulgar. There's a line within our culture, between sexy, being sexy is desirable and good, and being "over" sexy, which is too much. Some foreigners don't understand, sexy is outright sexy in their culture maybe, not here, so they don't understand that, so they come with that "over-sexy" and no other understanding that discos require, so this creates issues.[48]

I asked her to explain more about this fine line, and how a dancer would get that understanding.

> I'm Egyptian. That's it. I'm Egyptian, I understand. My people, the lines, the trend, the lyrics and music, the words, and the way to play with the crowd in each type of place. How I express myself through my charisma in line with the musical mood and the lyrics with the particular people around me to make it a shared charisma. That's it. It is a shared feeling through shared understanding—Egyptian understanding.

I tried enthusiastically to encourage her to elaborate on the role of understanding and interaction in discos, but she just kept shaking her head saying, "I'm Egyptian." I can imagine how difficult it is to try to put into words something that feels so natural, but it's important to note how incredibly innovative and clever Sahar is. For an Egyptian to come up in this environment across multiple elite strata of venues and be so successful for years highlights her skills and "scratchy" smarts beyond simply pulling on a naturalized identity. The nuance of her smarts will become more elucidated as the show progresses.

Quick Costume and Venue Change

Hang on—as the disco dancers quickly change their costumes for their second set, we need to change venues. Next up, for the final quick set, we have Najla Ferreira at Koo Lounge. OK, so arriving at Koo Lounge would practically take far longer than a dancer's miraculously rapid costume change. While discos proliferated throughout greater Cairo there were a number of them, such as Koo Lounge, that were on the farther outskirts of Cairo, in areas quickly becoming known for gated districts and development for the upper classes wanting an escape from the hustle and bustle of Cairo. Koo Lounge, for example, which had opened in April 2019, was located at the top of a building in the fifth settlement, about a half hour's drive from the main area of Cairo at a late hour after the traffic had dissipated. I could tell our ride was approaching Koo when the setting changed. Looking out the backseat window I no longer felt I was in Cairo. "It's more like Lebanon, right?" Ayman, my comrade for the evening, stated from the front seat. I nodded as my eyes gazed upon the tall buildings, department stores with shiny exteriors and bright lit-up names, and fashionable shopping malls. I'd never been to Lebanon, but the comment gesturing toward intra-MENA flows was interesting for the way that it complexified pan-MENA locals of perceived modernity as opposed to the unidirectional "Westernization" critique laden on elite youth and discos. Ayman explained that these areas outside Cairo were populated, or were soon to be, by the wealthier classes and designed by the state to get away from the grind of Cairo's density and gridlocked traffic while providing more modernized amenities and shopping.

I remembered researching literature on gentrification in Cairo, how during Mubarak's presidency large shopping malls and international coffee chains, plus these gated district compounds for the wealthy, were creating further cleavages in the already massive class inequalities, but also achieved greater gendered mobility for elite women.[49] We arrived, simply parking our car in what seemed a barren dirt lot, and walked up to the building entrance. A few guests and workers were smoking outside the building, but I didn't feel like anybody noticed me, and I was even less dressed up than when I went to Clubhouse. I remember Farah, who was also a featured dancer at Koo, explaining this to me when I was "okaying" my more business casual dress with her on a previous fieldwork night. She explained the variations of "A class" groups in Cairo, and how each disco tended to cater to a certain stratum. Koo catered toward the rich who lived in the fifth settlement and other outskirts, who didn't need to show off that they had money like other more newly rich (or not quite but perceiving to be) strata. So my jeans, boots, and fake leather jacket were perfectly fine. I shook my head at the flat social media policing and shaming that often solely focused on national identity and difference at the rich expense of the myriad ways class, gender, and nationality all function within Cairo. Not only were high profile dancers in elite sites the main sliver of access used by outsiders in the industry, but even within that sliver there was a great variety of how the upper classes identified, gathered, and geographically were located. My contrasting embodied experience entering the sites revealed as much.

We dropped our names to get into Koo, as I'd already spoken with the approachable owner about my research, and security escorted us up an elevator to the floor Koo Lounge was on. Even inside Koo, I felt far more comfortable than the handful of other discos I'd gone to in Cairo. I remember the owner explaining the open air roof is what made Koo unique. It did feel far less dense than other clubs, with bodies in general but also with the judgments of image-conscious glances. Perhaps the open-air concept correlated with the elite gated districts on Cairo's outskirts, the open "breath of fresh air" providing relief not just from the inconveniences of Cairo but also the need to set oneself apart in a packed club. (Unfortunately, this also relates to the lack of shared space with other classes; one of gentrification's selling points.)

I chuckled as I recognized one man dancing full out in the center of the disco; the owner of the place, Morad, was partying right alongside his guests. I pondered with amusement at his awesomely enthused moves; was he was simply enjoying the fruits of his labor or was this partially a business tactic as well? When I interviewed the owner previously, he explained to me, "These clubs are so popular now because it's a good business. Everyone is trying to escape the headache of life these days, so there are so many clubs opening up, not just clubs, the whole economy of Egypt is waking up; Egypt is finally waking up!"[50] I nodded, I found his correlation with the awakening of Egypt and the focus on economic improvement and "good business" typical of much mainstream thought at this time. This thinking aligned with the strategies and goals of the state government as well. I asked him why he chose this specific location. "I was always thinking to open here, me and my brother, in New Cairo, it was so empty and cheap before, but I always knew this area would be like a totally different country one day, not like Egypt, no, there's no noise, no traffic, no headache, so we need a place like this out here. We target the A-plus-plus class out here, ya know?"

I also asked about dancers, why they have been popularized again and how he chooses dancers for his club:

> Every club is about belly dancers now! After the Russian, French, Italian . . . these foreigners upgraded and revitalized the dancing and of course, we love Egyptian belly dancers too, I'm Egyptian, it's our culture. She has to look amazing; I only bring A-plus class-looking acts for the A-plus crowd. Also, the name dancers, her name is what brings my guests, I only bring the famous ones. Most important is how she interacts with guests like she is familiar with them, you would think they are so good friends. She must make this awesome interaction and play, sing, and dance with them. Did you try our sushi? We have amazing sushi, we upgraded everything!

Morad's discussion of dancers was intriguing for multiple reasons. First, historically it was not foreigners who popularized these sites, everything was by and for Egyptians. What does losing sight of this history enable? Second, two of the early Egyptian dancers who had popularized these sites (quoted earlier) have both now moved on, hinting at, or specifically referencing, "risqué decay" as a major reason; how does this intersect with the "lost" popularization "by and for Egyptians" narrative? Further, there was a tension in Morad's discussion of dancers; he began by stating the importance of a famous name and the foreign "upgrade," and mentioned the required "look"—referencing the "Westernized" refined elite look—thus seeming to side with privileges of foreign dancers. However, he then stated that the most vital factor in choosing dancers is guest interaction and exchange, facets that foreigners often lack in comparison to Egyptian counterparts due to language and cultural barriers and unfamiliarity. This tension ties back into what Zara dubbed the "rigged competition." *Oh.* I snapped back to the present as the owner saw me and waved merrily, but as I started walking over to greet him the entire crowd of socially dancing and drinking guests thronged over to the small, raised stage area in front of the DJ booth. A new hit *mahragan* song was playing and by the wave of energy, I could tell that the dancer had begun her set.

DISCOS 167

Figure 3.3 Najla Ferreira performs at a disco. Credit: Najla Ferreira

Set 2: Najla Ferreira at Koo Lounge

I was super excited to see Najla. The first time, I caught her mid-way through her short final set and was mesmerized by her charisma and interaction; I had to figure out who she was! Tonight, Najla was wearing spiked heels to help make up for the natural stage presence taller dancers like Sahar had. Her olive skin and long black hair moved sinuously with every movement like a mermaid. She was wearing a bright red designer bra and skirt costume, modern and beautiful but not at all boundary-pushing like many other super-sexy modern-style costumes worn on these same stages. Her skin-colored boy shorts shone beneath the otherwise sexy thigh cut-outs of her costume; clearly, she wanted everyone to know she was wearing them. Her full breasts reverberated beautifully with her shimmies as she playfully danced while joking with guests at the front of the stage.

However, despite how fluidly Najla moved her torso to the lyrics and melody of the song, it was her infectious facial expressions and personality that instantly made you fall in love with her. She completely enthralled the now gathered crowd. After spending so many nights in various discos, I had learned to feel which dancers were able to captivate the whole disco by this initial energetic "wave" that would magnetize and draw the crowd to rush the stage. Najla was definitely one of those dancers who had a greater than average magnetism.

Najla had impressive technique and musicality, and she didn't shy away from sprinkling in more "spectacular" technique that often reigned in social media clips from these sites; she tossed her long locks in a crazed figure-eight pattern when the song also went into a frenzy, and she had explosive chest pops that perfectly caught the percussive accents in the music. However, whether her breasts or butt were literally "in your face" due to the venue proximity, Najla never came across to me as vulgar or risqué, not from my perspective of witnessing in the flesh. Well, I guess that's part of it; witnessing isn't the right word. With dancers like Najla and Sahar you were pulled in and jumping and shimmying along with them. It always felt like more of an exchange and togetherness. Both dancers' technique, expert musical interpretation, glam costuming, and insanely gorgeous looks clearly set them apart as professional entertainers. Yet, at the same time, their charisma and interaction made you feel like they were your ideal party-going buddy that always got the nights lit.

Najla's eyes were constantly widening in innocent exaggeration as she'd laugh alongside her guests after doing a "cheeky" butt waggle or explosive chest pop. She'd belt out the lyrics of the song when she was particularly feeling it, often at the same time as the guests. My reading of her feeling it was through her all-out facial expressions, total embodied engagement with the music, and the sensed energy exuding from her pores. It was this embodied environment of unity some successful dancers were capable of cultivating that led to their sustainability; an embodied "sensed" environment that pulled in the flesh but was far harder to "read" in a social media clip.[51]

The women I was standing shoulder-to-shoulder with seemed to be feeling the charismatic energy too. A woman my age was filming Najla with her phone in one hand while her husband's arm was wrapped around her waist; she swayed side-to-side with him as they beamed up at Najla while singing along with the song. The woman turned the recording camera to face her and her husband, they leaned their heads in together and belted out the lyrics to whoever was watching on the receiving end. She then used the camera to record up and down her outfit while carefully pulling out her silver necklaces, brushing her hair back to show off her wrist full of bracelets and a designer watch alongside matching earrings that glinted in the disco lights. Her eyes softened and her lips slightly pursed; she seemed transformed and absorbed in the video capture, momentarily out of the groove we'd all just been enjoying. Taken all together, the woman's showing off of Najla's blinged-out costume, refined makeup, and looks suited to upper-class sensibilities, alongside her own designer jewelry, all while modestly enveloped by her husband and the coinciding protections of marriage and a high-cut top, allowed her to reap not only enthused energy but also social capital from proximity to Najla's dancing. Without the dancer's threat of risqué labeling, the woman raised her eyebrows slyly and again switched the camera, zooming in as Najla performed a deep backbend, with only Najla's full cleavage and the surrounding edges of her jewel-encrusted bra cups filling the screen.

Meanwhile, for me as a practitioner-ethnographer, no matter what body part of Najla was inadvertently in my face, particularly so close in a physically precarious position such as a backbend, I was more so captivated by the confidence these performers must have. To be so exposed, yet so self-assured, so close to bodies (also often image-conscious elite crowds with mobiles out and recording), the triple-threat of policing (self, society, state) always hanging over their heads, and on such tiny hard to maneuver stages or bars took guts. From her backbend, Najla plunged into a Turkish drop, expertly catching the end of the song. The crowd erupted as she slowly got up, still beaming and joking with the guests as if they were all best friends. I was always struck by how quickly the mini-disco sets flew by. Two security men flanked Najla and escorted her off from the tiny stage and they all disappeared into the throng of the crowd.

Figure 3.4 Najla Ferreira performs at a disco. Credit: Najla Ferreira

Wait, You Got to Get with the Vibe of the Place

Still seated and waiting. I was glad for my coffee obsession as I waited to meet up with Najla for our interview at an upscale coffee shop; the interview was supposed to have started well over an hour, and multiple lattes, ago. As much as I loved the dynamic contrasts in textures within modern *raqs sharqi* dancers, transitioning between super quick and articulated percussive accents right into sinuously slowed down and savory undulations and hip rolls, the same seemingly night-and-day contrast between ethnographic interviewing was sometimes hard to manage on a budgeted, tightknit schedule. I was either dealing with intensely improvisational, random, and innovative "on the fly" interviews like with Sahar, or found myself waiting and waiting for neatly arranged interviews that never seemed to materialize anywhere near the appointed time.

As I sat here, calmly enjoying the solitude of the non-smoking (and thus, non-occupied) upper section of the coffee shop, my thoughts turned to this familiar seated positionality. Grappling with my own kinesthetic activity within disco sites, I could not simply "have a seat" and observe, I was constantly, at the least, bopping or swaying along, if not yanked up and all out partying with the performers and my comrades of the evening. How was this ethnographic choreography conflicting with my positionality section I introduced myself to you all with, about "having a seat" and letting intra-MENA bodies take up the dance floor?

These thoughts and more stirred through my head as I enthusiastically waited for Najla. There had to be "something" to this differing choreography of mine as ethnographer in this specific site. My contemplation was cut off as Najla and another dancer-colleague arrived and plopped down across from me, ordering coffee and cheesecakes. I was immediately struck by how warm and engaging Najla was; that infectious charisma she had on stage was just an extension of her everyday persona. She happily shared about her background and beginnings, how her identity as half Brazilian and half Palestinian, but growing up mostly in the Emirates, shaped her character and approach to *raqs sharqi*. She came across as ambitious and full of life, her spirited gesturing and animated facial expressions with every twist of the tales she told keeping me eagerly anticipating whatever she'd share next. She explained that Rawi in the Sheraton hotel was her "home base" disco, and that as a non-Egyptian she didn't have the paperwork required to work on more elite sites such as the five-star hotels that only hired Egyptians. It was also a great opportunity to meet and hear from her fellow professionally disco-gigging colleague, also of MENA heritage.⁵²

In discussing the different sites of dance and paperwork Najla brought up a few differences between Egyptian and non-Egyptian dancers.

> First, many Egyptians won't want to work in discos because they have other options to make more money (hotels, cabarets), it's challenging for someone expert in embodying the complexities of Egyptian music to dance on these same flat songs for the whole set. I'm sure there are always more Egyptian professionals out there, we just aren't aware of them because they always keep it more hidden and off social media. There's always more risk for an Egyptian, with the cultural stigma and real repercussions, policing and shaming from all angles (family and society).⁵³

She then turned toward Sahar and her own identity and understanding of the dance in MENA context.

> Now Sahar, from what I know, Sahar is a celebrity, she must've given up everything to be a dancer, I don't know what problems she has with her family, I'm sure she has none (family), but she's one of the few risking it all to come out and up- which she has. I feel it's a real freedom for Sahar. That's what folks don't understand, there are so many Arab dancers, but you come out and throw stones at what you see us doing in clips from these discos, but we're saints compared to what goes on in *sha3bi* weddings and the majority of dance contexts, it's just never seen by you all. I'm half Arabic, have Arabic family, lived in the Middle East, worked as a dancer, to be honest I know what belly dancing is here, and it does not bother me. I know who I am. I know why I like to do this, I enjoy it, it pays me well, I don't care what people say, and believe me they say! Just because you put on a *badlat raqs, khalas,* you are this! I just wish people realized the reality . . .

I swallowed a lump in my throat. Some of the most profound embodied experiences I've had throughout my fieldwork were these interview moments. Most dancers' eyes would widen as they'd lean a bit forward as they so self-assuredly claimed ownership of who they were, without internalized acceptance of those thrown stones. This is why I've committed to teaching dance as well, to help facilitate the unloading of these stones in students, unburdening the self and society-imposed restrictions of respectability politics, "Oh, I wear mesh belly covers, I don't do floorwork, I don't take costume tips." So many limitations, and to ultimately appease what or whom? However, Najla gestures to the importance of the uneven weight and size of stones thrown at Egyptian dancers.

Najla continued elaborating on the realities:

This art form, mostly, we've all only seen it in cinema, you can't compare cinema to real life, those Golden Era dancers in movies weren't the same as in the flesh! Movies are fluffy, there's censorship and regulations! At the same time, even throughout that censored history, dancers have always been construed as husband-stealers and loose women, am I wrong? Even history makes it clear. We've all always been seen this way; it just gets super taken out of context in the West. Unfortunately, or perhaps, fortunately, we're getting films live from real life here, we're working dancers in a very serious business, in a specific environment; so what can you do in this environment? You must dance accordingly, and I'm not shy to say, I love dancing for Arab audiences, the energy's cyclical, *mahraganat* music is crazy, if you don't dance accordingly, you're dancing in limitation.

Ah, limitation, there's that linkage, perhaps the role of the risqué is to expose and flesh out what lies beyond the limitations we're all so entrapped beneath?

Our conversation turned toward perceived "problems" in Cairo *raqs sharqi*, particularly how dancers' technique and aesthetics were embodying *mahraganat*. "I think I'm considered one of the problems!" She threw her head back and laughed. "I don't think anyone likes this movement that's happening, but you can't stop it from happening." Her friend interjected, "Now there's this newer style of *raqs sharqi*, to music that the country is fighting, and nobody really accepts, *mahraganat*, but we're promoting it, so yes, we're also problem makers! I used to think it was a problem too until I had to work with it. This is the future, when a movement starts growing it's going to keep growing until it dies, *mahraganat* has proven that it's big, it's going, and we as club dancers promoting it won't stop either, because of our audiences, they want this."

I asked them both why they thought *mahraganat* remained so popular across classes if it was vehemently unaccepted at government and institutional levels. (During my fieldwork and writing the musicians' syndicate and other government officials waged multiple campaigns to constrain and ban the music and singers.)[54] Najla began enthusiastically: "It's fashion! When something new happens and the music is great, lyrics are fantastic . . . ." Her colleague then took over, leaning forward in zeal:

> Look, people are suffering; I feel these boys from the younger generation, some are uneducated, but they're hurting and suffering, they live in bad areas, they see there are lots of rich people, but they have nothing, streets piled in garbage, without proper sewage, and they're hungry. They start singing from pain, and they found success. Now their success is making them money and bringing them a lot. So now you want to stop them, they're suffering, they found their own way to survive, and now you want to cut them off? Why, are they not the kind of people you want to see thriving? Why does art have to be just one thing? Why does the government have to put guidelines on who is an artist and who is not? If you're creating something, and people love you, then you should be recognized by the state.

I asked Najla's friend why she felt the state wasn't recognizing this musical genre. "We can't know, we can speculate. I think they want to bring this country to a different class, a certain refined Egyptian. They don't want the people, which is the majority, to shine, they want to throw sand on that, cover it up. And the people have power, and that's the majority." I asked if she could talk more about the class aspects as I considered the paradoxes of the "refined" upper classes loving to enjoy *mahraganat* and wanting dancers who "get it" but simultaneously aren't given a chance to step on stage without a suitable class-sensible "look," versus the history of *mahraganat* from working-class *sha3bi* areas—people who could never afford to enter a disco. "Everyone has pain. When you sing about pain, me, you, the poor man, rich man, we all suffer. So yes, it resonates with everyone. Maybe not at the same level or in the same way, but we all felt injustice and pain. It touches everyone."

I asked more about the interaction with audiences in discos, and how they work with the music and dance to be successful. Now Najla stepped in:

> Look, not bragging, but understanding is what's key in discos. There's a difference between an Arabic-speaking native that grew up with this music at home, experiencing it at home, as a child, growing up through all your life experiences with it, verse someone who learned later in life or just gets translations. There are traditions and culture embedded in language, *ya3ny . . . saltana . . . al gharammm . . .* it tastes different when you were raised in that language, a different quality, Egyptians know that and want

Figure 3.5 Najla Ferreira performs at a disco. Credit: Najla Ferreira

that. The popular Egyptians and Arabs here follow certain trends. We pick music that's super trending, we understand the music so well, foreigners can't say these words, it's slang-slang, even for me it takes a while, it's street slang! Look at half Egyptian Linda, she doesn't do much at all, but she transmits so much, she is a monster and eats the crowd with her feeling. She memorizes and feels the music so deeply, Sahar the same, she feels the music and understands it so deeply, what's going on in the music, it is power.

I asked her about how she sees foreign dancers that are most visible in these sites. Her friend articulated:

Dancers that cannot do what Najla just said, or not as much, what they focus on instead is movement, like "wow" technique. Look at some of them, they're incredible acrobats and nobody can compete with their dexterity, some of them are just amazing, but in general, foreigners don't have that same quality of understanding that Linda, Sahar, Najla, and I have. I see us as distinguished in a different way. We don't have to do much, but the crowd is crazy, you can feel it. Another well-known foreigner, she dances so nice and the show's technically phenomenal, but you'll feel it, the energy's a little cold. It's success in a different way. So, you see, understanding in club sites is key. Otherwise, you must do things so over the top and crazy so people are like, "whoa."

Najla interjected: "But it is the understanding and charisma, they go hand in hand, that's key to success here. *Wallahi*, most of the time my heels and the floor are too high, I'm terrified of falling off haha, but it's the laughing, singing, knowing, the exchange—it is powerful."

Najla's colleague excused herself to catch an appointment in Mohandessin, so I asked Najla if she had any final thoughts to wrap up the invigorating interview. We had talked for hours yet it felt as short as a disco set due to Najla's charismatic vigor. Najla's tone calmed.

Ya know, I just feel so much love here. I feel I am at home with people who understand me. It's a different vibe than in the Emirates. At first, I thought I hated disco dancing ha, but I realized I feel more comfortable in this kind of place than in other sites of raqs sharqi. But I just want you to know, I really feel like there's not enough understanding. I think it's so disrespectful what I see online, if we believe in freedom, if "the West" believes in freedom because you are from the West, and I see many of these criticizers coming from there as well; practice what you preach! If you believe in freedom in your country, then let it be everywhere else in the world as well.

We both paused. Najla took a deep breath and continued, "So when I'm dancing in a club, what am I to do?! You got to get with the vibe of the place, that's what it is! We are with the vibe, and people cannot see vibe!" I felt chills run down my spine all the way to my seated hips.

Exposing in Order to Flesh Out

Disco *raqs sharqi* slides deeper into Rosemary Martin's argument to expansively theorize that the role of the risqué is to viscerally and vulnerably *expose* the non-emancipatory systems and structures that are safeguarded by policing at all triple-threat levels of state, society, and self. Simultaneously, if dancers can "get with the vibe" of the disco, and thus create a certain connection with audiences, they're also able to expose and embody alternative emancipatory relationalities at the cutting edge of society. The cultivation of "vibe" between bodies within the space as initiated by the always at-risk dancer is vital, for her risqué power to expose and embody exists in a liminal space dependent upon shared relational interplay. As I recalled my own hips, from stiffly waddling under scrutiny into Clubhouse versus their gooey circling alongside Sahar and Najla, to their now seatededness in deep listening, I leaned forward into the knowledge that vibe is an embodied environment cultivated through moving into a shared understanding. This vibe necessitates not only exposing but also embracing and exchanging risk embedded within the actions of risqué corporealities. However, as recounted, vibe isn't always achieved. In essence, the interplay of Najla and Sahar with their guests demonstrates how proximity to the risqué can be liberating and, or, create social capital. Ultimately, what meanings are generated depends on whether we're each able to get with the vibe of the disco.

Returning to the cunning of Ahmed Widan in opening up and popularizing discos in Cairo while still under precarity, these sites are, as he stated, "A good business," but also (*potentially*) "a type of unity." As the bejeweled lady beside me during Najla's show highlighted, the dancer's vulnerable and visceral exposing of the risqué in these sites can operate as "stigma-safe" social capital for the Egyptian elites. This proximity, without its vibing embrace, allows elite audiences to reify the privileges of entwined class, gender, and nationalist divisions and marginality within hegemonic structures and systems at self, society, and state levels. Meanwhile, the potential of alternative, albeit at-risk, liberatory knowledge circulating from the dancer's exposure remains gated and burdened upon the marginalized and policed dancer. This dynamic is epitomized by disco "success" garnered through spectacular techniques alongside consequential "cold" energy, wherein divisions often further cleave between corporealities; the risqué remains spectacularly dexterous and "wow," yet such choreographic tactics remain only available to a marginal percentage of bodies. It's not a unifying movement that just anyone can exchange and embody. Likewise, the already distanced and marginalized dancer remains further stretched into suspect sexuality and being. Meanwhile, the status quo, or center versus margin, remains distinct and unconnected as policing would have it. At the same time, audiences remain bejeweled in class, gender, and nationalist privilege and safety nets while "gated away;" predominantly unable to exchange in unison with such physically dexterous feats, but instead always being able to pay the high minimum fees to capture it on flesh and film as spectacle. Audiences remain untouched by the potential liberation of risqué corporeality.[55]

Certainly, working as a good business for the current patriarchal-capitalist system, "waking up," perhaps from the momentary upheavals of alternative revolutionary realities and emancipatory labors, in ways that maintain, and with policing protect, the already inequitable dominating systems and corporeal legacies. While this may still offer greater wiggle room in regard to elite women's gendered mobility, it's a non-revolutionary trade-off that further cleaves class divisions within inequitable structures. Similarly, this scenario is cautioned through the narratives of the two early Egyptian disco pioneers quoted earlier, who have since "moved up and on" from these sites that they too now admonish as "risqué decay."

Maya still performs at upper-class weddings, but her goals have changed. She now hopes for a family, and says she would never encourage her daughter to be a dancer because the dancer's life is too denigrated. She lovingly states that her daughter would suffer too much as she has, and she doesn't wish such hardships on anyone. She noted in our interview that society would have to change and see dance in a completely different way without stigma, and not be an industry dominated by power-hungry men.[56] The second anonymous early disco dancer, quoted earlier, also now says her dancing is more aligned with her goals to gain respectability for *raqs sharqi* (by performing only in elite contexts).[57] I do not condemn their "barters" with the hegemonic and violent system; this is their lived reality to navigate. At the same time, we cannot ignore how these barters further denigrate working-class communities and particularly women of color, the most marginalized and vulnerable in society. Due to my objective, aligning with Maya's stipulations, we must continue kinesthetically imagining and working toward more revolutionary worlds.[58]

However, if dancers and audiences are able to "get with the vibe," a type of embodied environment is cultivated wherein the proximity *with* the risqué exchanges potentially liberating possibilities and relationalities. Here, "vibe" circulates as a type of potentially emancipatory exchange and togetherness—"a type of unity." This is epitomized by disco "success" garnered not via the *extra*ordinary, but rather the ordinary, the vernacular exchange of gesturing, singing, and shared understanding that's expressed at a body level. This crystalizes in embodied exchanges such as those performed between Sahar and the birthday girl from Clubhouse, with the celebratory opening and shaking of chests breaking through such divisions and vibing in a shared understanding of alternative forms of community. In these cases, the risqué becomes untethered from specific corporealities that dominant hegemonies scandalize with intent to marginalize, police, and separate off, and is instead exchanged, embraced, and realized as a risk that any corporeality is capable of bearing; *no one* is truly free under non-emancipatory systems and inequitable structures. Meanwhile, this once marginal, yet now centrally exposed and shared "risqué" vibe, cultivates into a type of unity that's emancipatory through shared understanding and togetherness. All this vibing nudges us toward alternative emancipatory realities and relationalities. However, getting with "the vibe" is about more than a shared understanding that all bodies remain unfree and limited under inequitable hegemonies, its cultivation first necessitates exposure, a vulnerable and visceral labor requiring a courageous soul to risk it all by sliding down into and overtly shaking off normative ways of being and moving within policed reality and relationalities.

Conclusion: When the Disco Lights Cut On

The night's almost finished, so let's return to that vibe at Clubhouse. Although Sahar had likely packed her bag and moved on to her final gig an hour or two ago, my friends and I were still partying all out with the vibe she'd cultivated. I glanced over and saw the birthday girl still squealing in excitement as she tossed her long locks side-to-side with wild abandon while clasping hands with her female friends. Zara was all out shimmying her hips with the guys while I leaned back shimmying my shoulders toward Roberto; he reciprocated the gesture playfully while exhaling a plume of shisha smoke. I laughed, then *BOOM*—the disco lights cut on. At the same time, I spun quickly as Ahmed tugged down at the hem of my midthigh-length skirt, yanking its hem lower down over my thighs as I glared at him with a mixture of shock and irritation. He widened his eyes in innocence, instead tilting his head toward the surveillance camera in the corner of the building, now bearing full witness to my midthigh exposure. Did I get so lost in the music I didn't realize my skirt had hiked up a bit too high? Or did the "line" of acceptable flesh baring simply change when the lights cut on? Did I let loose too much; would I not be taken seriously in an interview now? Under the well-lit scrutiny of the surveillance camera and Ahmed's paternalism I found myself jolted back into a series of self-conscious insecurities; the vibe had been "cut off."

Writing now, I question the tangible power of the vibe beyond the corporeality of the risqué dancer. How much could guest proximity to the risqué enable if its potential vibe was so ephemeral? Furthermore, what's so empowering about a fleeting three-minute *mahraganat* song that means we can get away with sexy shaking in a hiked-up skirt, or fullheartedly singing along in a vernacular we'd dare not speak outside the disco walls, all the while partaking in embodied pleasures from places and people we'd never invite into our homes after the lights came on? Was disco *raqs sharqi* weighted more toward the role of the risqué as social capital for the already existing system rather than a vernacular-vibing liberation? I felt my heart sink. Sinking down into inequitable realities derived from constructed depravity. It was the narrative of Cairo *raqs sharqi*, but also the revolutionary aftermath.

I took a deep breath. No, there are always more steps to consider. I refocused on the powerhouse dancing of Najla and Sahar, their verve during interviews, and the cut-off yet resiliently resounding beats and lyrics of *mahraganat* as a movement that refuses to stop growing. However, I'm left questioning: if getting with the vibe is the first step, an exchange, albeit ephemeral on the part of guests . . . how do we move from ephemeral exchange to long-term embodiment that refutes being marginalized, gated, and cut off, and covered up via bright lights, disco walls, surveillance, gated communities, and policing? Perhaps, for now, it's best we continue listening deeper into the depths of Cairo *raqs sharqi* contexts and catch our next ride.

Taxi Transition: Pieces of Freedom

"*Midan Tahrir*?" The taxi driver nodded his head as I wrenched open the back door of the taxi and sunk into the tattered cloth seats. The driver lurched onto the main road as I coughed with the onslaught of thick secondhand smoke. The older driver adjusted the rearview mirror to catch my eyes with a cheesy grin, "Egypt nice! Welcome!" I forced a smile back at him with a gentle nod. I was spent from the lack of sleep between disco excursions and early afternoon Arabic colloquial language lessons. "Egypt people, good!?" he brightly enquired with an overly enthused "thumbs up." I nodded again, I lacked the energy for another superficial "tourist chat" over pyramids and camel-ride tropes. "From where?" he persisted as I muttered, "America" in exhausted honesty, instantly regretting that I probably just doubled the cost of my fare. "America, good!" He exalted as he turned onto the next street. Thankfully, the loud ring of my cellphone interrupted the chitchat. Heba, my Arabic teacher, had a scheduling mix-up and needed to reschedule our lesson times for next week. We spoke briefly about our classes and my evening plans. I didn't think anything of our conversation until I tucked my phone away and caught a very different glance in the rearview mirror.

The driver, Khaled, confirmed that I spoke colloquial Egyptian and inquired why I was in Egypt—his deepened Arabic tone relating that he knew it was no longer about pyramids and camel rides. I explained that I was doing ethnographic research and taking language classes (as usual, I thought it might be best to leave out the stigmatized dance aspect). Oddly, he didn't push further about my research, perhaps assuming from the language classes that I was interested in international relations work. The account that follows is my best translation of Khaled's Arabic, a one-sided impassioned lecture seared into my heart.

"Listen, I need to tell you about Egypt, America—the world! You think you have freedom in America! This is a big problem! For you and for the whole world! Americans always think they have complete freedom. Let me tell you straight; no American, no Egyptian, no citizen in this whole wide world has freedom! There is no full freedom. Not there, and not here. We might have pieces of freedom, *bess*! But, Americans never understand this. You Americans think you have freedom, and you can take this freedom and give it to others, but what you actually do in this blinded political madness, is take away the few pieces of freedom others might have to hoard for yourselves!" Khaled was nearly screaming, not in anger directed toward me, yet the urgency in his voice and gesturing as he repeatedly slammed his hands onto the steering wheel unnerved me. (Mind you, all of this was happening as he still wove and sped through the commotion of Cairo's city streets.)

"Look at the Palestinians! They are suffering and dying every day under occupation, they have the least freedom! The United States enables innocent people and children to die there every day to maintain power with the state of Israel!" As he steered with his left hand, his right hand's thumb and pointer finger now formed a gun, as he continuously mimed shooting himself in the head.[59] "Innocent children!" His body shook as he gestured, over and over. "Constant suffering, do you hear me?! Innocent children that will never even taste any freedom—because *you* let them suffer!" His voice cracked in anguish as his trembling gun-to-head gesture continued. "God save them; is that what freedom necessitates to you?! Does your country's freedom require the suffering and killing of others? Shredding away others' few pieces of freedom for your own, destroying lives and countries?!" My stomach churned as Khaled abruptly turned down another bumpy side street; my churning stemmed solely from the desperation of his raw address. I thought I was going to get sick and frantically wanted to roll down the backseat window, but I found my body frozen. Khaled gruffly pulled over; we'd reached my destination.

He turned to stare me dead in the eye. "Don't be blinded by political bullshit, you too only have shattered pieces, but your pieces have a relationship with all other broken pieces. How do your pieces relate to mine . . . to others? Look, if you have a shit president like this Trump, well okay Obama was shit too he just tried to show a nice face, *ya3ny*, maybe you have a shit president for four years, eight years . . . maximum! You can vote him out, resist, there are things you can do to change this! Here, it's a bigger problem, if we have a shit president, like we always do, we will have this same shit for the rest of our lives, maybe even part of our children's lives. This is the same shit that we both have, but there is a difference. You need to know which pieces of freedom you have and ask yourself, what will I do with the little freedom that I have? Every piece relates to all the others." His voice slowed, "What will you do with the pieces of freedom that you have?" He broke his gaze unexpectedly and gestured toward the door for me to get out.

I clambered out of the taxi after placing the fare on the front passenger seat; Khaled was no longer acknowledging me. I felt tasked with a life-long mission I hadn't yet committed deep enough to. I had been dropped off in Tahrir Square of all places: "liberation square," the most spatially significant city space in relationship to the 2011 revolutionary protests and their aftermath.

The overpowering viscerality of this taxi encounter was etched into my heart. It was an encounter that could have easily passed by as just another mundane ride. Walking through Tahrir Square, I couldn't feel the ground beneath my feet. Each step felt unstable and erratic. I couldn't feel the weight of my own body. Looking back, my sensation was a productive disassociative feeling of being taught how we don't realize the full weight our actions carry. I kept walking and replaying Khaled's plea in my head as my steps slowly stabilized.

Deep listening. I ruminated on how my Arabic learning signaled something in Khaled, something that triggered him to get straight to the gut of our ephemeral encounter's potentiality. Perhaps he assumed I was learning Arabic to work in government? I recalled being the only student in my undergraduate language class not learning for government or military work. Perhaps if I did mention my dance studies he would have kept with the superficial tropes, as dance is often dismissed as *hishek bishek* (an Egyptian idiom often referring negatively to dance or things empty of purpose). However, it was the heft of the somatic effect of this encounter that had the most meaningful impact on my future actions; such bodily-based areas of research dance studies centralizes in undermined value.

I thought about every other interaction that stayed on a level of superficial "tropes" founded on orientalist, patriarchal, or classist paradigms, engendering distance, disconnection, and as Khaled earnestly elucidates, biopolitics of life and death. I reflected on many other enlightening taxi rides. . . comparing when I first came and barely spoke any colloquial Arabic. . . but once you are able to listen more deeply and earnestly, a raw realness can coalesce, a necessary honesty.

Deep listening isn't a passive nor solitary act. I recommit this multiply moving ethnography and my myriad everyday imbricated movements as a dancer, writer, scholar, and human to critical ethnographer Soyini Madison's call for radical responsibility. Madison states, "art assumes responsibility for political effectiveness and communicates the principle that we are all part of a larger whole and are therefore radically responsible to each other for all our individual selves."[60] I further connect to the corporeality of such radical responsibility in centering the most marginal of human lives in our interwoven task of emancipatory revolutionary relationalities. It is the peripheral perspectives and persons, here embodied by both Khaled the taxi driver and the Palestinians he uplifts, that when listened to as central and with vulnerable viscerality, can enliven the core of our inherently interconnected freedom.

What are you doing with the pieces of freedom that you have?

4
Pyramid Street Cabarets
Negotiating Slippery Stages and Contradictory Competitions

I ordered three vanilla lattes at the Dunkin Donuts near my apartment as I waited for Karim to pick me up for the night's cabaret excursion. It was already one in the morning, and I wanted to make sure we would be wide awake to observe all the colorful commotion of the long night ahead. Despite the already late hour, the cabarets were just getting warmed up. The entertainment within would carry on well past sunrise. It was one of Karim's conditions that when we went to Pyramid Street cabarets, we had to take our own car, rather than an Uber or taxi; the other was that we would only go with one of his male companions tagging along for added "protection." I reluctantly agreed. I didn't feel the secondary male "protector" was necessary, but perhaps more so, the added personal expense of paying the entrance fee for this secondary male figure was straining on my largely self-funded fieldwork.

My phone rang to signal they were waiting outside. I plopped down awkwardly in the back seat, trying my best not to spill the lattes in the process. I smiled politely as Karim went through the procedure of trying to explain why my academic research included spending many nights observing dancers in cabarets to our third comrade for the night, Mido. My dance research was often met with strange curiosity and dismissal but explaining the importance of the cabaret field-site and its dancers, in particular, was always a particularly awkward conversation. This is due to how deeply marginalized and stigmatized these sites are within Egyptian society. "You know you will not find any dancing in these places, just drunks, drugs, and I'm sorry, but prostitutes," Mido, our "secondary security" for the evening lectured me. I took a long, slow sip from my latte as I glanced over at Karim. He understood my silent plea and took on the burden of further elaborating upon and defending my research. The constant dependence on male barriers and collaborators was both enabling and hindering to my research. Many times, it offered peace of mind for me knowing that I could let them be the barriers in dealing with all the practical fieldwork issues and obstacles, such as transportation and negotiating entrance fees and interviews. On the other hand, the barriers work both ways, and dealing with the imposed conditions and other controls on my project was sometimes tiring and costly.

Upon arriving at the stretch of cabarets sprawled across Pyramid Street, Karim and I started to deliberate on which one we would experience for that night. After settling upon a site, the men would park the car and wait for the doorman to greet them. Then, they'd step out of the car and begin the bartering negotiations for the cabaret while sharing smokes. Negotiations included how much we would each pay, what was included (usually a drink or two and a few table snacks), and what the cabaret had to offer compared to its various competitors just a short stroll down the road. Often Karim would disappear to take a look inside with the doorman as part of their negotiations. All the while, I sat patiently waiting in the backseat, sipping away at my latte. After a while, Karim would re-enter the front passenger seat, slam the door behind him, and give me the quick summary of the place and the deal. If I accepted, I'd then quietly dig into my wallet and covertly pass over the total amount, plus extra for tipping. This way, Karim could pass off the money as his own and not be embarrassed. As this chapter will come to dissect, this routine gesture of secretively passing off my money as his own within the cabaret field sites foreshadows the gendered economic politics of not only the site but also larger Egyptian and intra-MENA economic-political entanglements.

Initial preparations for cabaret nights were long and drawn-out affairs. It always took Karim at least an hour or two longer than he planned to secure a borrowed car for the evening, as he didn't own one himself. Additionally, the outside entrance price negotiations and site selection often took a good chunk of time, as well as a number of smoked cigarettes. However, after this preliminary preparation, physically entering the cabaret was swift. There was often little to no security outside to pass through, and after walking up or down a small flight of stairs or through a hallway, we'd arrive into the main seating area. This plain and prompt entrance sharply contrasted with the intensity we were confronted with upon stepping into the cabaret.

An explosion of sensory stimuli crashed over my body like a tidal wave, from the pulsating percussion-heavy *sha3bi* music thumping in my heart, to the dense layer of shisha, cigarette, and *hashish* smoke, to the multi-colored flashing lights dashing across the venue. Movement assaulted my vision from every direction. People were dancing socially throughout the stage as well as among the tucked-away back corner tables. Even waiters could often be seen bopping along and sharing in the excitement. Teenage boys were frantically crawling and squatting throughout the venue to hastily plow armfuls of five-pound notes together from off the floor to be collected than recirculated within the venue as tipping. Overly attentive waitstaff would suddenly lean across tables, rushing to light patron's cigarettes or open their beers alongside every table. Youthful women were planted strategically throughout the venue, often dancing socially amongst one another to advertise for the venue, or to please whichever male client was paying for their company. Of course, this is all not to forget the actual paper money sporadically exploding into the air here and there as if confetti being tossed on New Year's Eve. This money was often littered across the seating area and stage, making an increasingly slippery terrain for the dancer to negotiate.

We were seated along one of the back tables in the cabaret. As usual, Karim gestured for me to take the middle seat. This seating ensured I was safely "sandwiched" between their two male bodies. Though my comrades did not have the financial prowess that most of the other clientele in the cabaret had that evening, the way they interacted and situated themselves in relation to my own female body was similar to the more moneyed men seated throughout the venue with paid female company sitting, flirting, or dancing beside them. Not to dismiss the care and amiability within their sandwiching spatial configuration, but like the other men and their *reklam*, to differing degrees, they were performing and reifying their masculinity through relational power over the females beside them, whether as guardians, or for purchasable desirability, attention, or sex. Notably, these emblazoned masculinities could only be successfully realized because other male eyes were there to witness and often compete with these gendered power configurations. *Reklam* were women dominantly paid a small amount to sit and party with male clientele or amongst one another, this could include conversation, joking, flirting, sharing their food and drink, and often socially dancing at the table or on the stage. *Reklam* is one of the titles for the women that work this strongly stigmatized job within the cabarets, because they work as a type of advertising for the club to attract more clientele. Other titles these women's job title went by in English translation were "hostesses" or "service women."[1] However, to many outside the cabaret industry all these women are painted with the brush of "prostitute," even though they may, or may not, engage in sex work. While most *reklam* share gender and lower socioeconomic status, the reasons they engage in this work vary; many were single or divorced mothers taking care of children on their own, others enjoyed the exciting atmosphere and found this job to be the best for making quick money with their level of education, others simply took it as a job like any other, often with better income than what they could find elsewhere based on their experience and education.

At the same time, male eyes were not the only ones watching and making exchanges, as playful and strategic glances were made between working *reklam* throughout the venue. These less dominant but prevalent female–female exchanges highlight not only a layer of paid female sociability that the cabaret conditions nurture, but also gesture to non-dominant semiotics and solidarities circulating within the cabaret. Finally, there were workers who were contradictorily made most invisible within the space, despite their most pervasive, and invasive, physical presence crawling, running, crouching, and clambering around the stage, seating area, and table and chair legs beneath and around all of our feet. These almost exclusively young Egyptian men, mostly small in stature, were quick and constantly exerting robust physical labor to wind through the mass of feet, table, and leg chairs as if competing in a timed obstacle course. Their sole job was to collect the tip money (colloquially referred to as *keet*) as rapidly as possible from the floors, stage, and tables to ensure that it was ready to be re-circulated.[2] However, their labor was also to ensure the *keet* was staying in circulation and not being taken by any number of people who could potentially tuck away a few notes. I heard if the known amount of total *keet* was less than what the cabaret management had originally counted to begin the night with, it was these youthful men and boys who would take the fall, whatever that may entail. Judging by their frantic and grueling physical labor, this assessment seemed accurate.

Despite the youth's intense physical proximity to patrons, they were almost entirely ignored. This in/visibility contradiction gestures toward their low status on the hierarchy of bodies within the site. Their choreographies within the cabaret overlapped the gendered labor and economic conditions of Egyptian male youth at large, both pre- and post-revolution. Male youths scrambled for fewer and scarcer employment opportunities that mostly had a glass ceiling already based on their socioeconomic background. There structurally weren't opportunities to continue to move up if you just "worked hard." Yet, working hard was the only way to survive in the face of increasing inflation of basic goods and foodstuffs. Like Sisyphus forever rolling a boulder up a hill, these boys labored intensively to keep the *keet* off the floor, just to have it placed back into the already wealthy hands of those who would simply re-toss it. Within the dire economy and greater patriarchal norms, these youths found themselves at the bottom of the pile of those benefitting the least from these systems, alongside the working-class women. Yet, these structures not only demanded their physically exhausting and increasingly resourceful labor, but also held the greatest potential for policing and punishment. Despite how critical their work was to the overall system, it wasn't set up as a fair game, and ultimately, despite their toils, they received little sustenance or benefit from it.

My eyes continued to dart randomly throughout the packed venue. There was so much commotion I couldn't figure out what to focus on. Still attempting to take my seat, I was suddenly drawn to one corner of the venue where a handful of Egyptian men were dancing *sha3bi* socially amongst one another, Egyptian-brand Stella beers in hand, and laughing loudly. Simultaneously, a squabble was breaking out beside the door over pricing between the staff and some younger Egyptian men. Then suddenly, before my eyes could rest, a flash of red panties pulled my focus in yet another direction as a Lebanese man's hired "date" for the evening was suggestively swaying on the edge of the slightly raised stage. She was slightly biting her lower lip as she swerved her hips so vehemently that her dress hem would "swish" up just enough to provide provocative peeks at what lie underneath. Due to my lack of focus, I plonked clumsily into my rickety chair but was too distracted by the vast kaleidoscope of moving bodies all around to feel embarrassed. I ordered a Turkish coffee. I hoped its intensity would aid me in keeping up with the sensory surplus of the night, particularly as all this bustling movement and interaction was occurring just within the time it took to take our seats.

A dancer had just started her *nimra* (show number) and was circling the centralized stage's perimeter. She greeted and shook hands with the men surrounding the stage, though from their introductory exchanges she didn't seem too familiar with any of the clientele. This was a vast difference from the local all-Egyptian *sha3bi* cabarets found in areas such as downtown, where most clientele were regulars.[3] The dancer, announced with her stage name Suzy, smiled and nodded as she greeted the tables. Her entrance interaction delivered a sense of individualized importance to each front-row client, and, judging from a few of the exchanges of facial expressions and quite a few dirty jokes, set the tone of her performance. Her immediate physical contact with individualized guests differed from other entertainment establishments, as cabarets are the only site where the dancer regularly shakes guests' hands as she takes the stage. This entrance has combined class and sexual morality connotations, painting the dancer as just that, "*ra2asa*" (dancer). This label is colloquially juxtaposed with the designation of the "*fannana*" (artist), placed upon dancers working in other sites considered more respectable (such as hotels). The immediate physical contact between genders also gestures toward the purchasable physical contacts available to the male clientele in the cabaret, not necessarily with the dancer. Still, these transactions and relations are certainly significant draws. Many cabaret dancers throughout Cairo, but particularly along Pyramid Street because of the close-knit network of nearby cabarets, will work one *nimra* (a show number of about thirty minutes) after another, perhaps starting around midnight in one cabaret and hitting a handful more until eventually finishing her work between 4 and 6 am. Some working dancers in cabarets certainly engage in sex work, but not all; in my experience only a minority number of dancers did this, though they were highly likely to marry someone from the cabarets or within the cabaret work industry. However, the stigma of being a working dancer, particularly combined with this site of work, cast all dancers as "prostitutes" to significant sectors of the Egyptian public. The English word prostitute was often used in these contexts to discipline gendered laboring bodies through moral policing.[4] On the other hand, the apparent physical intimacy of the dancer's entrance, as well as the way spectators' attention was pulled in multiple directions, highlights another special signification of the site. Whereas spectators attend boat or hotel shows as a more passive audience, at the cabaret everyone becomes a part of the total event, because a night in the cabaret is about everyone in the space.

This chapter will focus on a typical Pyramid Street cabaret during the "Arab season" frequented by Egyptian and MENA men from the middle and upper classes, although primarily saturated with clientele from the Arabian Gulf. This Gulf saturation is especially prevalent during the lucrative Arab Season of the summer months. Pyramid Street, or Shari3 Haram, was originally built by Khedive Ismael to transport important dignitaries from Cairo for the opening of the Suez Canal in 1869. The first two elite casinos with *raqs sharqi*, Auberge and Shalimar, opened on the street when these sites were visited by the upper crust of local and international guests to see star dancers. During Nasser's era, the street became the bustling residential and commercial area it remains to this day.[5] Particularly during Sadat's era, with the Arabian Gulf oil boom, and continuing with the steep economic decline in Mubarak's era, the cabarets on Pyramid Street drastically changed. Major shifts and innovations also occurred within *raqs sharqi* during Sadat's era that tied directly into the overlapping hegemonies of the Saudi oil economy alongside Western neoliberalism's economic upheavals from the IMF and World Bank's structural adjustment policies and loans.

The Gulf oil boom, and particularly the oil embargo crisis of 1973, resulted in vast wealth for the Gulf countries, and their economic dominance in the region was visible through the drastic increase of Gulf tourists flooding into Cairo.[6] The embargo was targeted at nations perceived as supporting Israel during the Yom Kippur War, including the United States, Canada, Japan, and the United Kingdom. By the end of the embargo oil prices had risen drastically across the globe, and oil-exporting countries from the Middle East, such as Saudi Arabia, became extremely wealthy as well as recognized for their economic and resource power on a global scale. The economic power these Gulf tourists wielded was immediately felt in *raqs sharqi* as demands, backed by bursting thick wallets, for *khaleegy* regional music and dancing permeated venues.

The combination of petrodollars and Sadat's increasing regulation of dance re-oriented the structure of cabaret nightlife, particularly for Pyramid Street cabarets. In 1973 the *musannafat* under Sadat successfully prohibited the practice of *fath*. The crackdown was more intense than previous attempts to eradicate the practice, and this, combined with the influx of petrodollars and *khaleegy* clientele, resulted in a new system of competition within the male-dominated cabarets. Instead of *fatihat* women generating profit through male competition through the purchasing of alcohol, the competition was re-oriented toward highly performative tipping methods. Gulf clientele started to toss, throw, or "shower" money onto the stage and over the dancers, singers, *reklam*, and even other guests. Different male clients would compete with one another to see who was throwing the most money. This new influx of clientele and their methods of competition led to an immediate surge in cabarets throughout Pyramid Street, with well-known venues such as Lucy's Parisiana, El Leyl, and others popping up along the street to further capitalize upon this lucrative new opportunity and client base. As the *khaleegy* petrol-hegemony made its prowess known internationally, it was deeply felt across Cairo as *raqs sharqi* venue seats were filled with gulf clientele. And yet seats in Cairo homes were left empty as increasing numbers of working- and middle-class Egyptian men left to become Gulf migrant workers.

Since these times, cabarets became focused around the pinnacle objective of getting clients to throw money showers as tipping, known as *nu2ta* or *keet*.[7] Since this time, the cabarets have also been characterized by the *nimar* system, where multiple dancers perform a thirty-minute or so *nimra* in one costume before a brief transition and then the next dancer circulates in for her show.[8] Often a handful of dancers can be seen making their rounds up and down the street while performing throughout the night.

The *nimra* may start with a *mejance*, but afterward, the dancer must improvise according to the requests of the moneyed patrons and singer. Often the music is dominated by Egyptian *sha3bi*, where *mawwal* are quite popular.[9] Additionally, music such as *khaleegy*, with a smattering of other requests from Um Kulthum classics to Lebanese *dabka*, is also popular, depending on the biggest-tipping clientele of the evening.[10] The dancer doesn't know what will be played next. Sometimes dancers spend twenty-five minutes of their total show dancing one *khaleegy* song after another. Except for star cabaret performers such as Aziza or Nany, the majority of dancers work with a house band that is paid and hired by the venue.

Another key characteristic of cabaret performances is the constant interruption of the music, singing, and show for the *tahiyya*. A *tahiyya*, or greeting, is when the singer abruptly cuts off the show to say the name, region (country or neighborhood), and sometimes occupation of a client into the microphone. This salutation is done to show his importance to the rest of the venue, as well as simultaneously get him to cough up more tip money. Colloquially, this is akin to a pay-to-play "shout out." While the greeting is being pronounced, often the singer or client will be throwing, raining, or holding up and wagging *keet* for all to witness. This *tahiyya* works to encourage the masculinity-fueled tipping competitions that are the main objective of cabarets. For example, if one man's name and country are being praised, it challenges another man to show his importance and wealth as well. Nationality also is tied up in these equations as clients from the same country like to see their nation upheld as the most prominent or most generous. In contrast, other nationalities may enter into the competition to stake a claim in being recognized. These competitions can be invigorated with generosity as well, and often generosity and personalized importance are the smoke screens within and behind which the gendered-economic and nationalist rivalries operate. For example, on many nights I witnessed two Saudi men clinging to each other, hugging and non-stop kissing each other upon the cheeks, forehead, and tops of the head while raining and throwing money upon one another in drunken stupors of camaraderie.

Either way, these "tipping wars" are corporeally tied to notions of masculinity as entwined with economic and nationalist prowess. Tracing the roots and routes of this site-specific tipping practice is complex, and gestures to the entanglements of local Egyptian, intra-MENA, and global forces. The practice of guests providing *nu2ta* at local *sha3bi* wedding parties in Cairo is cited as one root of this, with the singer playing the role of *nabatshi*, or sometimes he is a separate figure within the cabaret; this is the man who does the *tahiyya* and holds up the tipped money. This local practice also intersects with the MENA oil boom and open-door economic policies of Sadat's era that resulted in the sudden proliferation of wealthy MENA male clientele within these clubs that started throwing and showering the money.

Cabarets are one of the original sites for housing *raqs sharqi* within Cairo. However, their reputations have made a one-eighty-degree turn from the monarchy era of being decadent sites where the upper crusts of celebrities, dignitaries, and even King Farouk can see the top star performers in the MENAHT world. Since the economic decline of the Mubarak era, cabarets still have hierarchies from low to high. Still, overall, all cabarets are considered by mainstream society and those within the dance industry as the "seediest" of sites where men go to drink, get high, and watch women's bodies. This combination of "drinking, drugs, and revealed female bodies" was consistently quoted to me by Egyptian friends and colleagues as well as those throughout the dance industry as reasons for the seediness or "lack of artistry" in cabarets. This particularly low ranking of cabarets on the already stigmatized dance work hierarchy is apparent in the way that many dancers who work across venues—meaning they don't specialize in just boats or cabarets—will hide their cabaret dancing because of the heightened stigma it brings. For example, Egyptian dancers will market their boat, hotel, and wedding gigs on social media but not their cabaret appearances. To give another example: during one taxi ride to a downtown cabaret, the driver and my male companions for the evening were chatting, but when they admitted they were headed to a cabaret the driver refused to drive us further as it was a "big shame" for my male friends to take a "nice girl" to that kind of indecent place. (Thankfully we were close enough that we could make the rest of the trip walking.)

Yet cabarets are one of the venues that largely carried on in the immediate aftermath of the revolution, when many boat cruises and hotels completely shut down or drastically cut their number of shows and journeys. This is not to say that Pyramid Street cabarets had smooth sailing in the wake of the 2011 revolution. Throughout their history cabarets have been targeted by certain sectors of society as being sites of decadent corruption or moral depravity.

A handful of cabarets were looted and vandalized after the revolution, but it's unclear as to the reasons. Many Egyptians reported it was common "street thugs" while others contended it was likely Brotherhood extremists. However, some cabarets did shut down, the reason possibly being tied to new strategies of erasing their "corrupt mark" on society. Post-revolution, Ragab el Sawerki, a strict Islamist businessman, bought up a few of these cabarets. He also owns department stores throughout Cairo that adhere to conservative Islamist practices.[11] While he has stores on Pyramid Street, these were not looted or vandalized as were the cabarets he was seeking to purchase after the revolution. A news article discussing this argues the concern of strict Islamists who use religion as a business and want to forbid art, tourism, and music, and keep women at home. The author contends that it would be bad if these people started running the country.[12] While these circulating theories cannot be confirmed, they're still useful for the politics they discursively set into motion.

Yet, with the resiliency of cabarets carrying on post-revolution, it would seem these ferocious "tipping war" schemes vicariously tied to men's sense of masculinity offer a sustainable system. Seated in the cabaret, watching Egyptian pounds fly around the room and be continually "scooped up" by tip collectors, busily gathering the notes like snow plows in a wintry storm, it would appear so. The dynamics of the cabaret system, with its primary focus on men, masculine competition, and the intense value pitted upon the thickness of one's wallet, bore strikingly similar parallels to the primary focus and objective of President Sisi's government. Here, intense concentration was also pitted on the masculine projects of national security and the economy as the primary path to Egypt's successful sustainability. Simultaneously, the intense number of cross-armed and suited Egyptian male security men staggered throughout the venue, there to keep watchful and policing presence over maintaining the primary *keet* flow, also reinforced the methods and values of Sisi's masculinized and autocratic military regime: top-down, linear, policed, and tightly controlled.

But as a feminist dance ethnographer, I must ask, is there more to the cabaret circuits than dominant understandings and bodies? What, or whom, is keeping the *keet* circulating? Are there other ways of being, knowing, and moving circulating within the cabaret? In an interview, the oral historian Sayyad H. explained to me that there was a time when all the tipping money in cabarets was real. However, after some time, the system changed, and cabarets began using fake notes or, primarily, used a strategic "purchasable ploy" to further amp up and hasten the tipping wars.[13] The primary way tipping works is that clients pay a set amount such as 100 Egyptian pounds, and depending on their perceived class status, personality, and street smarts, are given multiplied amounts in return, such as 500–1,000 Egyptian pound notes. Managers mentioned that it's never a far "pay-to-play" scheme, but that they try to be clever through the uneven distribution of money to amplify already prominent clientele's status and enjoyment within the venue.

This historic contextualization points out how the seemingly "sustainable" modern cabaret system is a façade in significant ways. Further, the tipping used to be split three ways: house, dancer, and band, but since the Mubarak era, all the tipping almost exclusively goes to the house. Thus, the competitive tipping war scheme that's become the main objective in cabarets is ultimately not a sustainable system. Furthermore, it's a system that's becoming increasingly and particularly precarious for the more marginalized Egyptian cabaret laborers. This knowledge gestures toward the necessity to look from more perspectives and positionalities to get richer understandings and more nuanced tactics to create better and more sustainable worlds, at both the micro-level of the cabaret as well as the macro-level of the national economy and gender dynamics.

I fretted uncomfortably in my seat. I wanted more time to think through all the commotion, literally and theoretically, that was engulfing me. A nearby waiter quickly turned his head so I wouldn't catch his smirking at me. *Ah, but he is right; my wishful thinking doesn't fit the cabaret*, because after the *mejance* entrance number (if there even is one), any song could play, anything goes. There is so much happening all at once. The song could cut at any moment, so as ethnographer, I must likewise pen and value the highly improvisational cabaret schema and just jump in to enjoy the show.

As if reading my thoughts, the center-staged dancer suddenly cast her gaze out upon the peripheries of the room. Despite the density of heavy smoke, money shower cascades, and an array of men and women dashing and dancing about the stage, she cut through the thickness and caught my eye. Suzy winked at me, followed by seductively blowing me a kiss. It was such a subtle gesture compared to the larger chaos engulfing the setting, but I found myself shyly smiling back at her. I was more emotionally captivated by her minute exchange than by the ostensibly more commanding forces and movement all around. *Tahiyya* Suzy! "The people judge and reject me because I reveal my body, but oh, if they could only know what I know, live what I live, feel what I feel, and do what I can *do* with this revealed body."[14] Cutting through the metaphorical and tangible smoke screens, she beckoned me to answer my own hypothesis about *keet* circulation and non-dominant semiotics through following her hips.

Nimra A: Suzy

After a brief pause to read her audience, Suzy continued to strut, languidly swaying her hips around the perimeter of the slightly raised stage for the crowd of men from across Egypt and the Arabian Gulf. Suzy was already well into her thirty-minute *nimra* as the music transitioned from *khaleegy* to a popular Egyptian *sha3bi* song. Unlike the majority of dancers working on boats and in hotels, Suzy, and many of the hostesses seated throughout the venue, are of a darker olive skin color and have thicker and more luscious figures. A heavy line of percussion kicks in, the dancer beams brightly, her previously limp arm now pumping overhead in the air as her opposite hip drops earthily down, down, down, matching the drumming's heavy downbeats. Her total change in energy and enthusiasm vividly demonstrated her happiness for the change to the songs she knew and loved, as opposed to the Arabian Gulf music that dominated that night (a standard becoming quite monotonous for the Egyptian workers and clientele). Following her excited lead, the Egyptian men, both those in the audience and those serving patrons tableside, exchanged a wave of energy with the dancer. Many broke from their conversations to exaggeratedly clap and shout out encouragement to her. With her grounded hip work and prideful Egyptian dancing and energy exchanged with the other Egyptians, Suzy embodies the characteristics and values of *bint al balad*, or the salt of the earth venerable daughter of the country. In doing so, she transmits a sense of solidarity and pride with the other Egyptians in the room, from the working-class musicians employed behind her, to the waiters busy pouring beers and keeping cigarettes lit, as well as the moneyed Egyptian patrons. The *bint al balad* persona in dance comes from the working classes and is often represented in dance with a strong incoming *masmoudi sagheera* rhythm or a genre of music (also known as *baladi*). The movements include heavy, earthy serpentine or percussive hip work as well as an extremely confidant and grounded character. The "daughter of the country," represents an Egyptian girl from the working class, often juxtaposed against the *afrangi* or "Westernized" Egyptian, and embodies wholesome local values and tradition. This labeling identifies a "village girl in the big city," but one who retains her traditional values and strong moral character. The song doesn't finish before the singer has the band abruptly cut it off to start playing more *khaleegy*, a nod to the biggest spending Gulf clientele in the cabaret that night.

As the music transforms, so does the dancer. Suzy redirects her energy, steps, and charisma, adjusting her breasts in her costume bra before exchanging a fiery glance toward a tipping male client from Kuwait. She tilts her torso forward slightly and begins to shimmy her shoulders loosely; this releases more reverberation, and an extra eyeful, of cleavage toward the tipper. Holding his gaze, she slightly parts her lips, taking her time for a lingering exhale as she does so. He grabs more stacks of money, mounted high on his table, to throw in her direction. Then the dancer quickly glances over at a Saudi man across the stage who had just beckoned his waiter to bring him another tray, stacked high with a mountain of money. She catches the male singer's eye and tilts her head subtly in his direction; he nods knowingly and begins belting out and praising the other man's name and country (*tahiyya*) and just like that—the tipping competition has commenced. The dancer keeps her body positioned toward the Kuwaiti. However, she begins to step, flat-ball-flat in the Gulf style, across the stage, her eyes remaining locked with the Kuwaiti's, although her hands slowly move down toward her hips to pull the lycra fabric of her skirt tighter against her backside. With the skirt pulled tight against her curves, she begins to layer subtle booty rotations over the *khaleegy* footwork—the Saudi's eyes follow her framing. He smiles. The minuscule yet alluring way she clings to her skirt lets him feel like she's dancing just for him. *Tahiyya* Ahmed, a stage manager.

> The most important thing about dancers is how they are smart on the stage, manage everything and everyone while she dances, to make each person feel good, so more money is thrown. How she makes each feel he is the best one in the cabaret, but somehow at the same time, so this starts the war between them. This is what I need, and the dancer makes this through small things with great power. She says a word here, gives a look there, move this way then that, *snaps finger* the money flies.[15]

The singer belts out another *tahiyya* as stacks of money are tossed and showered onto the stage, now flying through the air from multiple directions, just as Ahmed needs.

Suzy moves in closer to the Saudi man, her attention encouraging him to throw more money. But for every step closer she takes an elderly male Egyptian *duff* (frame drum) player from the band shadows behind her. His body serves a dual role. First and foremost, he sees himself as a male protector, a position that's rarely necessary, but this sense of purpose matters as he leers down at the drunken Gulf men throwing money as if children playing in piles of fall leaves. Likewise, he serves as another pair of policing eyes. He makes sure the dancer doesn't tuck away any of the bills into her costume, particularly tempting when the tipping wars get heated and the money escalates from Egyptian five-pound notes to U.S. hundred-dollar bills. (During this time in the summer of 2017, one U.S. dollar was worth 18 Egyptian pounds. Notably, this was when the IMF and World Bank policies had resulted in the "floating" of the Egyptian pound, wreaking devastating effects on an already dire economy. U.S. dollars were desperately desired and needed within the economy, thus resulting in an even greater class signifier for the man who could carry such bills. Trading currency through the precarious black market was common for many of my male colleagues throughout my fieldwork.)

The drunken client stumbles onto the stage and reaches for the player's *duff*; the musician pulls back defensively holding the *duff* close to his chest. The dancer turns around, now assertively embodying the *mi3allima* (boss lady persona), shoots him an angry glair and gestures to him with a quick twist of her hand: *What's the problem*?![16] The *mi3allima* is often represented as a working-class woman who owns her own small business and thus has to take on characteristics typically associated with men. Characteristics include those of assertiveness, strength, and toughness due to her role in the labor economy. Within *raqs sharqi* dance, this is when the dancer performatively represents the "one pulling the strings" economically or with power. For example, dancers often keep their male band members in line by embodying this persona due to the hierarchy of their labor roles, since it is the dancer who typically hires and fires the band. While many foreign dancers in Cairo spoke to me about playing the "innocent idiot" role off-stage to get their way with male employees and employers, most Egyptian working dancers said this wouldn't work with them, they must be "*mi3allima*."

The *duff* player grimaces under Suzy's intense gaze; he obliges the drunk yet high-spending client by handing over his instrument. His lips purse and his empty hands now begin to fidget nervously. The *duff* is his source of income and having it beaten on haphazardly as if a mere toy by the *khaleegy* was disgraceful. Suzy obliges the client for a moment longer, then pauses, and softens to redirect her focus, once again, from the drunken client to the *duff* player. She lightly places one hand on the *duff* player's upper arm, while her other hand raises to her temple as she pouts her lips. She endearingly pleads him for a tissue to wipe the sweat from her brow, now taking on the demeanor of *dalla3*. (This quality embodies and performs coquettish hyper-femininity and is very common in *raqs sharqi* performances with movements such as bashfully placing one hand on your cheek while rolling your shoulders back one after the other, or any sensual body movement where the dancer seems innocently surprised by her own beauty and charm.) The *duff* player nods assertively to her plea and dives into his pockets to produce a tissue that he hands to her with a slight bowing gesture. He felt important now too, useful as a provider. After dabbing her brow and neck with the tissue, she holds it to her heart in a small but significant gesture of gratitude. *Tahiyya* Suzy!

> What makes a good dancer? Most importantly, it's about how you interact with people, especially the bad men that want to define you, control you, give you order, shame you, or force you to retire. Do not accept them, just work harder, and this will give you a strong character. Dancing's not just about art or money like they think on the outside, it's about trusting yourself, and this is a big endeavor. After you trust yourself, you feel you are a big person, not a small person, and nobody can pick on you. You take what you want.[17]

As the *nimra* above highlights, the dancer has the capability to be powerfully center-staged within this masculine space. The dancer negotiates capitalizing on Gulf audiences with maintaining Egyptian masculinity and national pride by creating various connections of personalized importance, competition, solidarity, love, and gender in/dependence. She keeps these interactions flowing, so all feel they have their place within the space, but also so all feel individually important. She largely accomplishes this through embodying her gendered self as *dalla3*, *mi3allima*, and/or *bint al balad*. In doing so, Suzy constructs gender as fluid, dynamic, and multiplicitous, as well as inherently interconnected to other bodies, time, and space. However, while this multiplicitous gender construction and performativity may be enabling as an embodied political tactic not only within cabarets, but also larger state and social spheres, it's critical to remember that this is a heavy burden tethered and weighted down in larger inequitable patriarchal capitalist economies.

Interim

Suzy glanced down at her wristwatch, a common accessory for dancers working the cabaret circuits. She noted that her thirty-minute *nimra* was up, and with a quick signal to the band, she hiked up the long hem of her skirt and dashed off the stage and into the back changing rooms. There, she'd quickly throw on a T-shirt and jeans after taking off her skirt or simply wear an *3abaya* (modesty garment for outdoors) and meet her manager to drive speedily to the next cabaret to continue her rounds. As soon as Suzy glanced down at her watch, a plethora of other bodies, just previously spread throughout the venue, took the opportunity to step up onto the stage. The stage was only slightly raised, and had a step all around, making it easily traversable and accessible to all bodies within the room. *Reklam*, male clientele, and background *duff* players all swarmed the center of the stage, thereby leaving no gap in the dancing entertainment for customers.

Reklam were similar in often being mid-thirties and younger, and almost exclusively from lower socioeconomic backgrounds. However, the diversity in their bodies was a refreshing change from the white-skinned and often augmented or surgically enhanced thin or "hour-glass" paid dancing bodies almost exclusively hired for other *raqs sharqi* venues. A range of skin tones was paraded on stage as signifying beauty and desirability, and an equally wide spectrum of body types. Yet at the same time, the familiar site of heavy makeup, green or blue colored eye contacts, and long and thick hair extensions was still as prevalent.

Tahiyya Ahmed, a cabaret manager!

> Look, we choose the dancers and *reklam* by what clients want to see. There is not one type of sexy, all men have different styles and different tastes, some like thin, fat, dark, all these different things, so we bring a lot of different styles of women here. Different styles appeal to different tastes, so the more variety we have, the more happiness, the more happiness will mean more money. It's good business.[18]

Ahmed's "good business model" of having a stylistic spectrum of women as beautiful felt slightly refreshing from other Cairo venues, but that feeling soured due to the ever-present inequity of not just the cabaret but all *raqs sharqi* venue "business models." Compared to other commercial venues of *raqs sharqi* there was a greater diversity of skin tones and body types and sizes found within Cairo cabarets at the time of my fieldwork. However, the intense Cairo climate of color prejudice and anti-blackness still permeates these sites. For example, this is found in pay disparity for *reklam*. Managers regularly told me that *reklam* were all paid differently depending on "certain criteria." When pressed to elaborate, these criteria included classist and color prejudiced pay ranking based on how "nice" her teeth were (a huge class marker I noticed in Cairo), skin color (the lighter the skin the higher the pay), how nice (i.e. expensive) her jewelry or dress were, and overall attractiveness.[19]

My slight feeling of relief soured further upon recalling advertisements for skin whitening beauty products every time I opened my Facebook in Cairo. A diversity of bodies being paid and paraded as "desirable" helped chisel away at commercialized and homogenous beauty standards that increasingly called not only for only white Western models as ideal, but also for injections, surgeries, and other enhancements. These augmentations are rarely naturally attainable and thus require purchase power. At the same time, like green contact lenses and clipped-in hair extensions, purchasable beauty embedded within racial capitalist hierarchies had also attached and inserted itself to cabaret corporealities. Likewise, this is not to forget the overall purchasable gendered power dynamics of the women on stage and within the cabaret site at large.

The show was cut off as a strawberry unexpectedly blocked my view. The male waiter in charge of our table was holding out a strawberry on a toothpick, just about four inches from my face. I was startled, and with a big grin, he gestured for me to eat it. Apparently, I was so busy observing the entertainment that I hadn't touched the tray of snacks and fruits that comes with your two drinks. I politely declined, but he insisted, now gently wagging the strawberry, still awkwardly just inches from my face. I took it and ate, thinking it would get him to back off, but then he just leaned over, blocking my view entirely, because Karim had pulled out a cigarette to smoke and he had to be sure to light it for him. The hyper-attentiveness of waitstaff in cabarets was supposed to add to the air of client importance, but it always made me uncomfortable.

Karim tried to sneak a tip over to the waiter. He caught his eye and started slowly sliding his hand holding the folded bill under the tablecloth's hem. The waiter snatched it but was immediately "lasered" by one of the cabaret's security men (using a laser pointer to get his "points" across from anywhere in the venue). The waiter sighed than skulked over to hand over the tip. Karim always tried to tip the employees lower down on the pay scale but was caught ninety percent of the time despite his covert efforts. Policing eyes were everywhere, as management and security were also as strategically and abundantly planted throughout the site as were the hostesses.

My eyes re-focused on the stage as, perhaps, a more successful covert operation was occurring. A highly intoxicated man from the U.A.E. was on stage, stumbling through the motions of *khaleegy* social dancing footwork as five hostesses encircled him. The male singer across the stage squinted his eyes at the circle as two male *duff* players began marching over to the group. They exchanged stern glances that confirmed my thoughts that this "dance circle" might be used to block tipping that the women were tucking away. I smiled at their clever use of space, but more so for how they formed solidarity together to capitalize upon their situation. The women dispersed before the multiple policing men could confront their choreographed configuration, and the singer began playing to the drunk client, although he dismissed him away with a wave. He was more taken by one of the young hostesses from the circle.

A burst of laughter turned my attention to the band, where the Egyptian male *toura* (large finger cymbal) player Hamada was teasingly interacting with the array of older male percussion players. Male *toura* players were a common part of *raqs sharqi* bands in hotels and cabarets, but during my fieldwork I found some of the most playful *toura* performances in the cabarets. *Toura* traditionally existed in the liminal space between the starkly gender-divided male and female worlds of the Cairo entertainment system. Often the *toura* can be much more playful and performative than other band members, often leaving the band's position on the stage's perimeter to dance with the dancer, *reklam*, or clientele on or off stage. Egyptian dance ethnologist Sahra Carolee Kent historically elaborates on the role of the *toura* during an interview:

> He's the intermediary between the male and female world of the dancers. One thing I found out is that the *Usta* (from *awalim* and Mohamed Ali days) would have a *toura* who goes with her everywhere. He goes and plays but he is also her intermediary between the public male world. If she were to go alone and directly into this public male world there would be bad talk, so he goes with her and is the intermediary. When he plays and dances it's like *awalim* and *usta* style, I got so many moves from my *toura* guy, watching him dance in the hallways during our band rehearsals. So

my musicians told me (and I heard this from many musician interviews of my own as well), the *toura* may be considered either mentally deficient or homosexual. But I knew mine wasn't either of those, and they'd say well no, he isn't, but *toura* are, and I couldn't understand that contradiction. Several privately explained to me that no, Kassem isn't, but we have to pretend that he is. They see dancers as so powerful, so if an *Usta* can change a girl to a woman from the wedding *zaffa* (procession), she's powerful enough to play with men's minds, so he has to be one of those two things to be able to be close to her all the time and not fall in love or go crazy. He exists in that liminal space, because gender is so divided here, you need somebody in that liminal space, usually it's a young boy, but that doesn't really work for dance, you need a grown man. He can also be very protective of the dancer. It's a fascinating thing, I'm not as excited about the huge gender separation because I had to live it, but how he fills that gap, and watching my guy dance up and down the hallways was beautiful . . . if any woman danced like that here she'd be a star. So, he's a man that's allowed to dance like a woman.[20]

Hamada was in his thirties and wore his curly black hair slicked back into a long ponytail. An array of golden rings adorned all his fingers, but the large clashing finger cymbals with which he added percussive accents, energy, and flavor to the music were his most catching attribute. Despite his rings and multiple golden earrings, the rest of his attire was plain: he wore a black t-shirt and gray sweatpants with sneakers, differing from the dressier attire of the band.

Hamada moved with the grace and feminine-constructed *dalla3* of a *raqs sharqi* professional. He was percussively "tick-tocking" his extended tush to the band members while musically matching his movements with his cymbals. He looked over his shoulder bashfully then cast a demure glance to the musicians as he shimmied his butt from this slightly bent-over position. Shimmying just feet away from the drummers, their fits of laughter cut across the room as one musician grabbed *keet* off the floor to throw at Hamada's derrière while shouting flirty encouragement. Hamada slapped his backside playfully as he blew the musician a kiss. *Tahiyya* Yossry, a cabaret drummer!

Toura can be like you know, this way, or he cannot be that way. But in cabaret you have a different environment, it's catering to all kinds of people and kinds of tastes. Maybe some guests enjoy with the *toura* because he is playful, they take it as a comedy and fun, but other ones find it sexually enticing. For sure he adds an extra energy . . . you get all kinds of things in these types of places.[21]

Hamada's performance caught the admiration of a table of younger *khaleegy* men, who also began throwing *keet* at his "amazing ass" (which they shouted as they threw the tipping), as Hamada strutted over to them with swaying hips. He began performing *khaleegy* in front of their table.

He danced *khaleegy* footwork in the unisex "flat ball flat" style. Still, the way he layered stylistic elements typically only female dancers would made his performance not only beautiful but also disruptive to heteronormative gender and sexuality constructions. Hamada layered highly exaggerated and full booty circles and coquettish hand gesturing to the base footwork, which made the table of young men go wild. *Tahiyya* Hamada, the *toura* player!

My first love is *raqs sharqi*, I hope to work as a choreographer and dancer, but I do *toura* now because I cannot find work in this economy as a dancer. Most Egyptian and Middle Eastern people feel embarrassed or don't like it when a man dances. Especially if he is doing *raqs sharqi* in a feminine style, but then you start to get men working like this in touristy places like Sharm el Sheik, but the economy dropped since then. Most people look at both work, *toura* and *raqs sharqi* for men, as nothing but shit, but you know what? I stopped caring what the other people think, because I love this job, it walks in my blood. Sorry, but I dance *raqs sharqi* as a man better than women, so how can they say this is a women's dance only!? So, if you work hard, you can be anything, but you can't care what people say behind your back, do what you love and be who you are.[22]

Hamada points out another contradiction. On the one hand, the cabaret capitalizes upon and only allows strict homogenous heteronormative gendered labor roles, wherein women work as dancers and men as *toura*, musicians, and sex purchasers. On the other hand, this system allows for fissures in the structure that allow for multiplicitous spectrums of sexuality and gender expressions to enrich the environment and add special energy. Yet Hamada's statement also contains its own contradiction, as he works in *toura* though his unfulfilled aim is to be a *raqs sharqi* dancer, a role currently unavailable to him because of the economy. Hamada poetically points out that you have to create your own path through being who you are, and he has certainly found a creative niche that allows him space to dance on stage while making money as a *toura*. However, his claim to just "work hard" isn't necessarily fair as larger circumstances such as the national economy, and larger heteronormative gender and sexuality interpolations, also bear upon what opportunities are attainable or not.

Nimra B: Julia

If it had not been for the booming announcement from the singer, I wouldn't have noticed the next dancer, Julia, had taken the stage to start the next *nimra*. She had nearly finished making the round of handshakes and greetings before I could pull my attention away from Hamada's show. A few of the hostesses stepped down after Julia started her show. However, a few stayed on stage and swayed their hips to the music. Like Suzy, Julia was of a darker olive skin tone but extremely tall, her spike heels giving her even more of a towering presence. She wore an extremely full and voluminous wig of beautiful dark curly locks that cascaded down to her backside. She wore a mid-range bright red bra and tight mermaid-skirt costume, but without any jewelry accessories that helped give the image of star-status through the appearance of expensive adornments. However, what Julia clearly had invested in was extravagant breast enhancements, all the more advertised through her teensy costume bra out of which that her very full breast tissue was spilling.

Julia's technique heavily followed the percussion, including mostly rhythmic strutting about the stage as she trailed the male singer who was busy giving personalized attention to tipping clients. When they paused at different edges of the stage to provide catered attention to a table or client Julia shimmied her chest as she nonchalantly chewed gum and offered the occasional smile. Her other main movement included a variety of different sized hip circles. Still, she predominantly focused on strutting beside the singer and standing with her weight sunk into her right hip as she would twiddle with her long locks and joke with the clientele. She liked to bend over to exchange a few words with the clients and shimmy her chest as she rose back up, releasing provocative amounts of jiggly cleavage directly toward the tippers. She would then take her time gliding her index fingers along the edges of her bra cups to tuck back in her slightly exposed areolas.

Julia's allure particularly took one Saudi man. He scrambled onto the stage to dance with her; meanwhile, the singer was off giving a *tahiyya* to a table of businessman visiting from Upper Egypt. The client had a determined look in his eyes as he stared at Julia's breasts, not breaking from his covetous stare as he pulled out a couple of hundred-pound Egyptian notes from his wallet. Perhaps Julia sensed the precarity in his hungry gawking as she started looking around for the singer to help control the situation. However, the singer was preoccupied across the stage and the Saudi man was now only a foot from Julia's body. Julia smiled at him and bounced her chest percussively as she reached out to hold both his hands and socially dance. The client seemed hypnotized as he kept his stare but locked his hands in hers. Though he pressed his body toward hers, she used her outstretched arms as a barrier to keep him from touching her, and again looked over for her singer's assistance. The man broke from her grip and reached to place the notes between her breasts, and Julia quickly spun to prevent his touch without disturbing his sense of pleasurable entertainment. She used her own hands to gesture to him to toss the money over her head. In his alcohol-induced stupor he obliged her commands without thinking, lightly letting the notes fall, one after the other, onto her cleavage. She shimmied her breasts lightly while keeping her arms outstretched toward his body, ready to use as a barrier again if needed.

I empathized with Julia, recognizing her arm framing and spins as tactics dancers all over use to quickly dissipate a costume tipping situation that crosses our personal body boundaries. Here, however, it was not necessarily the dancer's boundaries, but the state's. Cabarets are the most notoriously policed venues. If the dancer steps off the stage, accepts body tipping, or is caught without wearing long enough undershorts or *shabka* (belly cover), she can be heavily fined or jailed. Yet the men that crossed onto the stage's boundaries and attempted to touch dancers or purchase women's company were not under such policing precarity and pressure.

Here I speak of policing in the sense of the *musannafat*, a government body enforcing laws and regulations during the time of my fieldwork and established since 1973. However, as mentioned earlier the policing of the dance by government bodies has been around as long as the dance itself, particularly within cabaret settings. While it's often more famous and foreign dancers who make official public headlines for their arrests and deportations while working in more elite venues such as disco-clubs, policing is heaviest albeit more hidden in socioeconomically lower Egyptian cabaret dancers and venues. These workers also have the least resources to negotiate their way out of fines, arrests, and policing, unlike their more economically well-off and connected counterparts in more esteemed venues. This information was witnessed as managers and dancers would frequently point out the multiple police waiting outside cabarets as well as through numerous interviews with managers, *impresarios*, and dancers that worked across venues. As one agent who would like to remain anonymous put it, "Of course, for dancers it's just expected you'll spend a month or so of every year in jail and regularly get fines if you're working in the downtown or Pyramid Street cabaret circuits. Mostly we can bribe our way out; but it's just a normal part of the job."[23]

Tahiyya Donya, a cabaret hostess!

I do not like this work, but there is no other job where I can make this kind of quick money without having schooling. I hate that all people think they can have sex with me and that I am such a bad person. The blame is always cast upon me, like I am the reason these places are shameful. But why don't the people ever think to point their fingers at these drunk vulgar men that come here to pay for these things?! I am raising my girls, *inshallah*, before they get too old I will have a decent apartment and will leave this work, but these men?! They have wives, children, and they come here and spend all the family money.[24]

As Donya points out, the working women within cabarets find their bodies bearing heavy weights not only to survive but also to try to gain financial capital while negotiating the sexually suspect criminality burdened upon their bodies. At the same time, these bodies also find ways to creatively capitalize within the space using their corporeality, as Julia's quick pivots and extended arm work highlight.

Tahiyya Bossy, cabaret dancer!

Of all venues to dance cabarets are the most difficult because you can get bad men that cross the line and want to touch you. The security in the cabaret is not the best either. So much is happening, and the staff cares mostly about keeping the money moving above all else. So, in these situations, if I can't take my protection from the management, I have to take my power myself. I take my power from my charisma and clever moves. Also, I learned to read the guests very well, I can judge by their eyes and their bodies what their intentions are, and then if they get too close I have to keep them happy, and act like I'm happy too, but really, I'm using the way I dance with them to keep the line from being crossed.[25]

While Bossy and Julia both expect the male management to offer protection in the cabaret system, mirroring the patriarchal gender system at large and what benefits it ought to provide, when it's not offered, they do not stand by idly or passively. Rather, they take matters into their own hands through corporealized cocktails of clever charisma and covertly coded choreographies. Bossy also highlights the danger of systems that prioritize accumulating capital at the expense of forgetting or sidelining bodies; in this, both genders become undermined and subject to violation.

A new *khaleegy* song began playing after the *tahiyya*. A table of Kuwaitis was throwing *keet* at one end of the stage, and the singer stayed near them, still leaving Julia to deal with the *khaleegy* client by herself. He grew impatient with raining the notes upon her quivering cleavage. He again took a few hundred pounds and lifted his eyebrow to her as he reached for her bra cups, she gestured for him to shower the bills as before, but he wagged the notes back and forth in a "no, no," refusal. She bent over into a full, deep, hip circle, but when she arose, he was still there with his hand outstretched. This time Julia shook her head from side to side, *la2*—no. The man burst into laughter and nodded, "yes, yes" as he dove back into his wallet and pulled out a few more hundred-pound notes.

He reached for her breasts so aggressively this time that she had to step back and swat his hand away. The man laughed again, now asking his waiter for stacks of pounds to be piled high on his table. As the waiter handed the client one rubber banded stack of money at a time, the singer and an accompanying *duff* player made their way over to the client to encourage his tipping, though Julia had already initiated that work. The singer began to praise the *khaleegy* man and attempted to dance with him. The client turned and violently threw a stack of still-banded notes at the singer; it thus flew dangerously all together as a projectile brick of money. The man started chucking hunks of bounded notes at the *duff* player and the singer, Julia backed up to give more room between herself and the man whose drunken stupor had turned aggressive.

The Egyptian singer and musician kept singing and praising the man as if he hadn't just incredibly disrespected them in the way he threw the *keet*. They were probably used to dealing with this kind of behavior, but I was feeling my stomach tie up in knots. Two of the managers made their way over to the hubbub to help control the situation, showing I wasn't the only one getting nervous over the increasing tension. However, for the management the primary goal remained keeping the *keet* in motion, not concern for the workers. I was disgusted that they were still focused on keeping the *keet* in circulation despite how disrespectful the man was to the Egyptian workers. Especially since it seemed this man could potentially turn violent at any moment, I thought he should be kicked out, or at least taken outside and calmed down. Karim must have noticed my concerned expression and assured me the management was used to handling this kind of behavior. "But he is treating them like they're shit!" I exclaimed. He laughed at me, "This the relationship between our two countries when one is rich, and one is poor. When one knows the other needs him . . . it is shit."

Tahiyya Ahmed, a cabaret singer!

> We must do whatever this rich clientele want, in cabarets you have to understand money is the main focus, and money happens through the *keet* wars. But, these guys still have to feel they are in my country, Egypt, and play with respect. If I feel someone is disrespectful, I will wait before signaling the musicians to make the rattle for the *tahiyya*. Just a momentary pause, but it's enough for him to feel a bit shaken from his status and know the ground beneath his feet is ours- Egypt.[26]

While the uneven macro relations of power between the macho-masculinities of the oil-rich Gulf nationalities and Egypt cannot be discounted, the subtle ways gendered bodies use their scant available resources and networks to challenge this hegemony, stake pride in their own bodies and homeland, and use time and space to create their own boundaries is significant. Specifically, these other sources of value, resistance, and validation are harvested from within the body itself, and the relations between other marginalized bodies when unified together.

Julia interjected in the bubbling tension of the man's aggression by performing a deep backbend in front of him, ending with her chest lifted and directly under his gaze as her head dropped back vulnerably and she fervently shook her chest from side to side. The Saudi relaxed a little, as he began taking great pleasure in holding the stacks of money high over her cleavage and letting the notes slowly spill down and bounce off her reverberating chest. Thankfully, her risky move worked to help dissipate the tension, because otherwise, she had put herself into an extremely vulnerable position, particularly considering his drunken aggression. He snapped his fingers to have the waiter continually re-supply his extended hand with money stacks to shower down upon Julia's body. He cackled as he towered above Julia and watched the notes glide and bounce off her shaking flesh.

Meanwhile, the waiter scurried back and forth, breathing heavily as he rushed to keep the Saudi's supply stocked. The Saudi didn't acknowledge his waiter; he just left his hand upheld and expected it to be continuously resupplied without even looking at, nevertheless thanking, the waiter. I felt my stomach churn—watching the young waiter rush to do his bidding without any acknowledgment, at the man's entitled cackling, and especially for Julia's core and thigh muscles, which must be burning from sustaining such a labor-intensive pose. It was the noxiousness of the toxic capitalist masculinity embodied within this performance that caused my stomach to twist and tie up in knots.

This *khaleegy* man vacationing in a developing country that significantly depended on his nation for financial aid and migratory work was exuding pleasure by dumping thousands of pounds, just for show, pleasure, and the performance of power it held, upon a pair of enormous fake breasts.[27] Julia's attentiveness to the man was also not genuine lust or attraction, but part of the show. This type of world, fueled by virile capitalist masculinity, in a sense, had to be performed on the stage; it was a sham charade and not a sustainable system. At the same time, the strained thighs of the working-class dancer, the heaving chest of the young working-class Egyptian waiter—these were the bodies bearing the brunt of the excessive labor to try to keep up this façade. Their labor and exertion were incredibly real. This capitalist masculinity was fueled by the paradigm ideology that a person was never enough, in senses of self that were founded upon loss and deficit. The incessant need to be more, where whatever "more" was, existed with an attainable price tag. Problematically, these attainable "mores" could only lead to worlds of aggressive hierarchal power relationships between bodies. Julia, physically bent over backward to uphold this inequitable matrix of power, had cultivated flexibility and sustained strength within this schema, but even strong lean muscles fatigue, strain, or injure after excessive exertion.

Suddenly, the rhythmic clanging of Hamada's *toura* was heard, as he and a hostess joined in Julia's choreography. Julia's hostess friend leaned forward to shimmy her chest above Julia's; meanwhile, Hamada kneeled and clanged his *toura* to match the shimmying energy of their chests from underneath Julia's arched back. After a moment, they all rose together and began dancing cheekily around the Saudi. The transition kept up the appearances of endless fictional enjoyment for the client while dissipating both the building aggression, as well as imminent muscle fatigue, of Julia's thighs and core. I was awestruck by how smoothly they handled the situation, but just as equally disenchanted by how unrewarded their efforts would be.

Tahiyya Mona, a former cabaret dancer!

> The cabarets have become so cruel financially. There was a time, ending during Mubarak's rule when cabaret money was all real, and we split the tips three ways; house, dancer, and band. Since the hard economic times and the new trick money system, it all goes to the house. Maybe a few star dancers like Aziza can negotiate a share of tips, but for us normal dancers, we have so much pressure to make the cabaret money that we get no share of. No matter how beautiful I dance, how I look, how I make the unique interactions with every guest to get all this flowing, at the end of the day the management only sees a number, did I make him enough *keet*? You just fight to make him more money, you don't fight to earn for yourself, you fight just out of fear of being fired. This makes everything feel so heavy and awful in the cabaret.[28]

Julia glanced down at her watch; her time was up. She made a quick circular motion with her hand to the band but couldn't wait for them to signal her exit. She sprinted off the stage to catch her next *nimra* down the street.

Despite the clever coalitions and choreographies performed within the cabaret, the overall structure steeped in powerful economic hegemonies of local scarcity and transnational dependency cannot be ignored. At the same time, the cabaret circuits offered glimpses of other worlds and other ways of being. Contradictorily creating opportunities for these alternative paradigms, these ulterior circuits and systems were constructed out of other bodily relationalities and value systems. In this tributary world, the shared space and traversable stage led to solidarities, relationalities, and coalitions that became stronger together, rather than competitive. Here, rather than understanding differences (in class, gender, or sexuality or status) as raw material for constructing isolating and competitive walls and dividers, these other networks utilized these foundations as valuable assets to create cohesively bridged community.

When Hamada, the hostess, and Julia physically lifted each other up to then dance together; or when the handful of hostesses worked together to round out their own desires in the interim; or when variously marginalized workers within the cabaret found themselves "not enough," as the dominant hegemony would have all bodies interpolated, they found recourse in one another. Rather than buy into schemes of being objects of purchasable pleasure or compete amongst one another for partial doses of spotlight or social capital, these laboring dancers found pleasure and profitable maneuvering in their own bodily networks and values of abundance, community, and corporealized creativity. While the marginalized cabaret workers' choreographies offer embodied insight into navigating local and larger globally inequitable systems, their heavy labor still operates within such systems, unable to yet transcend them.

Conclusion: Smoke Screens and Sunrises

Exiting the cabaret is just as speedy a process as entering it, and the transition just as jarring. Stumbling out of the cabaret sometime between 5 and 7 am, the dark and smoky atmosphere sporadically lit up by neon lights and disco balls contrasts sharply with the tranquil calm of a megacity just barely awakening from its slumber. Rose-gold rays of sunlight gently reach across and blanket the city in a mesmerizing shade as choruses of chirping birds enjoy their choirs before the bustling clamor of street traffic drowns out their tunes. We would usually walk a way down the road, stumbling a bit from pure exhaustion but also congenially joking and enjoying one another's company in the peaceful respite of daybreak. Those strolls back to our parked car are fond memories, occurring in a liminal time and space between yesterday and tomorrow, we would all agree they felt a bit like freedom. There was hardly anybody out in the streets to even cast their watchful gaze upon you, nevertheless bother you, an otherwise omnipotent reality of Cairo's public streets.

Mido commented on how the cabaret felt like a different world in an entirely different sense of time. Karim tilted his head thoughtfully. He responded, "Maybe it's not a different world, but it's like . . . *dunya ma2luba* [an upside-down world], because yeah there's like the creepy men and their money greed, but then there's like, all these stories we get to listen to from all these other workers there." He turned to face me.

> Do you remember the manager that lost his accounting job and his wife left him? Or Nashwa the *reklam* that kissed me when we came in, and I thought she's so bad, but then we heard how her husband died a revolutionary martyr, and she's raising all the kids in some weird underground garage?

She just wants her children to have an apartment to play in. I don't know. It's like there's the big story everyone knows, but then there are all these small stories inside that make me want to be—soft. I cannot explain it, as an Egyptian man in this shit (he gestures to the city around us), you never can walk around soft, you have to be so tough all the time, with everyone, but sometimes these stories give me a different feeling.

Mido hailed a taxi to give himself a ride home in the opposite direction to which we were headed. "Good, I hear Abdullah (the name of one of the *khaleegy* clients from the cabaret) likes to enjoy the soft ass!" he brashly joked as he facetiously policed Karim for his vulnerable expressivity. As the taxi door slammed and cut off his ensuing laughter, so too did the sense of liminality close off. It was a new dawn.

I found it intriguing that Karim didn't experience the cabaret as a different world. For him, it remained the same everyday world, but rather experienced from an alternative non-normative perspective (*ma2luba*). Furthermore, it seemed the competitions so critical to cabaret circuits might not be within the masculinity-fueled *keet* wars, but rather between the various worldly paradigms that the *keet* wars constructed. One was the dominant virile masculine-economic, while the second, beneath the *keet*-construed smoke screen, was the kaleidoscope of marginalized yet multiplicitous bodies and ways of being. The hegemonic matrix of men and money contradictorily encapsulated, yet enabled pauses and fissures, for the conditions of possibility for the upside-down world to be corporealized. As laborers within the cabaret experienced working in the chaos of non-normative directionality, from tip collectors crawling between table legs to dancers holding deep back-bends, these polyvalent workers found other ways to move through the world that meshed with their own objectives and desires, thus capitalizing upon an alternative wealth.

Paradoxically, the hegemonic Gulf oil-economies combined with virile power-hungry patriarchal masculinity create sites with incredibly shared spaces and traversable stages. In the cabaret, working-class Egyptian men from young to old, wealthy MENA men, *reklam*, dancers, musicians, and *toura* all intimately share the stage and overall space. This makes the cabaret a unique site within Cairo, a city that otherwise has staunch physical and ideological divisions between those of different social standings and classes.[29] The flat or only slightly raised stages, no photo/video policies, and *keet* wars encourage these crossings. Yet it is this precise diverse density of people and shared space that allows new circulations, coalitions, and collective possibilities to form in confrontation to this dominating system. Here, the variously marginalized workers—dancers, *reklam*, *toura*, and musicians—work better together to capitalize upon their own pleasure, belonging, job security, and dignity.

In previous chapters, many dancers working in other sites reified their social standing by placing deliberate divisions between their bodies and those sprawling across this chapter's pages. Down here in the depths, different directions are taken.

Tahiyya Zara, a self-proclaimed "zero-star to five-star" dancer (because she doesn't specialize in any venue but works gigs across the board).

> Do you know what I've learned by taking every type of gig, in seeing dance in all its form, color, and shapes? Wealth. What's the point of coming to Egypt and working only in one "top spot?" Number one, everyone thinks of dancers as sluts, why would I get off on being a five-star slut, or a bit less of a slut because I refuse cabaret work? Internal self-hating, I think a lot of dancers secretly hate being dancers. Of course, if you are a woman who slut-shames, that's also internalized misogyny. Audre Lorde, a black lesbian feminist, she knows about discrimination, she said the true revolution is in facing, I don't remember the exact words, but it's basically about getting through the oppression that lives inside you. A lot of dancers have issues with their own art because it's associated with sexuality and prostitution and using your body to make money, and actually, there's nothing wrong with any of that. I have no issue with my art, despite the whole world having issue with it.[30]

Zara doesn't just call attention to external physical and ideological divisions as oppressive and limiting. Rather, she specifically highlights the importance of deconstructing the most deeply held internal divisions we use to define and cultivate ourselves. Her powerful statement aligns with Suzy and Hamada. They both also came to accept, love, and trust themselves despite how their loves and labors misaligned with dominant gender, sexuality, and economic norms. Their experiences gesture toward a more genuine and sustainable wealth and value system founded within kaleidoscopes of colorful corporealities, rather than the *keet* strewn across the stage and flying through the air.

Taxi Transition: A Final Ride as Farewell Finale

Karim and I got into his car to start the drive back to my apartment. I felt ready to pass out from the long night, the last bits of energy from the Turkish coffees long past. I pulled the small notebook out from my purse and began quickly scribbling away raw field notes from the cabaret excursion. Usually, I would make a Nescafé at home and do this, but I knew as soon as I walked in the door I was headed straight to bed. We started driving down some smaller bumpy back roads, certainly a major detour from our normal route home from Pyramid Street. I looked up quizzically as Karim smiled and assured me not to worry.

We hit a particularly rough pothole that caused us both to wince in pain. I shook my head playfully and shut my notebook for the remainder of the ride. I figured the field notes would be pretty useless if they looked more like scribblings from a seismograph then legible handwriting. I peered out the front window and realized I had no clue where we were, but we should have been back to Dokki by now. Karim pressed his thumb and forefingers together and slowly drew his hand down, gesturing for me to be patient and wait.

Karim pulled off onto the side of the road to park. "Bring your notebook and come," he stated as he got out from the car with renewed vitality. We walked a short distance down the road and then came upon two beautiful vintage-style wrought-iron doors, which opened up to a charming al fresco courtyard café. The early morning's golden blanket of sunlight cast an ethereal warm glow throughout the brick-walled courtyard. A couple of birds cheeped about on chairs, and potted garden flowers and brush adorned all the courtyard walls. I gasped at how picturesque the café was, and nearly empty at this early opening hour. A waiter approached us. We sat at a corner café table and ordered two lattes and a light breakfast. My sleepy eyes were now wide-awake. Nothing invigorated me more than writing in beautiful outdoor cafes.

Karim smiled, "I knew you'd love it. I think you will write better stories from here." I took a sip from my latte and opened up my notebook. *Here.* Of course, he meant the physical "here" of the cafe we were sitting in, but as I began scribbling away on the blank pages, *here* came to embody a more rooted and personal meaning. I wasn't exactly sure where we were. I couldn't find this place on my own. In fact, the café was a brand-new addition to the bustling heart of downtown. If I'd driven by this spot during my initial fieldwork trips, I would have only seen an abandoned lot piled high with rubbish. Back then, the owners were still in the paperwork process of cultivating the abandoned lot into its full potential.

However, more so, I couldn't find this "here" on my own because there are so many wondrous aspects and parts of cities that are tucked away, around the bend, or just slightly far-off and only locally known. Often, these valuable and potential-full city spaces and niches are only revealed through coming into meaningful connection and relationships with other people. These people then generously share how they know the city, how they've moved through and come into being in the world through their own unique steps, streets, special hidden "spots," and stories.

People are like cities. Finding those secret spots of beauty tucked away, the resilience of flowers that sprout up through pavement cracks, the peace of hidden garden terraces, and coveted Nile views—the shrewdly shared streets and squares. You must really listen, walk through, and know them deeply to understand their beauty and hidden depths. The nooks of growing greenery and creative potential. This necessitates having to trust taking different routes than you're familiar with, getting lost and being pulled along into adventures because you trust that those people you're sharing this city with know the world in a richly, vividly, beautifully different way than you. Their paths have cultivated unique insight, stories, and ways of being and moving that show the city in richer, fuller, and more colorful perspectives.

This is why deep listening matters. Why going along for the ride and letting others take the wheel matters. To get a glimmer of the city through the music they choose, the roads they take, the way they navigate the chaos of traffic, road blockades, police checkpoints, and wrong turns. It unlocks the diverse ways different bodies move through and experience the world. What I've come to understand is that there is no "contemporary Cairo city." Rather, there exists a plurality of connected Cairos based on different perspectives, paths, and positionalities. Each version of Cairo cast new light on the others. Each has unique strengths and weaknesses that, when shared, can pull out potential and possibility in one another—this multiplicity matters. It's the core of what keeps the city moving, connected, and growing.

Circling Back and Dropping Off

Core Continuations and Connections

Centering Egyptian and MENA bodies, stories, sites, and significations while cultivating stronger, deeper, and more complexly entangled core connections to *raqs sharqi* within contemporary Cairo has been the primary aim of this ethnography. I hope I have done some slight yet significant justice to staging and sharing these stories such that the core connections result in deepened *ihsas* (feeling) for others as well. *Raqs sharqi* embodies how connections cultivated in meaningful feeling can move people into new ways of being, new nuanced relationships within themselves, as well as to other corporealities and spaces around them. It weaves a subtle yet significant power.

As I attempt to choreograph the conclusion of this writing, my body swirls with emotions and memories from my fieldwork. Crafting a "conclusion" to something that's constantly changing, moving, and always critically choreographing is a trying, contradictory, and sentimental labor. My memory settles on one particular insight from retired dancer Eman. When I first met with her about my project, she looked me up and down, "So, I hear you think there is some connection between dance and post-revolutionary politics?" She took a long, slow drag from her cigarette before continuing, "You are right." Before I was ready, she dove in, sharing a rich treasure-trove of dance stories with me. She interwove stories from both her time as a dancer, as well as back in her mother's time, as she was also a dancer. Criss-crossing throughout her story sharing were the over-arching political threads—from the decadence during King Farouk's era to her own bodily pain from frozen muscles that she experienced living during Morsi's rule. I remember the imagery of strong swaying trees when she talked about the 2011 revolution. As she recollected, Egyptian women at this time were like the trees. They fully realized their thick deep roots, and they grew tall.[1] Her eyes sparkled, and her chin lifted as she proudly re-embodied this historic moment. My heart swelled. *There it was*: that elusive corporeal quintessence

CIRCLING BACK AND DROPPING OFF   217

of connection. Connection I've been dancing my entire life in search of and in commitment to.

Eman paused. She nodded as she thoughtfully concluded, "But don't just think of it as the Egyptian revolution, because the thing is... there is a revolution inside every woman." Expanding upon Eman's assertion and conclusion, this ethnography has traced some of these revolutionary resonances within the various sites and corporealities of dancers throughout Cairo. Oscillating between the micro-individual level of the body, as well as the macro-level of Egyptian state, intra-MENA, and global politics, dancers such as Safiya, Randa, Farah and her *shabab*, Amina, Sahar, Najla, Suzy, Hamada, and Julia uniquely center insights and tactics for moving forward sustainably, productively, and with sensitive attentiveness to humanity in contemporary Cairo.

Circling Back

As the Nile cruising boat from Chapter 1 pulls into port, it brings along several key insights, tactics, and knowledge that become productive moving forward with the larger contemporary issues with which Egypt is grappling. Safiya, Randa, and Farah revolutionize understandings of the gendered self as *shamla* (whole, complete) and enough. They place and play with corporeal and physical-external borders and boundaries to increase their power based on their unique identities and particular positionalities. Farah and her *shabab* inspire audiences at large to not just look at issues from an outside representational perspective. Rather, they offer a new perspective on how to analyze, listen, and see through a focus on detailed "doings" of bodies and their interactions. Rather than seeing Farah as a vulnerably exposed woman entrapped by the multiple strong men around her, she and her crew suggest that focusing on the movements and relationships between corporealities moving within these seeming constraints offers critical intersectionally gendered knowledge and insightful ways of moving in the world. During their finale, when Farah accumulates power with percussive hip bumps from side-to-side, the men kneeling as their sticks "box" and "entrap" her, Farah feigns dismay and shock. Then, suddenly she reverts to moving her hips in a new and unexpected direction, surging forward to break free from the confines, bursting into powerful hip shimmies as the men recover around her.

As I reflected upon Farah's finale, I was captivated by the ways it paralleled current discourse about Cairo being one of the worst cities in the world for sexual harassment against women. This discourse on sexual violence and harassment was particularly marked after SCAF and President Morsi came into power in Tahrir Square immediately following the revolution.[2] I remember some U.S. dance practitioners pitying the women in the square. But what was the female body engulfed in this masculine and male military violence doing at a deeper and more detailed level?

Farah's hip bumps and directional "twist" speak to paying attention to subtle, ground-level details. In this case, the dynamic array of grassroots and women-led anti-harassment networks, campaigns, and organization that work on the ground, constantly buzzing and accumulating agency in how to "do" the gendered body differently in spaces of public protest.[3] These weren't the mainstream stories making international news. These were women-led and focused groups that collaborated with men, but in which men organized as background allies and trusted supporters in a dynamic paralleled by Farah and her *shabab*. These were bodies working within the over-arching masculine militarized violent constraints, which were doing phenomenal groundbreaking work in rearticulating gender relations. I wondered if the U.S. practitioners so concerned for women's well-being in the square were aware of any of this grassroots work. This matters, because as *raqs sharqi* dancers know, where we focus and frame our attention transmits particular feelings out to wider audiences watching and can move bodies into new ways of thinking and being. Or we can simply replicate the status quo.

There is no one *raqs sharqi* show or dancer, just as there is no singular "Egyptian" or "MENA" woman. Though they may share the same stage, each dancer has something unique to say on it through her dance. Farah and her crew teach audiences to look at these conditions from diverse and undermined new angles while forming relationships between genders and social classes built upon hybrid collaborations founded in trust and creativity. Randa and Safiya offer insight into how to craft successful strong female solos. Randa and Safiya's strong solos necessitate being built upon a dynamic, holistic, and varied foundation that one can quickly tap into improvisationally according to what best fits the music, mood, and context. This knowledge is based upon going with one's gut, a gut based on diverse experiences, hard work, and trusting in oneself to be enough. But to be *shamla* and have a strong solo, one needs to know what you're saying and creating with your dance, not just what you're negating (such as the cabaret circuit or sexual-labor stigma). What new possibilities, or ways of being in the world, are you embodying, creating, and transmitting? This foundational model, of crafting your show based on a holistic depth, not just of what you're resisting, but focused on what world you are creating, is pivotal to revolutionary politics moving forward.

Safiya embodies a multiplicitous world in her diverse range of musical and dance styles that she, and multiple local and international audiences, can take pleasure within. Randa performs and projects a world where a woman need never scale back her power to appease the fragile masculinity of men. Meanwhile, in the bathroom, Samia enables a world of prideful peace and agency in embodying her modest piety and dutifulness to family. All four women recognize the power of various boundaries and borders, both physically and ideologically, and the need to either step across, maintain and work within, or breakdown such edges. As Farah concluded our interview, she put it succinctly, "I'm growing as a person, as a woman, and as a dancer, especially in knowing my own character, in knowing things I didn't think I was able to do or say. So yeah, you have to get tough here and handle all your little heartaches. Today the money is gone, okay, we will deal with it, next?"[4] Through their verbal and danced discourse, all dancers argue that in moving forward, female corporeality must be contended with as a centrifugal force and that men need to take more background roles as supportive allies.

As I fondly recall checking in and out of five-star hotels alongside Amina for Chapter 2, my heart warmly expands with hope and faith for more fruitful futures. Amina's performance and labor reminds audiences to seek out abundance in the fissures and opportunities of what's dominantly read as demising in scarcity or death. She also demands intersectional and contextualized analysis and understandings that, in moving beyond dualistic conceptualizations of *aseel*, take their time to relish in the inextricably linked dynamics of gender, race, class, sexuality, and nationality within economic and political projects. Notably, the discourse surrounding the decline in five-star hotel shows as a sign of a troubled economy and lack of "artistic" dancers and audiences. Alongside this the tension between appearances versus actualities holds pertinent resonances with the larger political projects of the state regime under President Sisi.

Sisi's campaign and popularity are largely founded in the dual claims that he is capable of improving the economy as well as exterminating "internal and external threats" to the country. Many Egyptians do support Sisi and believe in his state and economic projects. Surface-level statistics and appearances would also validate his first claim, showing that Sisi has eliminated over 2,000 terrorists and arrested over 16,000.[5] However, economically there was backlash due to harsh the economic trade-offs of a 12 billion-dollar IMF loan in the fall of 2016, which resulted in the flotation of the pound and high inflation rates. For Sisi supporters, the revamping of the economy and elimination of "threats" to the country are deemed priorities in stabilizing the country and moving forward since the ousting of President Morsi and the Muslim Brotherhood regime. Time and time again, my colleagues in Cairo would tell me the economy and the safety of the country from "enemies" needs to come first, then we can get to "everything else." I often found myself nodding in agreement; after all, my own lack of economic prowess constantly frustrated me throughout my fieldwork. I kept thinking if only I had a generous grant or financial resources, "everything else" would be so much easier.

But Amina's performance gestures to the shaky foundation of this line of thinking, at both the micro-level of hotel shows and macro-level of political state-stability. Amina critically reminds us that understandings of contemporary contexts and conditions need sweetening with honey. In other words, her performance articulates the importance of richly grounded, holistic body-centric, and intersectional analyses that take their time to pause in and relish the inextricably linked dynamics of gender, race, class, sexuality, and nationality within economic and political projects and positionalities. Stating that my access and exclusion from elite sites was simply due to money would be to erase the complex ways my interpolated body was relationally tied to other gendered, raced, classed, sexualized, and nationalist bodies within those sites. From the stares of *khaleegy* men in the lobby to Yasser's violating butt-squeeze, and the "gentlemanly" arm-escort offered to Krystal, the interwoven power politics of gender, race, class, sexuality, and nationality must be accounted for to secure solid footing and move with integrity in any larger political projects of the country.

Amina's dancing also reminds us not to romanticize her performance. Her show necessitates confronting the excessive labor and burdens certain bodies bear, already uneven and heavy enough without dousing on profuse citrusy cleaning polish. Instead, her show argues for the futility in focusing on surface-level disembodied appearances at the expense of delving into the grueling labor of corporeal actualities. As Amina dabs at her sweaty brow and then holds out her sweat-stained *mandeel* for all to see, she likewise rubs away romanticism in favor of a messy reality grounded in the corporeality of labor.

A multiplicity of bodies needs to be at the helm of politics moving forward, from the economy to scapegoating authoritarianism with broad floating references to disembodied "threats" to the country's safety. Amina's choreographic analysis demands a grounded exposure and analysis fleshed out with the meat, bones, sweat, tears, and blood of variously marginalized and centralized corporealities. For example, in actuality, the successfully eliminated and arrested "terrorists" are not specific to violent terrorists. Rather, in Sisi's state of exceptionalism a "terrorist" or "threat" can be any person that dares speak out against the state, or move through the world in a way misaligned with a militarized patriarchal heterosexual authoritarian regime. President Sisi continues to use the pretext of existential threats to clamp down on dissenters. This category increasingly includes other peaceful political opponents, civil society actors, human rights activists, journalists, LGBTQ+ citizens, as well as other everyday non-violent Egyptians, including many youths involved with the 2011 revolution.[6] Applying Amina's performance knowledge points to how the state's project reifies a violent system at the cost of marginalized corporealities and actualities.

Amina challenges all of us to oscillate between the body-politics of both intangible appearances and corporeal actualities to ask not only where and which bodies are valued in these broad political projects, but also which are centered, and which are marginalized? Finally, in addition to deeply dissecting our understandings of politics and power plays to include an intersectional *aseel* analysis, Amina offers rich probing moving forward. As Amina stands with her hands on her hips, *mandeel* still in hand, looking out upon her spectators, she daringly demands a foremost focus on cultivating her complex redefinition of *aseel* relationalities. In Amina's redefinition of *aseel* relationalities—demonstrated between her and her musicians—bodies that bear the often overlooked abor, marginalization, and violence of dominant discourses must instead be centralized in their full creative and commanding potential. Applying this insight and tactic to state economic projects redirects resources and funding from dominant militarized patriarchal systems and instead to the most marginalized of communities and corporealities living and laboring in the actualities on the ground.

Further, as DJs play their final mix in the discos of Chapter 3, dancers Sahar and Najla Ferreira take on the risk of exposing how self, societal, and state policing marginalize and cut off core aspects of our bodily identities and communities at the expense of more unifying vernacular vibes. As "risqué" dancing women who throw down working-class *mahraganat* vernacular to elite audiences up close and personal, they urge us all to "get with the vibe." Nonetheless, as hard as they fist pump and jump in the air to audience excitement, journalists still rush to type up articles on the latest societal "problem makers," whether that be the latest attempts to ban a working-class *mahraganat* singer or arrest a risqué dancer based on a viral video. Yet as Sahar and Najla remind us, the power of music and dance is in how they are both able to touch everyone, albeit in different ways. As stated, the people have power, and that's the majority. While many artists call for recognition from the state, perhaps there's even more revolutionary possibility within movements deemed "risqué?"

It's time to share a story you would have missed if we had remained scrutinizing social media or callously digesting prolific articles of arrests and deportations rather than deeply listening. During my fieldwork, Egyptian star Layla was only spottily performing in discos and had no social media presence. Layla's home base is as a cabaret circuit queen.[7] She dominates this circuit as a powerhouse dancer, her high reputation spreading through word of mouth on the circuit. In other words, you wouldn't find her if you hadn't taken the time to reach these ethnographic depths. This story stems from a long-anticipated interview we had in the middle of the night in a *reklam*-filled cabaret office as Farah Nasri, Ahmed, and I gig-hopped Layla's cabaret circuit. During our invigorating conversation, she discussed her rare appearance in the discos.

"I don't prefer discos too much because I prefer in-depth shows with a live band. But I like that *raqs sharqi* has grown a new context, and a real artist caters her dance to the context. The problem is if you *only* can dance disco style without any other understanding, so you solely rely on seduction, with overdone facial expressions and movements. I know some foreigners get deported for this; Egyptians that go too far get arrested. But to be honest, the reality is no, I am not for special laws against dancers and deportations or arrests. I want dancers to present art, to understand more without just relying on seduction, but there's no need for laws, deportations, and arrests for this-absolutely not. Understand, the "laws," limits, and levels of creativity and expression, this already exists in the dancing itself. It's all embedded within the dance; the education is the dance. There's no need for policing that we have now, for anyone. Yes, things that make sense I agree with, like wearing undershorts, but what doesn't make sense is men making rules against women. I don't mind foreigners being here, of course not, but this, this better way I envision will happen by and through Egyptians. It's all on us." Ahmed shouted his praise for her again, complimenting her as a strong pioneering woman. "I am strong enough to do it, yes, but we all need to be united together. *Musreen o bess.*"[8]

As a strong Egyptian dancer working within the most heavily policed venues, Layla's risqué corporeality has taken the next step in dance scholar Martin's calling for new communities, whilst uplifting my heart from its qualms as the disco lights cut on at the end of Chapter 3. Rather than debate the line and bounds of "acceptable" policing like most dancers I interviewed, Layla's embodied knowledge has led to alternative realities and relationalities, ones in which policing as we now experience it is thrown out altogether, and wherein embodied lived education and creativity founded on in-depth understanding take a lead. She digs into Martin's policing scholarship to highlight the already ever-present possibilities for being together that don't reinforce inequitable systems and instead center the creative and potentially more emancipatory communities and corporealities that policing scandalizes as risks to the current system. The biggest "threat" is that these exposed alternative realities and relationalities are far more unifying and emancipatory for the majority, the everyday people.

Like vibe, this "better way" is not visually clear or easy to manifest. It remains hard to see, much less embody, amidst smoky darkened discos and wider society, but it is worth the risk of leaning into. Listening to Layla alongside Sahar and Najla's danced discourse, we must all get vulnerable enough to strip off our "stones," of policing as well as privileged separations. Otherwise, we remain weighted down in nonrevolutionary trade-offs and barters for sequestered mobility within inequitable systems, allowing proximities and ephemeral vibes but never full embodied liberatory unity. In other words, we need to not only "get with" the vernacular vibe but rather make it viscerally corporealized into vibrant new communities, relationalities, and ways of being together in a shared understanding that serve the majority, the people.

Meanwhile, as the sun rises upon another night at a Pyramid Street cabaret within Chapter 4, Suzy, Julia, and the other cabaret workers spotlight alternative wealth harvested within solidarities and corporeal collaborations and choreographies that cut across dominant social divides, stigma, and structures. This body-focused dynamic expands upon scholarship by Middle Eastern political theorist Timothy Mitchell on carbon democracy and transnational capitalist and petrol-hegemonies.[9] Mitchell argues that fossil fuels create both the opportunities for forms of modern democracy as well as their limits. This carbon democracy is a global process wherein one country's form of politics is in relationship with various other transnational politics.

In dissecting global capitalism's successful hegemony through oil economies, he discovers that purposeful divisions and separations were the main means by which multinational oil corporations succeeded in controlling uprisings and protests for more democratic rights. Corporations utilize divisions between classes, nationalities, and ethnicities, as well as physical divisions of the processes of production and transportation of oil, to disrupt workers' chances for collective action.[10]

"McJihad" is Mitchell's theory that global capitalism can only function in different localities (such as key oil-producing Middle Eastern countries) by fusing with local social forces and moral authorities.[11] These fusings may or may not mesh with global capitalism and empire's same methods and goals, and their pairing is often rife with tension and contradiction. Mitchell argues that it is within these hybridized local forms of McJihad that people must look for the vulnerabilities and weaknesses within the system to be exploited by workers to argue for more democratic claims to life. Applying his theory to the microcosm of the cabaret, it is in the way that bodies use the materiality of the shared space, stage, and *sala* (seating area) that the creation and vulnerabilities within the localized and hybridized McJihad process are found. However, Egyptian-English dancer Zara pushes forward Mitchell's theory through her class-crossing "zero to five star" embodied dance experiences to point out that the core of these divisions, thus the core of potentiality, lie deepest within corporealities.

Mining the micro-roots of these processes, and how they're played out across cabaret bodies, illuminates larger ways in which class, gender, sexuality, and nationality as corporealities are at the core of macro-level political and economic dynamics affecting Cairo. Focusing on insights and tactics from Suzy's *nimra*, as well as the choreographed cooperation during the interim and Julia's *nimra* are in conversation with ways gender and women's issues have been dealt with drastically differently by both the autocratic State and certain revolutionaries within Tahrir Square in 2011. Both pre- and post-revolution, women's issues were limited within state-feminism, critiqued as monolithic, top-down, and controlled.[12] Despite this being the critiqued model during Mubarak's years, it has been re-instated with the National Council of Women under President Sisi. At the same time, Sisi's increasing autocratic grip over independent organizations has led to a stifling of the polyvalent and grassroots, women-led and focused coalitions and missions started by revolutionaries in Tahrir Square, during and in the wake of the 2011 revolution.[13]

This theme recurs throughout Egypt's history. Women's roles and rights have continually been appropriated to serve regime needs first and foremost. It is also noteworthy how moments of revolutionary and nationalist ruptures, such as the 2011 revolution but also including the 1919 revolution, followed by Nasser's state-formation in 1952, all resulted in fissures of the hegemonic patriarchal order.[14] These fissures resulted in the proliferation of diverse women's movements, demonstrations, and expanded gender roles in domestic and public spheres that fostered revolutionary sociopolitical transformations.[15] However, following such ruptures, the state seized up and consolidated power once again, and women's roles and rights were one of the first and most evident areas to be controlled and policed. (Note that this pattern of women's expanded gender roles and power, followed by tight conservative suppression, during times of greater political shifts is not unique to Egypt or the MENA. For example, in the United States during World War 2, women's roles and activities expanded to include what was previously in the "masculine" domain such as working in industry and heading households. Following the war, the "honey, I'm home" lifestyle became promoted and normalized, with women urged to return to their homes and identify within the domestic sphere as housewives and mothers.)

Yet during the 2011 revolutionary rupture, like others before, a different world was realized because gender was done differently. In conversation with certain female revolutionary movements within Tahrir Square, what Suzy's *nimra*, where she performs her gender fluidly and polyvalently, argues for is to cultivate worlds and politics where gender is not only centralized, but wherein gender is understood as dynamic, multiplicitous, and inherently intersectional and connected with all other bodies and political dynamics. It demands ground-level and fleshed-out bodily contextualization to be better understood and to best pragmatically serve a wide array of female corporealities across the socioeconomic spectrum. Further, and again expanding upon the gender and corporeal relationalities cultivated by revolutionaries within Tahrir Square, the interim and Julia's *nimra* also contend that moving forward will mean moving together. Julia and the other laboring bodies within the cabaret worked in cross-aligned solidarities and creative coalitions that swerved multidirectionally.

Thus, Suzy and Julia's corporealities and choreographies offer tactics that may disrupt and re-direct the unidirectional and top-down directionality of power dynamics that both dominant petrodollar-fueled heteromasculinities and iron-fisted autocracies, attempt carving into the larger social system and citizen subjectivities. At the same time, we mustn't forget that these cabaret workers are so heavily policed because their corporealities challenge larger state and patriarchal visions of normative and idealized subjectivities while their choreographies offer embodied insight into alternative ways of being together. While the cabaret workers' tactics and insights apply at the macro-political structural levels, Zara, Hamada, and Suzy also remind us that this work dually begins deep in one's own being and body. Focusing on insights, cautions, and tactics from the cabaret is to argue that moving forward sustainably will mean moving together in multiplicity and multidirectionality.

Dropping Off

All these dancers, along with the taxi transition drivers, offer more nuanced, richer, and beautiful interpretations of Cairo's city rhythms. They teach academic and practitioner audiences alike nuanced ways to interpret, feel, and move to the music—if we have been listening. They task each of us with the responsibility and tools for deepening the depths of our listening. This is a task I too urge every academic, audience member, and practitioner to continually dedicate and commit themselves to. Listen. Listen deeply and with visceral vulnerability. Listen to continually learn, to love, and to cultivate connections that will continue to deeply move us all.

While the autocratic state of Egypt continues to carve unidirectional, top-down, and narrow ways of being, knowing, and moving into its citizen-subjects, this ethnography's performers, from dancers, taxi drivers, venue staff workers, hostesses, and musicians, have choreographed and mapped out other multidirectional, multiplicitous, and meandering routes, roads, rhythms, and ways of being. Ultimately, they all come together in offering this: moving forward will mean moving together in new and nondominant ways that cultivate more meaningful and multiplicitous core connections, wherein the concept of "core" is grounded in the understanding, analysis, and valuing of bodily realities and knowledge as a centrifugal nexus. These core connections enrich the way bodies know themselves, one another, but also how they move through the city . . . and potentially into revolutionary new realities and relationalities. The ways that bodies move matter. They embody, choreograph, and create the worlds we live in. *Here*, these are worlds of multiply moving possibility, potentiality, and poignant plurality.

Well, this is where we part ways. At least for the time being. Thank you for coming along for this enriching backseat ride throughout Cairo with four site-specific show stops. I always feel bittersweet, yet deeply touched, bidding farewell to Cairo. I am curious; as you step out from this ethnographic ride, what world are you more consciously stepping into? If a few well-placed words, shared stories, and well-paced steps can nudge the world a bit, what will your next move be? After all, we're all wrapped up in this together. I'm hopeful. Still, as we began, so I part from you with similar encouragement; listen. Listen deeply and lovingly. Keep moving. Stay open to connection.

And when that invitation arises, connect at the core.

Notes

Introduction

1. For more, see Gelvin, *The Arab Uprisings: What Everyone Needs to Know*.
2. Al-Youm, "Egyptian President Sisi Extends Emergency State by Three Months," Youness, "Egypt Renews State of Emergency for 10th Time," and Human Rights Watch, "Egypt: A Move to Enhance Authoritarian Rule." For more on the political contexts and conditions of Egypt since the 2011 revolution up until 2018, see Şahin, "Core Connections: A Contemporary Cairo Raqs Sharqi Ethnography," 84–109.
3. Zaki, "El-Sissi's Women? Shifting Gender Discourses and the Limits of State Feminism," and Hafez, *Women of the Midan: The Untold Stories of Egypt's Revolutionaries (Public Cultures of Middle East and North Africa)*.
4. The National Interest, "How Sisi Could Wreck the Egyptian Economy," and Khalaf, "Sisi's Egypt: The March of the Security State."
5. For more detailed information on the development of *raqs sharqi* at this time, including farther back histories related to *awalim* and *ghawazee* entertainers, please see: Nieuwkerk, *A Trade like Any Other: Female Singers and Dancers in Egypt*, Şahin, "Core Connections: A Contemporary Cairo Raqs Sharqi Ethnography," 59–109, and Ward, *Egyptian Belly Dance in Transition: The Raqs Sharqi Revolution, 1890–1930*.
6. Said, *Orientalism*, 5.
7. Said, *Orientalism*. For Middle Eastern feminist scholars that have expanded upon Said's Orientalism with more intersectional and dynamic studies, please see Abu-Lughod, ed., *Re-Making Women: Feminism and Modernity in the Middle East*.
8. To provide a sense of diversity, belly dance styles may include Turkish, Egyptian, Lebanese, American cabaret, transnational fusion (formerly "tribal style"), and even gothic steampunk.
9. Here I speak of policing both in the sense of a government body enforcing laws and regulations as well as sociocultural "policing" judgments and gatekeeping by various non-governmental communities, such as those within and outside of the dance industry in Cairo. For more information on the historic policing and regulation of *raqs sharqi*, please see Nieuwkerk, *A Trade like Any Other*, Roushdy, *Femininity and Dance in Egypt: Embodiment and Meaning in al-Raqs al-Baladi*, and Morley, "Dancers Inciting Debauchery: Policing Raqs Sharqi to Legitimize the Egyptian Regime."
10. For more on dance studies theory intervening in the mind/body split, please see Desmond, "Embodying Difference: Issues in Dance and Cultural Studies."
11. Abu-Lughod, *Veiled Sentiments*, xv.
12. Abu-Lughod, "Writing against Culture."

13. I feel it is important to acknowledge and honor my early dance teachers here: Ann Distafano, Shahrzad (United States), Lynda Latifa Wilkinson, Faten (DC), Artemis Mourat, and Sahra C. Kent.
14. For more on the various circulations of power and political dynamics encountered within mostly white U.S. studio classes to be compared with Arab-American and MENAT performance contexts discussed here, please see Bock and Borland, "Exotic Identities: Dance, Difference, and Self-Fashioning," Dox, "Dancing Around Orientalism," Haynes-Clark, "American Belly Dance and the Invention of the New Exotic: Orientalism, Feminism, and Popular Culture," Jamarkani, "Dancing the Hootchy Kootchy: The Bellydancer as the Embodiment of Socio-Cultural Tensions," Kraus, "Becoming a Belly Dancer: Gender, the Life Course and the Beginnings of a Serious Leisure Career," Kraus, "Transforming Spirituality in Artistic Leisure: How the Spiritual Meaning of Belly Dance Changes Over Time," McDonald, *Global Moves: Belly Dance as an Extra/Ordinary Space to Explore Social Paradigms in Egypt and Around the World*, Moe, "Beyond the Belly: An Appraisal of Middle Eastern Dance (Aka Belly Dance) as Leisure," and Sunaina, "Belly Dancing: Arab-Face, Orientalist Feminism, and U.S. Empire."
15. For an in-depth analysis of each of these discursive approaches, see the literature review section in my doctoral dissertation: Şahin, "Core Connections: A Contemporary Cairo Raqs Sharqi Ethnography," 3–37.
16. Roushdy, *Femininity and Dance in Egypt*, or her shortened version, Roushdy, "Baladi as Performance: Gender and Dance in Modern Egypt."
17. Nieuwkerk, *A Trade like Any Other*.
18. Emerging belly dance scholarship focuses on the MENAHT within globalized contexts. Cairo becomes the next main focal point of dance, but investigations that center Cairo tend to avoid the trappings of Western works that refer to it as an "authentic" dance locale (which calls attention to their colonialist nostalgia) and instead offer Cairo as one of many centers of globalized *raqs sharqi*. For examples, please see Potuoğlu-Cook, "Beyond the Glitter: Belly Dance and Neoliberal Gentrification in Istanbul," Lorius, "'Oh Boy, You Salt of the Earth': Outwitting Patriarchy in *Raqs Baladi*," and Arvizu, "The Politics of Bellydancing in Cairo."
19. For a sampling of belly dance globalization studies, please see McDonald, *Global Moves*, and McDonald and Sellers-Young, *Belly Dance Around the World: New Communities, Performance and Identity*.
20. Said instead forwards that all cultures are impure and based on fluidity, hybridity, and based on inter-relationality to all other people, places, and politics. He urges scholars to avoid dominating forms of duality and division and instead centralize multiplicity. See Said, *Culture and Imperialism*.
21. Most of the research concluded that belly dance embodies orientalism while adding complexity to the discourse in dissecting how and why dancers engaged with an embodied and representational "exotic other" to craft more empowering versions of themselves. See Bock and Borland, "Exotic Identities: Dance, Difference, and Self-Fashioning,", Carlton, *Looking for Little Egypt*, Dox, "Dancing Around Orientalism," Keft-Kennedy, "Representing the Belly-Dancing Body: Feminism, Orientalism, and

the Grotesque," Shay and Sellers-Young, *Belly Dance: Orientalism, Transnationalism, And Harem Fantasy (Bibliotheca Iranica. Performing Arts Series)*, and Vermeyden, "The Popularization of Belly Dance in Toronto, Canada (1950–1990): Hybridization and Uneven Exchange."
22. Najwa Adra's chapter on *baladi* (social dance) also offers a critical intervention into the field by asserting that social dance is not a homogenous and static "authentic" base to the dance, but rather is dynamic and polysemous. However, despite her efforts to center *baladi* dance and the agency of MENA subjects, her chapter appears in a formidable belly dance anthology, edited by Shay and Sellers-Young, that frames her introductory article as the "foundation" upon which all other orientalist explorations of the dance will be situated. Thus, even as she labors to deconstruct orientalist notions of MENA dance, she operates within an already orientalist structure due to the anthology's framing. See Adra, "Belly Dance: An Urban Folk Genre."
23. Foster, *Corporealities: Dancing Knowledge, Culture and Power*, xi.
24. García, *Salsa Crossings: Dancing Latinidad in Los Angeles (Latin America Otherwise)*, 15.
25. I started my fieldwork as a graduate student in the University of California Riverside's Critical Dance Studies Ph.D. program in 2015. Because my fieldwork was almost entirely self-funded, I would continually dance and T.A. (sometimes on the east coast, sometimes the west coast) until I saved enough money to go to Cairo for another 1–4 months at a time. After completion of my Ph.D. in 2018 and starting part-time lecturing at California state universities in San Diego alongside dance gigging, this trend continued, albeit still on a meager contingent faculty budget. Altogether, I spent just over two years in Cairo spread out between 2015 and 2020.
26. While I attended a plethora of weddings with and without hired dancers, I didn't feel I had enough access and experience to include these sites with integrity. Further, weddings are more differently social-ritual and family-centered rather than commercial, a trait linking my other sites. Notably, weddings are a highly valuable site for centering Egyptian contexts, meanings, and bodies and I hope other scholars will explore this further in the future.
27. For more information on the deep societal stigmatization of *raqs sharqi* performers and female entertainers see Nieuwkerk, *A Trade like Any Other* and Nieuwkerk, *Performing Piety: Singers and Actors in Egypt's Islamic Revival*.
28. Jarmakani, *Imagining Arab Womanhood: The Cultural Mythology of Veils, Harems, and Belly Dancers in the U.S.*, and Sunaina, "Belly Dancing."
29. Adra, "Belly Dance," 47.
30. Hafez, *Women of the Midan*, Hafez, "Bodies That Protest: The Girl in the Blue Bra, Sexuality, and State Violence in Revolutionary Egypt," Hafez, "No Longer a Bargain: Women, Masculinity, and the Egyptian Uprising," and Hafez, "The Revolution Shall Not Pass through Women's Bodies: Egypt, Uprising and Gender Politics."
31. *Reklam* will be discussed in more detail in Chapter 4.
32. For more information on the cultural, dance, and musical context of *ihsas* or "feeling" in *raqs sharqi*, please see Bordelon, "'Finding the Feeling' Through Movement and

Music: An Exploration of Tarab in Oriental Dance." For a richer exploration of the role of feelings, music, and states of ecstasy in Arab music, please see Racy, *Making Music in the Arab World: The Culture and Artistry of Tarab (Cambridge Middle East Studies, Series Number 17)*, 2004, and Farraj and Shumays, *Inside Arabic Music: Arabic Maqam Performance and Theory in the 20th Century*.

33. Abu-Lughod, *Remaking Women*, 25.
34. A focus on circulations of dance resonates with my dance form and project and is also informed and in conversation with key models from Dance Studies. Please see Potuoğlu-Cook, "Beyond the Glitter," Srinivasan, *Sweating Saris: Indian Dance as Transnational Labor*, García, *Salsa Crossings*, Kwan, *Kinesthetic City: Dance and Movement in Chinese Urban Spaces*, and McMains, *Spinning Mambo into Salsa: Caribbean Dance in Global Commerce*.
35. Abu-Lughod, *Remaking Women*, 25.
36. Historically, entertainers of all genders such as *awalim*, *ghawazee*, *gink*, and *khawals* performed in Egypt and throughout the MENAHT. Men and those of multiplicitous gender subjectivities have always been integral to this dance form, but in the context of my research they are largely made invisible in commercial performance venues. While there is no law or regulation stipulating men cannot perform professionally as *raqs sharqi* dancers in these sites, they would fall prey to the same tactics of policing as dancers, with claims of inciting debauchery, eliciting prostitution, and so on used to enforce their invisibilization. Dancer licenses were also not given out for male *raqs sharqi* performers during the period my fieldwork (Roushdy, Femininity and Dance in Egypt, 4). Male identifying professionals do perform in Cairo for international belly dance festivals and slightly along the Northern Coast tourist areas such as Sharm al Sheikh, which largely cater to international tourists. I do attend to other critical, yet peripheral, dancing male bodies, and non-dance male choreographies and bodies, within and between *raqs sharqi* venue spaces. In doing so, my ethnography explores gender dynamically in the ways both male and female identifying bodies co-constitute gender and gender politics. At the same time, the reality in my research contexts is that gender is heavily practiced with binary usage at this time. For further reading visiblizing the male dancing body, please see Shay, *Choreographic Politics: State Folk Dance Companies, Representation, and Power*, Shay, *The Dangerous Lives of Public Performers: Dancing, Sex, and Entertainment in the Islamic World*, Shay, "The Male Dancer in the Middle East and Central Asia," and Karayanni, *Dancing Fear and Desire: Race, Sexuality, and Imperial Politics in Middle Eastern Dance (Cultural Studies)*.
37. For example, a U.S. dancer may reflect upon their performance as successful due to how "spot on" their technique was that night, or how satisfied they personally felt, whereas a Cairo dancer may judge their performance by how many audience members began to sing along and wave their hands to the music as well as the overall mood that was created.
38. Please see Lazreg, *The Eloquence of Silence: Algerian Women in Question*.
39. Anthropologist Karin Van Nieuwkerk similarly argues that the performing arts in Cairo, and female celebrity figures in particular, actively shape, and are being shaped,

by larger Islamist, economic, gendered, and national forces. She contends that there is no "pure" body that is not already interpolated by larger systems of power, that bodies shape, and are shaped by, larger systems. *Performing Piety*.

40. Hafez, *Women of the Midan*.
41. Abu-Lughod, *Remaking Women*, 12.
42. *Raqs al 3asaya* translates as "stick dance" and is commonly performed within a larger *raqs sharqi* repertoire to reference the *tahtib* stick martial arts movement practice of men in the *Sa3id* region of lower Egypt. This dancing has strong signifiers to Egyptian culture and nationality.
43. Safiya is a stage-name pseudonym used for anonymity purposes and to comply with IRB and ethics protocols. Anonymity is the default within this project as per IRB and ethics protocols. Safiya means pure. All dancers referenced in this text use stage names due to their highly publicized and stigmatized dance work, however for more at-risk Egyptian or MENAT dancers stage names are shortened (first stage name only) and/or changed.
44. Dina, interview by author, Cairo, July 12, 2016.
45. Norland, "Saudis and the Last Egyptian Belly Dancer."
46. Amina is a stage-name pseudonym used for anonymity purposes and to comply with IRB ethics protocols. Amina means honesty.
47. For an exemplary example of binary orientalist representations of the Arab world and peoples, see: Jarmakani, *Imagining Arab Womanhood: The Cultural Mythology of Veils, Harems, and Belly Dancers in the U.S.* Jarmakani discusses how representations such as the sexy belly dancer are mapped onto larger power discourses of an imperialist U.S. nation and its progress and imperialist self-definition.

Chapter 1

1. For broader relevance of terrorism within Egypt at this time, and how overbroad definitions of terrorism have been used to undermine essential rights in the name of national security, please see Chiha, "Redefining Terrorism under the Mubarak Regime: Towards a New Definition of Terrorism in Egypt."
2. These Nile tour cruising boats were often referred to colloquially as either *safeena al siyaha* and less commonly, *marakib*.
3. For a vivid example illustrating professional dancers, *awalim*, being hired for boat parties, see Mahfouz, Hutchens, and Samaan, *The Cairo Trilogy in 3 Volumes: Palace Walk, Sugar Street and Palace of Desire*.
4. For more on the transition and relationships between *awalim* and *raqs sharqi* female dancers in Egypt, see Nieuwkerk, *A Trade like Any Other: Female Singers and Dancers in Egypt*.
5. The *tanoura* may refer to the performer but is also the name of the practice as well as the heavy colorful skirt the performer whirls and manipulates into various visual designs and shapes throughout the performance. Each color within the *tanoura* skirt

refers to a particular *Sufi* order. Though there are female professional performers, *tanoura* is dominated by male performers in Cairo.

6. More recently there has become a style of boat sites that remain docked and function more like upscale restaurants and nightclubs for Egyptian and intra-MENA audiences, such as the *Blue Nile* and *Nile Lounge/Nile Dragon VIP*. This chapter speaks about cruising tour boats only, these other types of stationary boats don't fall into this category.
7. *Tanoura* shows rarely if ever occur in the five-star hotel or cabaret *raqs sharqi* shows. While *tanoura* are overwhelmingly male, there are always a few exceptions, for example a female-*tanoura* named Hanna who performs regularly on boats. However, during the holy month of Ramadan nonsexually stigmatized *tanoura* performances are prolific across many additional commercial sites wherein *raqs sharqi* performances nearly cease.
8. Yet this still contrasts to wedding, cabaret, disco-club, and hotel gigs where the Egyptian and intra-MENA clientele overwhelmingly make up the dominant audiences.
9. Said, *Orientalism*, 58–59.
10. Wynn, *Pyramids and Nightclubs: A Travel Ethnography of Arab and Western Imaginations of Egypt, from King Tut and a Colony of Atlantis to Rumors of Sex Orgies, Urban Legends about a Marauding Prince, and Blonde Belly Dancers*, 4.
11. García, *Salsa Crossings: Dancing Latinidad in Los Angeles (Latin America Otherwise)*, 128.
12. Samia, personal correspondence, Cairo, January 2, 2017.
13. For more on the politics of the Golden Era of Egyptian cinema please see: Shafik, *Popular Egyptian Cinema: Gender, Class, and Nation*, and Shafik, *Arab Cinema*.
14. Reminder, Safiya is a stage-name pseudonym used for anonymity purposes and to comply with IRB ethics protocols. Anonymity is the default within this project as per IRB protocols. Safiya means pure.
15. Samia, personal correspondence.
16. Borelli traces the genealogy of the *mulata* dancer in Cuba in order to explore how she choreographs her racialized and sexualized identity through her articulate hips. While focusing on a particular female body part, such as the swaying hips, would typically read as fetishization and objectification, Borelli challenges this immobilized reading and instead posits that hips (that know their history and potentiality) can demonstrate just how powerful a force the moving body is in producing alternative knowledge and self-authorship while further embodying larger subaltern histories. Borelli, *She Is Cuba: A Genealogy of the Mulata Body*.
17. The informal interview with Safiya occurred on January 22, 2017 at a dining table inside the *Nile Maxim* banquet room after the evening's cruise had finished following one of her many performances. My friend and research collaborator Karim was also present to help me with any interview translation issues (questions I needed help phrasing correctly or translating parts of Safiya's response that I didn't catch, although I understood and led most of the interview). Although Safiya's conversational in English, the interview mostly occurred in colloquial Arabic. The interview was recorded and then I transcribed it myself back home in the United States.

18. *Sha3bi* is a term with many meanings dependent upon context. It translates to "of the people" or indicates "popular culture" but often is colored with working-class or local connotations. The term can be one of pride but also wielded with classist condescension. Here, it is referred to a music and dance genre.
19. Roushdy, *Femininity and Dance in Egypt: Embodiment and Meaning in al-Raqs al-Baladi*, 42.
20. Star dancer Fifi Abdou became a popular emblem of *baladi* and *sha3bi* styles during this time, particularly her *tableaus* incorporating the *mi3allima* (boss lady) persona and *baladi* movements while wearing the white *galabeya* as opposed to the two-piece bra and belt/skirt costume.
21. For more on how political and economic policies effected the Egyptian people, particularly with a focus on gender, see Botman, *Engendering Citizenship in Egypt* and Hafez, *Women of the Midan: The Untold Stories of Egypt's Revolutionaries*, ch 2.
22. Safiya, interview by author, Cairo, January 2017.
23. A deeper dissection of the gender, sexuality, and nationalist politics of state theatricalized folklore troupes will be covered in the second section of this chapter. For more information on the Reda Troupe and its relationship with nationalism, gender, and sexuality, please see Fahmy, "The Creative Development of the Mahmoud Reda—Contemporary Egyptian Choreographer," Vermeyden, "The Reda Folkloric Dance Troupe and Egyptian State Support During the Nasser Period," and Shay, *Choreographic Politics: State Folk Dance Companies, Representation, and Power*.
24. For more on the entwinement of laws and regulation since the inception of *raqs sharqi* performances in Egypt, please see Ward, *Egyptian Belly Dance in Transition: The Raqs Sharqi Revolution, 1890–1930*, Şahin, "Core Connections: A Contemporary Cairo Raqs Sharqi Ethnography," 59–84, Nieuwkerk, *A Trade like Any Other*, 40–49, and Roushdy, *Femininity and Dance in Egypt*, 1–46. For a broader account of policing on MENAHT dance historically, please see Shay, *The Dangerous Lives of Public Performers: Dancing, Sex, and Entertainment in the Islamic World*.
25. The history as well as dance and state politics of *fath* will be returned to in-depth in Chapter 4. Nieuwkerk, *A Trade like Any Other*, 40–49.
26. *Fitna* is an Arabic term that loosely refers to social chaos, temptation, or disorder. Its definition often depends on the specific context of usage; in the case of female professional dancers it's used to refer to the social disorder/chaos a women's sexual power and perceived deviancy may elicit. For more on *fitna* as related to sexuality, see Ahmed, *Women and Gender in Islam: Historical Roots of a Modern Debate* and Mernissi, *Beyond the Veil: Male-Female Dynamics in Modern Muslim Society*, 4.
27. Safiya, interview.
28. Samia, personal correspondence, Cairo, February 4, 2017.
29. This duo-informal interview with Randa and Tito occurred on February 14, 2017 in the hotel lobby of the Barcelos Hotel in Cairo. I recorded the interview and transcribed it myself back in the United States. The interview was conducted in English and Arabic that Randa was able to translate when I didn't comprehend. Randa spoke primarily in English while Tito primarily in Arabic, which I was mostly able to understand. The interview was graciously arranged by Sara Farouk Ahmed, one of the festival organizers and a dear colleague and source of knowledge during my fieldwork.

30. Randa, interview by author, Cairo, February 2017.
31. Throughout this book I respect and write the personal dance histories as dancers choose to tell and generously share them, even if the actuality is different.
32. For example, a dear dancer-friend of mine that worked in Cairo in earlier decades had a male friend who used to work in a cabaret but had since moved on to own a small business. He was apparently so adamant about hiding his cabaret history that he had his friends tell my dancer friend he died rather than say he was working down the street.
33. Interview with belly dance festival director by author, February 2017.
34. Randa, interview.
35. Nieuwkerk, *A Trade like Any Other*, 59. For more detailed information on the history of *awalim* (and *ghawazee*) and their relationship to the development of *raqs sharqi* at this time, please see Nieuwkerk, *A Trade Like Any Other*, Şahin, "Core Connections," 59–109, and Ward, *Egyptian Belly Dance in Transition*.
36. Nieuwkerk, *A Trade like Any Other*, 49.
37. *Tableau* refers to dance numbers that have a narrative or story line based in or referencing any number of regional folklore dancers theatricalized by the national troupes or other Egyptian contextualized narratives and settings, such as smoking shisha at a coffee shop.
38. Samia, personal correspondence. February 17, 2017.
39. In Golden Age films, soloist dancers such as Samia Gamal and others can be seen performing with a background of male and female dancers behind them, and early cabaret clubs had background chorus line female dancers as well. However, the collaborations seen since the 1970s in commercial *raqs sharqi* venues are more closely tied to the national folklore troupes and Nagwa Fouad. By the 1970s Egyptian-Palestinian Nagwa Fouad was considered one of the greatest *raqs sharqi* artist performing in the MENA. For more information on Nagwa Fouad and her legacy as a star dancer, see Shereen, "An Uncommon Woman Nagwa Fouad, Queen of Oriental Dance."
40. For more on the role of Egyptian women as 'mothers and daughters' of the nation, see Botman, *Engendering Citizenship in Egypt* and Hafez, *Women of the Midan: The Untold Stories of Egypt's Revolutionaries*, ch 2.
41. Hafez, "The Revolution Shall Not Pass through Women's Bodies: Egypt, Uprising and Gender Politics," 180.
42. For more information on the Reda Troupe and its relationship with nationalism, see Fahmy, "The Creative Development of the Mahmoud Reda: Contemporary Egyptian Choreographer," Vermeyden, "The Reda Folkloric Dance Troupe and Egyptian State Support During the Nasser Period," and Shay, *Choreographic Politics*.
43. Fahmy, "The Creative Development of the Mahmoud Reda."
44. Vermeyden, "The Reda Folkloric Dance Troupe," and Shay, *Choreographic Politics*.
45. Shay, *Choreographic Politics*.
46. Shereen, "An Uncommon Woman," 118.
47. Shereen, "An Uncommon Woman," 118. Nagwa Fouad added innovative changes to the structural performance of *raqs sharqi* that had lasting significance until the present

day. Nagwa Fouad was the first dancer to have atleast a somewhat-choreographed *mejance*, or entrance opening piece, composed specifically for her dance performance, allowing her to create a dramatic choreographed spectacle for her show's opening.

48. Shereen, "An Uncommon Woman," 118.
49. Sahra C. Kent, interview by author, Cairo, February 2017. Sahra was one of the first to get a higher degree in dance ethnology doing ethnographic dance research in Cairo while also working as a professional dancer in the 1990s. She has been a highly respected teacher and mentor throughout my dance career as well, with her courses on Egyptian dance ethnology fueling my own eventual fieldwork path. I am deeply grateful and indebted for her knowledge and mentoring.
50. Farida Fahmy, interview by author, Cairo, March 28, 2017. My informal interview with Farida Fahmy occurred in English in her Zamalek apartment. The full interview was conducted in English and I recorded and transcribed it myself back in the United States.
51. However, *funun al sha3biyya* are still sometimes requested and used at Egyptian weddings for the middle classes and up that can afford to hire them to fill up the show time and space as well as highlight the wedding party's wealth. However, this social context is quite different from commercial venues and out of scope for this project.
52. Vanessa Friedman, interview by author, Cairo, February 2017. Vanessa was a wonderful friend and research collaborator during my stay in Cairo. I had many long interviews with her after her show in the five-star Sofitel Moroccan restaurant where she generously shared her vast knowledge of the professional working *raqs sharqi* scene. Interviews occurred in English at a table after her show in the restaurant, and we were either alone or with her then husband Yasser, who also worked in the national troupes and often participated in the interviews with his unique insight. I recorded the interviews and transcribed them myself back in the United States.
53. *Mizmar* is a traditional wind instrument known for Nile Valley *Sa3idi* music.
54. An exception to this is the cabaret circuit, where rather than dancers largely going off stage to interact with guests, guests are often welcome and invited up onto the stage with the singers and dancers to socially dance. These dynamics will be discussed more in Chapter 4 in the context of cabarets.
55. While dancers may not have surgical enhancements, most working dancers, anywhere in the world, will modify their costuming and looks to better fit an idealized male gaze aesthetic. Modifications run the spectrum from wearing a padded push-up style costume bra to enhance the breast shape and size to costumes fitted to accentuate hip and butt curves. In the Cairo entertainment industry, across venues, it is common to enhance one's look with enlarging the breasts (through whatever method), enhance the face such as larger pouty lips, defined eyebrows, and false eyelashes, as well as long thick and full hair wigs or extensions.
56. While Safiya and Randa did not engage in the ubiquitous photo-taking that often took up a large chunk of the second part of the *raqs sharqi* show, Farah, and most other dancers working across boats in Cairo do. While the *Nile Maxim* has a hired boat photographer to take guest/performer photos with Sukre, the *tanoura* performer,

most other boats commonly have this photographing occur with both the *tanoura* artist and the dancer during the second more folkloric-inspired part of her set. These enlarged photos are then purchasable by guests for around 30–50 pounds, but cell phone photographs and quick video clips are also extremely pervasive during this part of the show.

57. In 1973 the *musannafat*, a male-dominated government organization established toward the end of Nasser's era and in charge of licensing and regulations for *raqs sharqi* professionals, continues to create and enforce policing of dancers with these and other regulations related to movements, costuming, use of space, and audience interaction. For more please see: Nieuwkerk, *A Trade like Any Other.*

58. The informal interview with Farah Nasri occurred in her dressing room on the *Nile Maxim* after one of her shows on January 18, 2017. I recorded the interview and transcribed it myself back in the United States. The informal interview with Farah's crew happened below deck on the *Nile Maxim* on March 21, 2017. Farah and Karim were also present to assist with the interview and any necessary translating. The interview was recorded and transcribed into English by myself back in the United States. Farah suggested I pay each musician and dancer 20 pounds for quick interviews. Her *funun al sha3biyya* crew primarily worked in Dream Park, similar to a small amusement park geared toward Egyptian children that hosted *funun al sha3biyya* shows. Her crew dancers worked in both Reda and *komiyya* troupes but all worked in Dream Park and I heard from many dancers that this was one of the best places to see a strong *funun al sha3biyya* show where they really shone; notably *raqs sharqi* dancers do not work in Dream Park.

59. It's also important to note, as Farah Nasri pointed out, that Randa, Safiya, and Samia are all much older women compared to the other dancers featured in this book. Farah is significantly younger than them and their ages also affect their life experiences and how they choose to craft their shows on stage. Additionally, Farah performs all over Cairo as a highly in-demand soloist, mostly performing solo *raqs sharqi* shows, so she is able to adapt her show to both kinds of styles and does not exclusively perform with her *shabab*.

60. Shereen, "An Uncommon Woman," 118.

61. Ahmed, interview by author, Cairo, March 2017.

62. Salah, interview by author, Cairo, March 2017.

63. For a greater discussion of women's modernity projects tied to various feminisms in Egypt and how they simultaneously created both new potential and opportunities for women, as well as new forms of control and surveillance, see: Abu-Lughod, *Re-Making Women: Feminism and Modernity in the Middle East.*

64. Farah, interview.

65. Ahmed, interview.

66. Samah, interview by author, Cairo, March 2017.

67. Samah, interview.

68. For more on the history and politics of Egyptian and other MENAHT male social and professional dancing that debunks such biological determinism, please see Karayanni, *Dancing Fear and Desire: Race, Sexuality, and Imperial Politics in Middle*

Eastern Dance (Cultural Studies), Shay, "The Male Dancer in the Middle East and Central Asia," 2006, and Shay, *The Dangerous Lives of Public Performers*.
69. Hafez, "The Revolution Shall Not Pass through Women's Bodies," and Botman, *Engendering Citizenship in Egypt*.
70. Botman, *Engendering Citizenship in Egypt*.
71. Farah, interview.
72. Farah, interview.
73. Ahmed, personal correspondence, Cairo, January 27, 2017.
74. Mahr, "Bread Is Life: Food and Protest in Egypt," and The New Arab, "Will Egypt's Bread Riots Be Met with Tank Barrels?"
75. An example of Sisi's economic endeavors to better the economy while simultaneously being stifled by the military's deep-state grip over the government and the regime's own economic interests is discussed in Economist, "The Price Is Wrong: What Fuel, Bread, and Water Reveal about How Egypt Is Mismanaged." See also Bush and Greco, "Egypt under Military Rule."
76. Brown and Bentivoglio, "Egypt's Resurgent Authoritarianism: It's a Way of Life," and Hamzawy, "Egypt after the 2013 Military Coup."

Chapter 2

1. For more information on this and other historic sites along the Nile, see Wilkinson, *The Nile: Travelling Downriver Through Egypt's Past and Present*.
2. This information is from the archived hotel site history document from the Marriott company; see Marriott Hotel, *Cairo Marriott Hotel History*.
3. Wynn, *Pyramids and Nightclubs: A Travel Ethnography of Arab and Western Imaginations of Egypt, from King Tut and a Colony of Atlantis to Rumors of Sex Orgies, Urban Legends about a Marauding Prince, and Blonde Belly Dancers*, p. 14.
4. Ramadan is the holy month of fasting from sunrise to sunset in the Islamic faith, a sacred time for becoming closer to God and committing good deeds. Most venues stop having *raqs sharqi* shows in Cairo, and many fasting practitioners abstain from food, drink, and other activities deemed *haram* (shameful)—a category into which watching dancers could easily fall.
5. This information is from the archived hotel travel site history document from the Semiramis hotel company: Gerber, "Intercontinental Semiramis History."
6. For an in-depth elaboration of human rights violations and violence against Egyptian citizens, particularly minorities, journalists, LGBTQ+ citizens, and peaceful dissenters, please see Amnesty International: *Egypt*. My fieldwork encompasses the years 2015–2020, which can be looked up on this website. See also Human Rights Watch, *Egypt: Events of 2019*.
7. I use the term prostitution because this is the word used in the laws. For more on the complexity and history of the term prostitute as it is used legally as well as socioculturally within Cairo from an anthropological perspective, please see Wynn, *Love, Sex, and Desire in Modern Egypt: Navigating the Margins of Respectability*, ch. 6. The

statement that sex work has been on the rise post-revolution was reported to me by many members of the dance industry at large (cutting across classed venue types), particularly by managers and impresarios, as well as in the following source focused on five-star hotels: Johnson, "Egypt After The Revolution: There's Not Much To Sell But Sex."

8. Starting in 2013 in the immediate wake of the revolution and up until 2017, punishments related to prostitution, sexual difference, "habitual practices of debauchery," and "licentiousness" have risen by nearly five times, following a focus of cracking down on sex workers and LGBTQ+ individuals in response to Egypt's Law No. 10/1961, on the Combating of Prostitution (1961). Sex workers today are at risk of legal criminalization, facing up to three years in prison as well as additional fines. Additionally, the government's efforts to protect sex workers are minimal, raising the risk of rape and violence against them while clients paying for sexual services are not prosecuted but rather often serve as a witness for the prosecution. See: Abdel Hamid, "The Trap: Punishing Sexual Difference in Egypt," and Mohamed, "Patriarchal Society Alienates Sex Workers in Egypt."

9. Early cabarets were also critiqued from the perspective of the socialist nationalism that was ushered in with the Nasser era. This socialist nationalism stigmatized these venues as sites of extravagant class excess and elitism related to the old monarchy and colonial rule. Cabarets will be discussed at length in Chapter 4.

10. For more information, see Nieuwkerk, *A Trade Like Any Other: Female Dancers and Singers in Egypt*, and Şahin, "Core Connections: A Contemporary Cairo *Raqs Sharqi* Ethnography."

11. An *usta* was the female leader of a group of female *awalim*. She had male assistants to help her with business negotiations that occurred in coffee houses around the Mohamed Ali Street area, but this business system was predominantly a female-run and informal arrangement that *awalim* held as a monopoly business along this street. For more information on the *usta* business system, please see Nieuwkerk, *A Trade Like Any Other*, ch. 3.

12. For more, please see Nieuwkerk, *A Trade Like Any Other*, ch. 3. For more on the role of gender politics and roles within Nasser's presidency, please see Botman, *Engendering Citizenship in Egypt*, ch. 3.

13. Sara Farouk Ahmed, interview with the author, Cairo, February 2, 2017.

14. Notably, the influx of foreign dancers in Cairo did not permeate the thriving cabaret scene, only those venues classified as more "elite, reputable, and clean"—that is, boats and hotels. Many foreign dancers reported not having any interest in what they deemed the "low class" cabaret scene; likewise, most who did audition for these jobs were not desired or hired by the venues due to their lack of understanding of cabaret performances values, aesthetics, and goals (see Chapter 4).

15. At the same time, not all foreign dancers operate on the same axis of privilege and circumstance. For example, many Russian and other Eastern European dancers, also coming from harsh economic circumstances, greatly benefit from the financial gains of working in Cairo as a primary benefit as opposed to the social capital of the

international teaching circuit that is available to women who are often more economically secure and come from Western nationalities. For more on foreign dancers working in Cairo, see McDonald, *Global Moves: Belly Dance as an Extra/Ordinary Space to Explore Social Paradigms in Egypt and Around the World.*
16. Nieuwkerk, *Performing Piety: Singers and Actors in Egypt's Islamic Revival*, p. 3.
17. As a reminder, Amina is a stage-name pseudonym used for anonymity purposes and to comply with IRB ethics protocols. Anonymity is the default within this project as per IRB protocols. Amina means honesty.
18. For example, when my Egyptian male friend, who was supposed to meet me for coffee in the Semiramis lobby before I went to Dina's show, was a no-show. He failed to ever show up because he worked overtime in the Khan al Khalili trying to secure more business at a time when tourists were still just trickling through the giant tourist souk. He didn't feel comfortable meeting me in the space without going home first to shower and change into nicer clothes, but because of working later he knew he couldn't make the time. He told me later that he thought the entrance security wouldn't let him through dressed in his work clothes even if he tried.
19. Krystal is a stage-name pseudonym used for anonymity purposes and to comply with IRB ethics protocols. In this case, I hope foreign dance readers listen for "likeness" with Krystal, as this case study offers an opportunity to gain critical self-awareness and growth in regard to uneven axes of intersectional race, gender, class, and nationalist political relationships.
20. Krystal, personal correspondence, Cairo, January 19, 2017.
21. Revealingly, a common way to teach this close-legged mermaid dancer stance in the United States that directly relates to kinesthetic class-policing is by the instructor telling students to "imagine they are holding a 100$ bill between their thighs."
22. Yasmina, interview by author, Cairo, April 29, 2017.
23. Yasser, personal correspondence, Cairo, February 16, 2017.
24. Alexandrian *melaya luff* dances are more of a character dance than a regional dance, and their innovation and popularity are owed to the Reda Troupe.
25. This musical information on *baladi* was taught to me by many musicians in Cairo as well as dance teachers. For more textual information on *baladi* progressions and their history and relationship with dance, see Hilal, "'Baladi Personae in Egyptian Dance and Music.'"
26. Although I never secured a full-length sit-down interview as desired with Amina, we had many conversations (with her manager present) in her dressing room before her shows. In conversations, she never shied away from where she came from, who she was, and how hard she was willing to work. Our conversations helped ground my interpretation of her performance.
27. Srinivasan, *Sweating Saris: Indian Dance as Transnational Labor.*
28. Roushdy, *Femininity and Dance in Egypt: Embodiment and Meaning in al-Raqs al-Baladi*, p. 11.
29. Ghannam, *Live and Die Like a Man: Gender Dynamics in Urban Egypt*, 67.
30. Abu-Lughod, *Veiled Sentiments 2nd Edition (1999) by L. Abu-Lughod*, xxii.

Chapter 3

1. These sites are called discos (*discohat* in Arabic plural), but the term is sometimes synonymous with club/s by members of the upper classes, particularly those with abroad experience. Throughout this chapter some collaborators may refer to these sites as discos, disco-clubs, or clubs, all these terms refer to the same site. Discos/*discohat* is the term most widely understood by all class levels for this site.
2. For more on the scandalous and censored politics of these music videos please see: Arvizu, "The Politics of Bellydancing in Cairo," Morley, "Dancers Inciting Debauchery: Policing Raqs Sharqi to Legitimize the Egyptian Regime," and Adum, "'Raqs Sharqi Dancers Reject Wahda We Nos Channels.'"
3. *Mahragan* means festival (*mahraganat* festivals) in Arabic but also is a slang Cairo term referring to things that are boisterous, loud, extravagant, colorful, and sometimes messy. Golia, "Egypt's Mahragan: Music of the Masses." The musical genre can be referred to by either the singular or plural by those within the industry interchangeably. Elshamy, "'Mahraganat': New Hybrid Music Wave Sweeps Egypt."
4. Golia, "Egypt's Mahragan."
5. State Information Service: "CAPMAS: Poverty Rates in Egypt Decline to 29.7% within Year."
6. For more on the political, class, and gender dynamics of *mahraganat*, this English close-captioned interview is a great resource: Världskulturmuseerna, "Interview Mai Amer - Mahraganat & Gender | مقابلة مع د. مي عامر حول فن المهرجانات وأين صوت النساء؟," May 24, 2022. For more on *mahraganat* and the economic situation of the working-classes, please see Zeid, "Songs from Egyptian Slums to Media."
7. Mekky, "Sheikhs against Shakes: Egypt Belly Dancing Channel 'Arouses Viewers.'"
8. In Egyptian Arabic "Chinese" is used as an adjective to describe something as cheap, fake, or of poor-quality reproduction. The dancer quoting this prefers to remain anonymous.
9. Zara describes this dynamic with the metaphor of a race where Egyptians have a million hurdles to navigate and foreign dancers have none, but rather, foreigners show up in the best and most enabling tracksuit and sneakers and are cheered on by family and friends while Egyptians are booed, kicked out of home, and worse. Zara, interview by author, Cairo, December, 2019.
10. Gant, "Russian Belly Dancer Is Jailed for a Year in Egypt after She Was Filmed Dancing in a Nightclub."
11. For more on the similarities and differences between local and foreign dancers working in Cairo in earlier times, see McDonald, *Global Moves: Belly Dance as an Extra/Ordinary Space to Explore Social Paradigms in Egypt and Around the World*.
12. For a few examples, please see Egyptian Streets, "Russian Belly Dancer 'Johara' Deported, Charged with 'Inciting Debauchery,'" Egyptian Streets, "Two Egyptian Belly-Dancers Sentenced to Prison Over 'Debauchery' in Music Videos," Egypt Independent, "Egypt Imprisons Belly Dancer Sama Al-Masry for Indecency," and Al Sherbini, "Egypt Bellydancer Outrage Cuts Party Short."

13. For more on the history of dance policing, please see Nieuwkerk, *A Trade like Any Other: Female Singers and Dancers in Egypt*, and Roushdy, *Femininity and Dance in Egypt: Embodiment and Meaning in al-Raqs al-Baladi*.
14. Please see Ward, "Rewriting History: Respectability Politics and Revisionist History in Contemporary Egyptian Belly Dance."
15. Martin, *Women, Dance and Revolution: Performance and Protest in the Southern Mediterranean*, and Martin, "Dancing in the Spring."
16. Martin, "Dancing in the Spring," 213.
17. Morris and Giersdorf, *Choreographies of 21st Century Wars*, 19.
18. Hafez, "No Longer a Bargain: Women, Masculinity, and the Egyptian Uprising," 40. For more on this and other incidences of gendered violence during the revolutionary aftermath, see Hafez, "The Revolution Shall Not Pass through Women's Bodies: Egypt, Uprising and Gender Politics."
19. Hafez, "The Revolution Shall Not Pass through Women's Bodies," 173.
20. Hafez, "Bodies That Protest: The Girl in the Blue Bra, Sexuality, and State Violence in Revolutionary Egypt," 23.
21. Hafez, "Bodies That Protest," 25.
22. Name changed for anonymity.
23. When discos first popularized, they were for the elite upper classes, colloquially referred to as the "A-plus" or "A-plus-plus" class. Over the time of my fieldwork and writing, there were discos for middle, upper-middle, elite, and "A-plus-plus" elite classes. Each disco tended to cater to a certain social stratum, although those strata could shift over time. (Primarily only in discos catering to the lower-level strata might an exception be made for audiences and discos desiring a more voluptuous Egyptian dancer aesthetic more akin to cabaret ideals discussed in Chapter 4).
24. Roberts, "Cairo Clubs: Don't Forget to Take Off Your 'Hat.'"
25. For more, please see Daly, "What I Learned as a Door Selector at a High-End Bar in Cairo," September 10, 2021.
26. Farah Nasri, interview by author, Cairo, December 2019.
27. This chapter speaks toward the contemporary model of disco-club sites. Oral historian Sayyad H. informed me that discos during the Mubarak era were also sites of socialization for Cairo's youth, with live bands or cassettes playing Egyptian and international music that would go until around midnight, from there the venues would transform into a cabaret for older family audiences with a *raqs sharqi* performance. Sayyad H., interview by author, Cairo, December 2019.
28. Kandil, "Why Muslim Brotherhood's Morsi Failed to Complete Presidential Term," and Hafez, "The Revolution Shall Not Pass through Women's Bodies."
29. Hafez, "The Revolution Shall Not Pass through Women's Bodies," 180.
30. Moghadam, "Explaining Divergent Outcomes of the Arab Spring: The Significance of Gender and Women's Mobilizations," 675.
31. Pratt, "Gendered Paradoxes of Egypt's Transition."
32. "Annual Report: Egypt 2013," and Pratt, "Gendered Paradoxes of Egypt's Transition."
33. Mekky, "Sheikhs against Shakes.'"

34. Farah Nasri, interview by author, Cairo, December 2019.
35. Egyptian dancer, interview by author, Cairo, March 2017. My informal interview with this dancer (who in 2020 correspondence preferred to be anonymous as she has since disassociated from the disco circuit) occurred after one of her five-star hotel shows. I recorded the interview and transcribed it myself back in the United States. The interview was in English.
36. These musical genres and styles are not exhaustive; there could be an "oldie" like "Shik Shak Shok" or a drum solo thrown into the dancer's set. This site is also the most likely for fusion props more typical outside of Cairo to be utilized, like LED Isis wings. The dancer might also perform with the singer.
37. Maya, interview by author, Cairo, December 2019. This interview occurred in Egyptian Arabic in a five-star hotel lobby before one of Maya's upper class wedding performances. I recorded the interview and translated it into English back in the United States.
38. Farida Fahmy, interview by author, Cairo, March 28, 2017.
39. For more about gender and modernity in post-revolutionary Egypt, please see Hatem, "Revolutions, Crises of Modernities, and the Production of Gender Subjectivities in Egypt," and Hafez, "Gender and Citizenship Center Stage: Sondra Hale's Legacy and Egypt's Ongoing Revolution."
40. Zara, interview by author, Cairo, December 2019.
41. For a sound example of this within *raqs sharqi* and *sha3bi* aesthetics, please see Lorius, "'Oh Boy, You Salt of the Earth': Outwitting Patriarchy in *Raqs Baladi*," October 1996.
42. For an in-depth analysis on this, please see Zuhur, *Popular Dance and Music in Modern Egypt*.
43. Sellers-Young, *Belly Dance, Pilgrimage and Identity*, 109–128.
44. Ward, "Rewriting History."
45. Zara, interview by author, Cairo, December 2019.
46. Stallybrass and White, *The Politics and Poetics of Transgression*, 5.
47. Foucault and Miskowiec, "Of Other Spaces."
48. Sahar, interview by author, January 2020. I interviewed Sahar with the accompaniment of my male colleague Ayman in Egyptian Arabic. I recorded the interview and translated it into English in the United States.
49. Singerman and Amar, *Cairo Cosmopolitan: Politics, Culture, and Urban Space in the New Middle East*.
50. Morad, interview by author, Cairo, December 2019. I interviewed Morad in English in the quietest corner of his disco.
51. However, I would argue that a few dancers such as Najla are able to somewhat capture this in their social media video clips. I feel Najla highlights this dynamic in many of her shared clips, focusing more on performer-audience "exchange," just as much as the spectacular "wow" technique; this serves as exemplary marketing for her.
52. This other dancer prefers to remain anonymous due to her greater at-risk background.
53. Najla Ferreira, interview by author, Cairo, January 2020. This interview was conducted in English.

54. Youssef, "The Controversial Street Music That Won't Be Silenced," and Rafik, "Egypt's Musicians Syndicate Temporarily Suspends Mahraganat Music."
55. An important note is that these two options are not tied to the foreign versus Egyptian/MENAHT debate. Dancers from any background may or may not be able to achieve vibe as theorized here.
56. Maya, interview by author, Cairo, January 2020.
57. Egyptian dancer, personal correspondence, March 2020.
58. Kinesthetic imagination comes from dance scholar Ann Cooper Albright, referencing the necessity of creating possibilities (theoretically or materially) with and through embodied experience. Albright, "Tracing the Past: Writing History Through the Body."
59. For more resources on the Palestinian occupation please see: Khalidi, *The Hundred Years' War on Palestine: A History of Settler Colonialism and Resistance, 1917–2017*, 2020. The IMEU (Institute for Middle East Understanding) is an accessible non-profit organization that offers journalist facts, analysis, experts, and digital resources on the occupation of Palestine and the Palestinian liberation movement (please visit IMEU.org for more information).
60. Madison, *Critical Ethnography: Method, Ethics, and Performance*, 2011, 193.

Chapter 4

1. *Reklam* is originally a Turkish word meaning "advertisement" that has been adopted into Egyptian vernacular. I am still investigating the origins and popularization for the word *reklam*. In older times similar women would sit and drink with customers known as *fatihat*. I also asked colleagues in Turkey about cabaret hostesses akin to *fatihat* and *reklam*; they were intrigued by the use of a Turkish term because they said for similar work in Turkish (Ankara) cabaret environments they use an adopted Turkish word *konsomatris* from the French *consommatrice* (definition: [feminine] 1. Consumer or 2. Someone who eats or drinks in a public establishment).
2. *Nu2ta* is the singular colloquial Arabic, and *keet* the plural used in cabarets, for the specific kind of tipping money circulated within cabarets.
3. There are multiple types of cabaret circuit in Cairo; this ethnography analyzes the Pyramid Street strip of cabarets. Cabarets in downtown Cairo are vastly different, catering to a primarily working-class Egyptian audience, and would warrant an analysis all their own, out of the scope of this chapter. Newer cabarets established on stationary boats (not the cruising tour boats of Chapter 1) are another type of cabaret related to the gentrification of Cairo city-space and also are out of the scope of this chapter.
4. For more on the sociocultural usage of the term prostitute in Cairo, please Wynn, *Love, Sex, and Desire in Modern Egypt: Navigating the Margins of Respectability*, ch 6.
5. For more of the history of Pyramid Street and the changes it experienced over time, please see Nieuwkerk, *A Trade like Any Other: Female Singers and Dancers in Egypt*

and Şahin, "Core Connections: A Contemporary Cairo Raqs Sharqi Ethnography," 84–109.
6. The 1973 oil crisis began in October 1973 when the members of the Organization of Arab Petroleum Exporting Countries proclaimed an oil embargo.
7. For more on the macro-level economic and political effects of the oil embargo and Saudi Arabia petro-dollars in general, see Mitchell, *Carbon Democracy: Political Power in the Age of Oil*.
8. *Nimar* is the plural of *nimra*.
9. A *mawwal* is a genre of vocal Arabic music that demonstrates strong vocal abilities and improvisational skills. The *mawwal* occurs before the actual song and relates to poetry traditions wherein the lyrics may have deep meanings that audiences can mutually relate to.
10. *Dabka* is popular form of social line dancing and music from the Levantine regions of the Middle East.
11. For example, he does not hire women or Christians and work halts during prayer times.
12. Adum, "Farewell to the Al Gandoul Nightclub on El Haram Street."
13. I talked with Sayyad H. and several cabaret managers about tipping practices and history. I interviewed Sayyad H. several times throughout my fieldwork at open coffee shops in Cairo with our mutual trusted and generous friend Khaled (August 2015, August 2016, March 2017, and December 2019). Sayyad H. is an oral historian from a famous Mohamed Ali Street musician family that played the accordion. Some cabarets, Lucy's famous Parisiana being one example, may use fake notes (hers are shaped like pounds but feature a Santa Claus face in the center of the bill and the words "special coupon" under the amount).
14. Suzy, interview by author, Cairo, February 2016. A cabaret waiter, Ali, was a key collaborator in procuring interviews with dancers, entertainers, and musicians after their shows in the alleys/parking areas just outside of the noisy cabarets. Karim was present for these informal interviews, and the dancer's male manager or agent was always present. The interviews included paying a small amount to both Ali and the dancer, usually between 50 and 100 pounds, for quick interviews before they had to run to catch their other cabaret shows elsewhere. The interviews in Arabic were recorded and I transcribed them myself back in the United States.
15. Ahmed, interview by author, Cairo, April 2017. I had a dual interview with star cabaret dancer Aziza and her husband Ahmed before their nightclub shifts got started around midnight at a café down the street from their show. Karim was assisting in translating the informal interview which I recorded and then transcribed back in the United States. I had many inspiring opportunities to attend Aziza's live shows and study dancing with her; those experiences and her in-depth interview were extremely useful for nuancing my background knowledge of cabaret circuits.
16. Fifi Abdou, a famous dancer popularly performing from the 1970–1990s was known to embody this character with her shisha water-pipe dance and white *galabeya baladi* number.
17. Suzy, interview by author, Cairo, February 2016.

18. Ahmed Cabaret Manager, interview by author, Cairo, March 2017. I interviewed Ahmed with Karim present in his office at the cabaret in Arabic. I recorded the interview and transcribed it back in the United States.
19. For more on the complex historical and contemporary climate of color prejudice and anti-blackness within Cairo, please see Poole, "'Brown Skin Is Half of Beauty': Representations of Beauty and the Construction of Race in Contemporary Cairo" and Sabry, "Anti-Blackness in Egypt: Between Stereotypes and Ridicule- An Examination on the History of Colorism and the Development of Anti-Blackness in Egypt."
20. Sahra C. Kent, interview by author, Cairo, February 2017. The interview was in English.
21. Yossry H, interview by author, Cairo, April 2017. I interviewed well-known drummer Yossry in his Pyramid Street music studio. He held a long career playing in an assortment of venues and worked with hundreds of dancers over the years in Cairo and international dance festivals. He also helps train up and coming cabaret dancers. Karim assisted me with translating the informal Arabic interview, it was then recorded, and I transcribed it by myself back in the United States.
22. Hamada, interview by author, Cairo, February 2017. I held an informal interview in Arabic with Hamada the *toura* player during the breaks between his performances in the parking lot area just outside the venue. Ali the waiter arranged the interview and they both were paid 50–100 pounds. Karim assisted with translating the interview and I recorded it and then transcribed it myself back in the United States.
23. Cabaret dancer agent, interview by author, Cairo, December 2018. This interview was in Arabic and transcribed back in the United States. For more information on the contemporary public policing and regulation of *raqs sharqi*, please see Morley, "Dancers Inciting Debauchery: Policing Raqs Sharqi to Legitimize the Egyptian Regime."
24. Donya cabaret hostess, interview by author, Cairo, July 2016. I paid her 50 pounds for the Arabic interview and Karim assisted with translating. I later transcribed it by myself in the United States. Interviewing hostesses within cabarets were some of the hardest interviews to procure as many women did not give us permission to ask questions, and other times primarily the management would not allow it. In this case, Donya granted us permission but made sure it was also okay with the management as well. Many cabaret staff were concerned I was working for the police or government and were concerned I would only want to report negative things about their work. Every time we did procure cabaret interviews, we were also invited at some point into the manager's office to talk about my research and hear the managements' life stories.
25. Bossy, cabaret dancer, interview by author, Cairo, August 2016. I held an informal Arabic interview with Bossy after her *nimra* in a small alley outside the cabaret. Karim was assisting with translating and her manager/husband was also present. I recorded the interview and transcribed it myself back in the United States.
26. Ahmed cabaret singer, interview by author, Cairo, April 2017. I held an informal Arabic interview with cabaret singer Ahmed after his show at a cabaret. Karim assisted with translating and I recorded the interview and transcribed it myself back in the United States.

27. My interpretation for his motivation is based upon numerous exchanges with the dancers, *reklam*, waitstaff, managers, and Gulf clientele of cabarets. My aim is not to reify stereotypes of the *khaleegy* "lusty sheihk," but to center what cabaret workers want this chapter to "do." The uneven power dynamics between *khaleegy* petrol hegemonies and their own laboring Egyptian corporealities were centered in my conversations with workers, as well as the stigma they faced in their own culture. I do encourage readers to read Wynn's ethnography that explores Gulf Arab tourism in Cairo at far more heterogeneous levels than this Pyramid Street cabaret specific fieldwork to further disarm any chances of reifying stereotypes. Wynn, *Pyramids and Nightclubs: A Travel Ethnography of Arab and Western Imaginations of Egypt, from King Tut and a Colony of Atlantis to Rumors of Sex Orgies, Urban Legends about a Marauding Prince, and Blonde Belly Dancers.*
28. Mona G., interview by author, Cairo, March 2017. Mona G. is a Hungarian-Syrian dancer who has been working in Egypt for over a decade. The informal English interview occurred in her apartment and was recorded and transcribed by myself back in the United States.
29. For a series of Cairo case studies exploring the role of physical city-space structural organization, layout, and redesign as related to class and modernity politics, please see Singerman and Amar, *Cairo Cosmopolitan: Politics, Culture, and Urban Space in the New Middle East.*
30. Zara, interview by author, Cairo, September, 2017. I held an informal interview with Egyptian-English dancer Zara and her then manager at an open *baladi 2ahwa* (coffee shop) during a long break between her gigs. The interview was in English and I recorded it and transcribed it myself back in the United States. The full quote Zara was referencing by Audre Lorde is as follows: "The true focus of revolutionary change is never merely the oppressive situations which we seek to escape, but that piece of the oppressor which is planted deep within each of us, and which knows only the oppressors' tactics, the oppressors' relationships." Lorde, *Sister Outsider: Essays and Speeches.*

Circling Back and Dropping Off

1. Eman, interview by author, Cairo, August 2016.
2. For more on gendered violence during the aftermath of the revolution, see Hafez, "Bodies That Protest: The Girl in the Blue Bra, Sexuality, and State Violence in Revolutionary Egypt," and Hafez, "The Revolution Shall Not Pass through Women's Bodies: Egypt, Uprising and Gender Politics."
3. For more context, information, and to give voice to these movements and coalitions, please see Allam, *Women and the Egyptian Revolution: Engagement and Activism during the 2011 Arab Uprisings,* and Hafez, *Women of the Midan: The Untold Stories of Egypt's Revolutionaries (Public Cultures of Middle East and North Africa).*
4. Farah Nasri, interview by author, Cairo, January, 2017.

5. McManus, "Measuring Success in Egypt's War on Terror."
6. McManus, "Measuring Success in Egypt's War on Terror," and Magdi, "'We Need to Talk' about al-Sisi's Twisted Take on Human Rights."
7. Stage name changed for anonymity.
8. Layla, interview by author, Cairo, January 2020. However, in the meantime, Layla practically offers other tactics; simultaneously calling for "wiggle room" within the current system through her suggestion of a syndicate led by strong female Egyptian dancers, and more general state support and recognition.
9. Mitchell, *Carbon Democracy: Political Power in the Age of Oil*.
10. Mitchell, *Carbon Democracy: Political Power in the Age of Oil*.
11. Mitchell, *Carbon Democracy: Political Power in the Age of Oil*, 213.
12. Hafez, "The Revolution Shall Not Pass through Women's Bodies: Egypt, Uprising and Gender Politics," 181.
13. Pratt, "Gendered Paradoxes of Egypt's Transition."
14. For more, please see Baron, *Egypt as a Woman: Nationalism, Gender, and Politics*, and Hafez, "The Revolution Shall Not Pass through Women's Bodies: Egypt, Uprising and Gender Politics."
15. For more, please see Hafez, *Women of the Midan: The Untold Stories of Egypt's Revolutionaries (Public Cultures of Middle East and North Africa)*, and Botman, *Engendering Citizenship in Egypt*.

Bibliography

Abdel Hamid, Dalia. *The Trap: Punishing Sexual Difference in Egypt*. (Al Qahirah: Egyptian Initiative for Personal Rights, 2017), https://eipr.org/sites/default/files/reports/pdf/the_trap-en.pdf.

Abu-Lughod, Lila. *Remaking Women: Feminism and Modernity in the Middle East*. Amsterdam: Amsterdam University Press, 1998.

Abu-Lughod, Lila. *Veiled Sentiments: Honor and Poetry in a Bedouin Society*. Berkeley: University of California Press, 1999.

Abu-Lughod, Lila. "Writing against Culture." In *The Cultural Geography Reader*, edited by Timothy Oakes and Patricia Price. 62–71. London: Routledge, 2008.

Adra, Najwa. "Belly Dance: An Urban Folk Genre." In *Belly Dance: Orientalism, Transnationalism, and Harem Fantasy*, edited by Anthony Shay and Sellers-Young Barbara. Costa Mesa, CA: 28–50. Mazda Publishers, 2005.

Adum, Priscella, trans. "Farewell to the Al Gandoul Nightclub on El Haram Street." *Shira.net*, October 21, 2011. http://www.shira.net/about/el-gandoul-nightclub.htm.

Adum, Priscella, trans. "'Raqs Sharqi Dancers Reject Wahda We Nos Channels.'" *Shira.net*. November 4, 2011. http://www.shira.net/about/tet-channel.htm.

Ahmed, Leila. *Women and Gender in Islam: Historical Roots of a Modern Debate*. Reprint, New Haven, CT: Yale University Press, 1993.

Alaa El-Din, Menna. "Cairo Taxi Drivers Call for Protests to Ban Uber, Careem Services." *Ahram Online*, February 3, 2016. https://english.ahram.org.eg/NewsContent/1/0/186586/Egypt/0/Cairo-taxi-drivers-call-for-protests-to-ban-Uber,-.aspx.

Albright, Ann Cooper. "Tracing the Past: Writing History Through the Body." In *The Routledge Dance Studies Reader*, edited by Alexandra Carter and Janet O'Shea. 2nd ed., 101–10. London: Routledge, 2010.

Allam, Nermin. *Women and the Egyptian Revolution: Engagement and Activism during the 2011 Arab Uprisings*. Cambridge: Cambridge University Press, 2017.

Al Sherbini, Ramadan. "Egypt Bellydancer Outrage Cuts Party Short." *Gulf News*, October 29, 2018. https://gulfnews.com/world/mena/egypt-bellydancer-outrage-cuts-party-short-1.1489206.

Al-Youm, Al-Masry. "Egyptian President Sisi Extends Emergency State by Three Months." *Egypt Independent*, October 26, 2019. https://egyptindependent.com/egyptian-president-sisi-extends-emergency-state-by-three-months/.

Al-Youm, Al-Masry. "Russian Belly Dancer Johara Sentenced Year in Prison." *Egypt Independent*, April 10, 2019. https://egyptindependent.com/russian-belly-dancer-johara-sentenced-year-in-prison/.

Amnesty International. "Annual Report: Egypt 2013." *Amnesty International*. May 17, 2013. https://www.amnestyusa.org/reports/annual-report-egypt-2013/.

Amnesty International Report 2020/2021*Egypt*. *Amnesty International*, 2020. Amnesty International Report 2020/21: The state of the world's human rights - Amnesty International

Anderson, Benedict. *Imagined Communities: Reflections on the Origin and Spread of Nationalism*. Rev. ed. London: Verso, 2016.
Arvizu, Shannon. "The Politics of Bellydancing in Cairo." *The Arab Studies Journal* 12/13, no. 2/1 (2004–2005): 159–81.
Baron, Beth. *Egypt as a Woman: Nationalism, Gender, and Politics*. Berkeley: University of California Press, 2007.
Behar, Ruth. *The Vulnerable Observer*. Amsterdam: Amsterdam University Press, 2014.
Bock, and Borland. "Exotic Identities: Dance, Difference, and Self-Fashioning." *Journal of Folklore Research* 48, no. 1 (2011): 1–36.
Bordelon, Candace. "'Finding the Feeling' Through Movement and Music: An Exploration of Tarab in Oriental Dance." PhD diss., Texas Woman's University, 2011.
Borelli, Blanco Melissa. *She Is Cuba: A Genealogy of the Mulata Body*. Oxford: Oxford University Press, 2015.
Botman, Selma. *Engendering Citizenship in Egypt*. New York: Columbia University Press, 1999.
Brown, Nathan, and Katie Bentivoglio. "Egypt's Resurgent Authoritarianism: It's a Way of Life." *Carnegie Endowment for International Peace*. October 9, 2014. https://carnegieendowment.org/2014/10/09/egypt-s-resurgent-authoritarianism-it-s-way-of-life-pub-56877.
Bush, Ray, and Elisa Greco. "Egypt under Military Rule." *Review of African Political Economy* 46, no. 162 (October 2, 2019): 529–34. (Link no longer available, last accessed May 2019).
Carlton, Donna. *Looking for Little Egypt*. Bloomington, IN: International Dance Discovery, 1995.
Chiha, Islam Ibrahim. "Redefining Terrorism under the Mubarak Regime: Towards a New Definition of Terrorism in Egypt." *Comparative and International Law Journal of Southern Africa* 46, no. 1 (February 28, 2013): 90–121.
CNN.com. "Three Bombs Rip through Egypt Resort," April 24, 2006. https://edition.cnn.com/2006/WORLD/meast/04/24/egypt.blasts/index.html.
Daly, Moustafa. "What I Learned as a Door Selector at a High-End Bar in Cairo." *Egyptian Streets*, September 10, 2021. https://egyptianstreets.com/2021/09/10/what-i-learned-as-a-door-selector-at-a-high-end-bar-in-cairo/.
Desmond, Jane. "'Embodying Difference: Issues in Dance and Cultural Studies.'" In *Meaning in Motion: New Cultural Studies of Dance*, edited by Jane Desmond. 29-54. Durham, NC: Duke University Press, 1997.
Desmond, Jane. *Meaning in Motion: New Cultural Studies of Dance*. Durham, NC: Duke University Press Books, 1997.
Dox, Donnalee. "Dancing Around Orientalism." *TDR/The Drama Review* 50, no. 4 (December 2006): 52–71.
Economist. "'The Price Is Wrong: What Fuel, Bread, and Water Reveal about How Egypt Is Mismanaged.'" *The Economist*, February 10, 2018. https://www.economist.com//news/middle-east-and-africa/21736552-egyptians-are-addicted-subsidies-make-them-poorer-what-fuel-bread-.
Egypt Independent. "Egypt Imprisons Belly Dancer Sama Al-Masry for Indecency." *Egypt Independent*, June 27, 2020. https://www.egyptindependent.com/egypt-imprisons-belly-dancer-sama-al-masry-for-indecency/.
Egyptian Streets. "Russian Belly Dancer 'Johara' Deported, Charged with 'Inciting Debauchery.'" *Egyptian Streets*, February 8, 2018. https://egyptianstreets.com/2018/

02/08/russian-belly-dancer-johara-deported-after-being-charged-with-inciting-deb auchery/.

Egyptian Streets. "Two Egyptian Belly-Dancers Sentenced to Prison Over 'Debauchery' in Music Videos." *Egyptian Streets*, September 3, 2015. https://egyptianstreets.com/2015/09/03/two-egyptian-belly-dancers-sentenced-to-prison-over-debauchery-in-music-videos/.

Elshamy, Mosa'Ab. "Mahraganat: New Hybrid Music Wave Sweeps Egypt." *Al-Monitor*, March 22, 2021. https://www.al-monitor.com/originals/2013/05/egypt-new-music-mahraganat-sadat-electro-shaabi.html.

Fahmy, Melda (Farida). "The Creative Development of the Mahmoud Reda—Contemporary Egyptian Choreographer." MA thesis, University of California Los Angeles, 1987.

Farraj, Johnny, and Sami Abu Shumays. *Inside Arabic Music: Arabic Maqam Performance and Theory in the 20th Century*. Oxford: Oxford University Press, 2019.

Foster, Susan. *Corporealities: Dancing Knowledge, Culture and Power*. London: Routledge, 1995.

Foucault, Michel, trans. Jay Miskowiec. "Of Other Spaces." *Diacritics* 16, no. 1 (1986): 22–27.

Gant, James. "Russian Belly Dancer Is Jailed for a Year in Egypt after She Was Filmed Dancing in a Nightclub." *Mail Online*, April 12, 2019. https://www.dailymail.co.uk/news/article-6916277/Russian-belly-dancer-jailed-year-Egypt-filmed-dancing-nightclub.html.

García, Cindy. *Salsa Crossings: Dancing Latinidad in Los Angeles*. Durham, NC: Duke University Press Books, 2013.

Gelvin, James. *The Arab Uprisings: What Everyone Needs to Know*. 2nd ed. Oxford: Oxford University Press, 2015.

Gerber. "Intercontinental Semiramis History." *Cosmopolis Travel*, 2012. https://cosmopolis.ch/travel/intercontinental_cairo_semiramis.htm. (Link no longer available, last accessed June, 2018.)

Ghannam, Farha. *Live and Die Like a Man: Gender Dynamics in Urban Egypt*. Stanford, CA: Stanford University Press, 2013.

Golia, Maria. "Egypt's Mahragan: Music of the Masses." *Middle East Institute*, July 7, 2015. https://www.mei.edu/publications/egypts-mahragan-music-masses.

Hafez, Sherine. "Bodies That Protest: The Girl in the Blue Bra, Sexuality, and State Violence in Revolutionary Egypt." *Signs: Journal of Women in Culture and Society* 40, no. 1 (2014): 20–28.

Hafez, Sherine. "Gender and Citizenship Center Stage: Sondra Hale's Legacy and Egypt's Ongoing Revolution." *Journal of Middle East Women's Studies* 10, no. 1 (2014): 82–104.

Hafez, Sherine. "No Longer a Bargain: Women, Masculinity, and the Egyptian Uprising." *American Ethnologist* 39, no. 1 (2012): 37–42.

Hafez, Sherine. "The Revolution Shall Not Pass through Women's Bodies: Egypt, Uprising and Gender Politics." *The Journal of North African Studies* 19, no. 2 (2014): 172–85.

Hafez, Sherine. *Women of the Midan: The Untold Stories of Egypt's Revolutionaries*. Bloomington, IN: Indiana University Press, 2019.

Hamzawy, Amr. "Egypt after the 2013 Military Coup." *Philosophy & Social Criticism* 43, no. 4–5 (2017): 392–405.

Hatem, Mervat F. "Revolutions, Crises of Modernities, and the Production of Gender Subjectivities in Egypt." *Review of Middle East Studies* 50, no. 1 (February 2016): 48–54.

Hawthorn, Ainsley. "Middle Eastern Dance and What We Call It." *Dance Research* 37, no. 1 (2019): 1–17.

Haynes-Clark, Jennifer Lynn. "American Belly Dance and the Invention of the New Exotic: Orientalism, Feminism, and Popular Culture." MA thesis, Portland State University, 2010.

Heistein, Ari, and Mor Buskila. "How Sisi Could Wreck the Egyptian Economy." *The National Interest*, May 5, 2017. https://nationalinterest.org/feature/how-sisi-could-wreck-the-egyptian-economy-20497.

Hilal, Suraya. "Baladi Personae in Egyptian Dance and Music." *Middle Eastern / Belly Dance Academic Research and Sources Facebook Group*, 2008. (Link no longer available, last accessed February, 2016).

Human Rights Watch. "Egypt: A Move to Enhance Authoritarian Rule." *Human Rights Watch*, October 28, 2020. https://www.hrw.org/news/2019/02/12/egypt-move-enhance-authoritarian-rule.

Human Rights Watch. *Egypt: Events of 2019*. Human Rights Watch, 2020. https://www.hrw.org/world-report/2020/country-chapters/egypt.

Jarmakani, Amira. "Dancing the Hootchy Kootchy: The Bellydancer as the Embodiment of Socio-Cultural Tensions." *The Arab Studies Journal* 12/13, no. 2/1 (2004–2005): 124–29.

Jarmakani, Amira. *Imagining Arab Womanhood: The Cultural Mythology of Veils, Harems, and Belly Dancers in the U.S.* Basingstoke: Palgrave Macmillan, 2008.

Johnson, Robert. "Egypt After the Revolution: There's not Much to Sell but Sex." *Business Insider*, April 5, 2013. https://www.businessinsider.com/prostitution-in-caro-egypt-2013-4?international=true&r=US&IR=T.

Kandil, Amr Mohamed. "Why Muslim Brotherhood's Morsi Failed to Complete Presidential Term." *Egypt Today*, June 30, 2019. https://www.egypttoday.com/Article/1/72268/Why-Muslim-Brotherhood-s-Morsi-failed-to-complete-presidential-term.

Karayanni, Stavros Stavrou. *Dancing Fear and Desire: Race, Sexuality, and Imperial Politics in Middle Eastern Dance*. Waterloo, Ont.: Wilfrid Laurier University Press, 2004.

Keft-Kennedy, Virginia. "Representing the Belly-Dancing Body: Feminism, Orientalism, and the Grotesque." PhD diss., University of Wollongong, 2005.

Khalaf, Roula. "Sisi's Egypt: The March of the Security State." *Financial Times*, December 19, 2016. https://www.ft.com/content/8127ef6e-c38e-11e6-9bca-2b93a6856354.

Khalidi, Rashid. *The Hundred Years' War on Palestine: A History of Settler Colonialism and Resistance, 1917–2017*. Metropolitan Books, 2020.

Kraus, Rachel. "Becoming a Belly Dancer: Gender, the Life Course and the Beginnings of a Serious Leisure Career." *Leisure Studies* 33, no. 6 (2013): 565–79.

Kraus, Rachel. "Transforming Spirituality in Artistic Leisure: How the Spiritual Meaning of Belly Dance Changes Over Time." *Journal for the Scientific Study of Religion* 53, no. 3 (2014): 459–78.

Kwan, SanSan. *Kinesthetic City: Dance and Movement in Chinese Urban Spaces*. New York: Oxford University Press, 2013.

Lazreg, Marnia. *The Eloquence of Silence: Algerian Women in Question*. 2nd ed. Abingdon: Routledge, 2018.

Lorde, Geraldine Audre. *Sister Outsider: Essays and Speeches*. Berkeley, CA: Crossing Press, 1984.

Lorius, Cassandra. "'Oh Boy, You Salt of the Earth': Outwitting Patriarchy in *Raqs Baladi*." *Popular Music* 15, no. 3 (1996): 285–98.

Madison, Soyini. *Critical Ethnography: Method, Ethics, and Performance*. 2nd ed. Thousand Oaks, CA: Sage Publications, 2011.

Magdi, Amr. "'We Need to Talk' about al-Sisi's Twisted Take on Human Rights." *Human Rights Watch*, November 20, 2017. https://www.hrw.org/news/2017/11/20/we-need-talk-about-al-sisis-twisted-take-human-rights.

Maged, Mira. "Belly Dancer Safinaz May Face Deportation for Contentious North Coast Video." *Egypt Independent*, August 15, 2019. https://www.egyptindependent.com/belly-dancer-safinaz-may-face-deportation-for-contentious-north-coast-video/.

Mahfouz, Naguib, William Maynard Hutchens, and Angele Botros Samaan. *The Cairo Trilogy in 3 Volumes: Palace Walk, Sugar Street and Palace of Desire*. New York: Everyman/Knopf, 2022.

Mahr, Krista. "Bread Is Life: Food and Protest in Egypt." *TIME*, January 31, 2011. https://science.time.com/2011/01/31/bread-is-life-food-and-protest-in-egypt/.

Marriott Hotel. *Cairo Marriott Hotel History*. n.d. http://www.marriott.com/hotelwebsites/us/c/caieg/caieg_pdf/History of the palace.pdf. (Link no longer available, last accessed May, 2019).

Martin, Rose. *Women, Dance and Revolution: Performance and Protest in the Southern Mediterranean*. London: I.B. Tauris, 2016.

Martin, Rosemary. "Dancing in the Spring." In *Choreographies of 21st Century Wars*, edited by Gay Morris and Jens Richard Giersdorf, 207–21. Oxford: Oxford University Press, 2016.

McDonald, Caitlin. *Global Moves: Belly Dance as an Extra/Ordinary Space to Explore Social Paradigms in Egypt and Around the World*. Vancouver: Leanpub, 2012.

McDonald, Caitlin, and Barbara Sellers-Young. *Belly Dance Around the World: New Communities, Performance and Identity*. Jefferson, NC: McFarland & Company, 2013.

McMains, Juliet. *Spinning Mambo into Salsa: Caribbean Dance in Global Commerce*. Oxford: Oxford University Press, 2015.

McManus, Allison. "Measuring Success in Egypt's War on Terror." *The Tahrir Institute for Middle East Policy*, July 27, 2017. https://timep.org/commentary/analysis/measuring-success-in-egypts-war-on-terror/.

Mekky, Shounaz. "Sheikhs against Shakes: Egypt Belly Dancing Channel 'Arouses Viewers.'" *Al Arabiya*, February 19, 2013. https://english.alarabiya.net/articles/2013/02/19/267118.

Mernissi, Fatema. *Beyond the Veil: Male-Female Dynamics in Modern Muslim Society*. Rev. ed. Bloomington, IN: Indiana University Press, 1987.

Mitchell, Timothy. *Carbon Democracy: Political Power in the Age of Oil*. London: Verso, 2013.

Moe, Angela M. "Beyond the Belly: An Appraisal of Middle Eastern Dance (Aka Belly Dance) as Leisure." *Journal of Leisure Research* 44, no. 2 (2012): 201–33.

Moghadam, Valentine M. "Explaining Divergent Outcomes of the Arab Spring: The Significance of Gender and Women's Mobilizations." *Politics, Groups, and Identities* 6, no. 4 (2017): 666–81.

Mohamed, Sara. "Patriarchal Society Alienates Sex Workers in Egypt." *Egyptian Streets*, March 4, 2021. https://egyptianstreets.com/2018/07/12/patriarchal-society-alienates-sex-workers-in-egypt/.

Morley, Margaret. "Dancers Inciting Debauchery: Policing Raqs Sharqi to Legitimize the Egyptian Regime." Paper presented at Contra: Dance & Conflict, Dance Studies Association Conference. Malta, July, 2018.

Morris, Gay, and Jens Richard Giersdorf. *Choreographies of 21st Century Wars.* Oxford: Oxford University Press, 2016.
New Arab. "Will Egypt's Bread Riots Be Met with Tank Barrels?" *The New Arab*, April 1, 2017. https://www.newarab.com/analysis/will-egypts-bread-riots-be-met-tank-barrels.
Nielsen, Hans C. Korsholm, Jakob Skovgaard-Petersen, and Danish Institute in Damascus. *Middle Eastern Cities, 1900–1950.* Amsterdam: Amsterdam University Press, 2001.
Nieuwkerk, Karin Van. *Manhood Is not Easy: Egyptian Masculinities through the Life of Musician Sayyid Henkish.* Cairo: The American University in Cairo Press, 2019.
Nieuwkerk, Karin Van. *Performing Piety: Singers and Actors in Egypt's Islamic Revival.* Austin: University of Texas Press, 2013.
Nieuwkerk, Karin Van. *A Trade like Any Other: Female Singers and Dancers in Egypt.* Austin: University of Texas Press, 1995.
Norland, Rod. "Saudis and the Last Egyptian Belly Dancer." *Newsweek*, May 31, 2008. https://www.newsweek.com/saudis-and-last-egyptian-belly-dancer-89525.
Poole, Maurita. "'Brown Skin Is Half of Beauty': Representations of Beauty and the Construction of Race in Contemporary Cairo." PhD diss., Emory University, 2011.
Potuoğlu-Cook, Öykü. "Beyond the Glitter: Belly Dance and Neoliberal Gentrification in Istanbul." *Cultural Anthropology* 21, no. 4 (November 2006): 633–60.
Pratt, Nicola. "Gendered Paradoxes of Egypt's Transition." *Open Democracy*, February 2, 2015. https://www.opendemocracy.net/en/5050/gendered-paradoxes-of-egypts-transition/.
Pratt, Nicola. "Women in the Egyptian Revolution and Their Resistance against Violence" *Politics, Popular Culture and the 2011 Egyptian Revolution*, 2020. https://egyptrevolution2011.ac.uk/exhibits/show/women-and-the-revolution/women-and-the-revolution.
Racy, A. *Making Music in the Arab World: The Culture and Artistry of Tarab.* Cambridge: Cambridge University Press, 2004.
Rafik, Farah. "Egypt's Musicians Syndicate Temporarily Suspends Mahraganat Music." *Egyptian Streets*, October 17, 2022. https://egyptianstreets.com/2022/10/17/egypts-musicians-syndicate-temporarily-suspends-mahraganat-music/.
Roberts, Kate. "Cairo Clubs: Don't Forget to Take Off Your 'Hat.'" *Egyptian Streets*, February 8, 2019. https://egyptianstreets.com/2019/02/08/cairo-clubs-dont-forget-to-take-off-your-hat/.
Roushdy, Noha. "Baladi as Performance: Gender and Dance in Modern Egypt." *Surfacing* 3, no. 1 (2010). 71–99.
Roushdy, Noha. *Femininity and Dance in Egypt: Embodiment and Meaning in al-Raqs al-Baladi.* Cairo: The American University in Cairo Press, 2014.
Sabry, Islam. "Anti-Blackness in Egypt: Between Stereotypes and Ridicule- An Examination on the History of Colorism and the Development of Anti-Blackness in Egypt." MA thesis, Abdo Akademi University, 2021.
Safy, Shereen. "'An Uncommon Woman Nagwa Fouad, Queen of Oriental Dance.'" *The Best of Habibi Online* 18, no. 3 (2001). http://thebestofhabibi.com/vol-18-no-3-march-2001/nagwa-fouad/. 1-8.
Şahin, Christine. "Core Connections: A Contemporary Cairo Raqs Sharqi Ethnography." PhD diss., University of California, Riverside, 2018.
Said, Edward. *Culture and Imperialism.* Vintage, 1994.
Said, Edward. *Orientalism.* Zaltbommel, Netherlands: Van Haren Publishing, 2014.

Said, Maha El, Lena Meari, and Doctor Nicola Pratt. *Rethinking Gender in Revolutions and Resistance: Lessons from the Arab World*. London: Zed Books, 2015.

Sellers-Young, Barbara. *Belly Dance, Pilgrimage and Identity*. London: Palgrave Macmillan, 2016.

Shafik, Viola. *Arab Cinema*. Cairo: The American University in Cairo Press, 1998.

Shafik, Viola. *Popular Egyptian Cinema: Gender, Class, and Nation*. Cairo: The American University in Cairo Press, 2007.

Shay, Anthony. *The Dangerous Lives of Public Performers: Dancing, Sex, and Entertainment in the Islamic World*. London: Palgrave Macmillan, 2014.

Shay, Anthony. *Choreographic Politics: State Folk Dance Companies, Representation, and Power*. Middletown, CT: Wesleyan University Press, 2002.

Shay, Anthony. "The Male Dancer in the Middle East and Central Asia." *Dance Research Journal* 38, nos. 1–2 (2006): 137–62.

Shay, Anthony, and Barbara Sellers-Young. *Belly Dance: Orientalism, Transnationalism, And Harem Fantasy*. Costa Mesa, CA: Mazda Publishers, 2022.

Singerman, Diane, and Paul Amar. *Cairo Cosmopolitan: Politics, Culture, and Urban Space in the New Middle East*. Cairo: The American University in Cairo Press, 2009.

Srinivasan, Priya. *Sweating Saris: Indian Dance as Transnational Labor*. Philadelphia, PA: Temple University Press, 2011.

Stallybrass, Peter, and Allon White. *The Politics and Poetics of Transgression*. Ithaca, NY: Cornell University Press, 1986.

State Information Service. "CAPMAS: Poverty Rates in Egypt Decline to 29.7% within Year." State Information Service, October 19, 2021. https://www.sis.gov.eg/Story/159611/CAPMAS-Poverty-rates-in-Egypt-decline-to-29.7%25-within-year?lang=en-us.

Sunaina, Maira. "Belly Dancing: Arab-Face, Orientalist Feminism, and U.S. Empire." *American Quarterly* 60, no. 2 (2008): 317–45.

Världskulturmuseerna. "Interview Mai Amer - Mahraganat & Gender | مقابلة مع د. مي عامر حول فن المهرجانات وأين صوت النساء؟". May 24, 2022. YouTube video, https://www.youtube.com/watch?v=4BebdCl66S8.

Vermeyden, Anne. "The Popularization of Belly Dance in Toronto, Canada (1950–1990): Hybridization and Uneven Exchange." PhD diss., The University of Guelph, 2017.

Vermeyden, Anne. "The Reda Folkloric Dance Troupe and Egyptian State Support During the Nasser Period." *Dance Research Journal* 49, no. 3 (December 2017): 24–37.

Ward, Heather. *Egyptian Belly Dance in Transition: The Raqs Sharqi Revolution, 1890–1930*. Jefferson, NC: McFarland & Company, 2018.

Ward, Heather. "Rewriting History: Respectability Politics and Revisionist History in Contemporary Egyptian Belly Dance." *Belly Dance with Nisaa*, 2022. https://www.bellydancewithnisaa.com/onlinelectures. (Link no longer available, last access February, 2022).

Wilkinson, Toby. *The Nile: Travelling Downriver Through Egypt's Past and Present*. Reprint. New York: Vintage, 2015.

Wynn, L. *Love, Sex, and Desire in Modern Egypt: Navigating the Margins of Respectability*. Austin: University of Texas Press, 2018.

Wynn, L. *Pyramids and Nightclubs: A Travel Ethnography of Arab and Western Imaginations of Egypt, from King Tut and a Colony of Atlantis to Rumors of Sex Orgies, Urban Legends about a Marauding Prince, and Blonde Belly Dancers*. Austin: University of Texas Press, 2007.

Youness, Ahmed. "Egypt Renews State of Emergency for 10th Time." *Al-Monitor*, March 2, 2021. https://www.al-monitor.com/originals/2019/10/egypt-sisi-renew-state-of-emergency-constitution.html.

Youssef, Adham. "The Controversial Street Music That Won't Be Silenced." *BBC Culture*, June 14, 2012. https://www.bbc.com/culture/article/20210608-the-controversial-street-music-that-wont-be-silenced.

Zaki, Hind Ahmed. "El-Sissi's Women? Shifting Gender Discourses and the Limits of State Feminism." *Égypte/Monde Arabe*, no. 13 (2015): 39–53.

Zeid, Dina Farouk Abou. "Songs from Egyptian Slums to Media." *Global Media Journal* 17, no. 32 (2019): 1–6. http://www.globalmediajournal.com/open-access/songs-from-egyptian-slums-to-media.php?aid=87445.

Zuhur, Sherifa. *Popular Dance and Music in Modern Egypt*. Jefferson, NC: McFarland, 2021.

Index

For the benefit of digital users, indexed terms that span two pages (e.g., 52–53) may, on occasion, appear on only one of those pages.

Figures are indicated by *f* following the page number

3aeesh, 100–1

Abu-Lughod, Lila, 10–11, 22, 25–26, 27, 137–38
Adaweya, Ahmed, 55
Adra, Najwa, 18, 231n.22
Ahmed, Sara Farouk, 110
Ali, Ahmed, 150–51, 156–57
Arab nationalism, 71–72
Arab season, in Egyptian tourism industry, 104, 189–90
Arab Spring, 1–2, 16
Arab tourism, in Egypt, 48
aseel, 128–30, 134–35, 219, 221
Auberge, 189–90
awalim, 5–6, 44, 67, 109, 123, 201–2

badlat raqs, 50
baladi, 5–6, 55, 62, 72–73, 80–81, 123, 128–32, 133–35, 195–96, 231n.22, 235n.20
bint al balad, 195–96, 198
Borelli, Melissa Blanco, 54, 234n.16
Botman, Selma, 94
bread riots of 1977, 100

Cairo, 42*f*
　cabarets, 65–66, 109
　five-star hotels in, 102–3, 104, 105, 106–8
　6th of October bridge, 103*f*
Cairo Marriott Hotel and Empress Nightclub, 102–4, 107*f*, 114–15, 117–35
Cairo *raqs sharqi*, 9, 129*f*
　Arab season for, 104
　criminalization and dangers faced by dancers, 144–45, 146, 147, 205–6, 223
　ethnography of, 19–35, 38–39
　on Instagram, 141–42
　male-female duets in, 62
　in music videos and, 139, 140–41
　on Nile tour boat cruises, 44, 46, 48
　recentering, 13–19
　sexual harassment and, 47–48
　social media posts about, 142, 144, 145, 146
　Sofinar in popularizing, 140
　2011 revolution and, 48–49
　venue system, 65–66
　wide-legged stance in, 123–24
　Zara Dance performing, 142–43, 143*f*
Cairo *raqs sharqi*, in disco clubs, 33–34, 141–42, 162–63
　Clubhouse Disco, 149–62, 151*f*, 164–65, 179–80
　Ferreira performing, 164, 167–69, 167*f*, 170*f*, 171–77, 175*f*, 180, 221–22, 223
　foreign dancers performing, 142–44, 145, 176
　Koo Lounge, 164–66, 167–69
　mahraganat and, 146, 147, 157–58, 159, 160–62, 173–74, 180, 221–22
　Sahar performing, 157–62, 163, 172, 174–76, 177, 179–80, 221–22, 223
　sha3bi and, 154–55, 159, 160–62
　vibe in, 177, 179, 180
　Zara Dance on, 156–57, 161–62, 166, 179–80, 224
Cairo *raqs sharqi*, in five-star hotels, 32–33, 58–59, 65, 103–4, 108, 135
　Abdou performing, 111*f*
　Amina performing, 114–15, 116, 117–35, 219, 220–21
　class and, 109, 110

Cairo *raqs sharqi*, in disco clubs (*cont.*)
    khaleegy audiences for, 110–11, 220
    male staff and management and, 115–16
    during Mubarak era, 108–9, 112–13
    tipping dancers, 125–27
    after 2011 revolution, 111–12, 113, 114
Cairo *raqs sharqi*, in Pyramid Street cabarets, 34–35
    Hamada performing, 201–4, 209–10
    Julia performing, 204–11, 223–24, 225–26
    keet and tipping in, 187, 190–92, 193–94, 196–97, 203, 207–8, 212, 213
    khaleegy audiences for, 190, 195–96, 197–98, 201, 203, 207, 209
    Layla performing in, 222–23
    mi3allima in, 197, 198
    nimra in, 188–89, 190–91, 195–98, 199, 204–11, 224, 225
    reklam in, 186–87, 190, 199–200, 222
    Suzy performing, 188–89, 194–98, 199, 223–24, 225–26
    toura players and, 201–4, 209–10
Cairo *raqs sharqi*, on *Nile Maxim* boats, 31–32, 48–49, 217
    bathroom attendants and, 50–51, 53–54, 55, 62–64, 65, 67–68, 70
    Farah Nasri performing, 69–96, 78*f*, 81*f*, 217–18
    Randa performing, 59–69, 60*f*, 63*f*, 218–19
    Safiya performing, 51–59, 61, 218–19
Cairo Sheraton hotel, 111*f*
capitalism, 56, 142–43, 178, 198, 200–9, 212, 223–24
carbon democracy, 223–24
circularity, 13, 24–25, 28–29, 30–31, 61
class. *See also* gender, class and
    bodies and, 108
    Cairo *raqs sharqi* in disco clubs and, 161–62, 164–65
    Cairo *raqs sharqi* in five-star hotels and, 109, 110
    mahraganat and, 140
    sexuality and, 123–24
    working-class cabarets, 19, 30, 35, 96, 127, 161–62
    working-class dancers, 96, 114, 123, 127, 133, 144–45, 160–61, 209, 225–26

Clubhouse Disco, 149–62, 151*f*, 164–65, 179–80
colonialism, 7
corporeality, 15–16, 161–62, 200, 206, 220, 225–26
    risqué, 177–78, 223
    womanhood and, 18, 89

dalla3, 52, 54, 56–57, 58–59, 68, 124, 133, 197–98, 202
Dance Studies, 15–16, 17–18, 21–22, 27
deep listening, 1, 19, 20, 22, 23, 39, 177, 183, 215, 226–27
Diebitsch, Carl von, 103

"El3ab Yalla," 136
embodied experience, 15–16, 164–65, 172–73, 224
embodied knowledge, 8–9, 16–17, 19–20
embodied *raqs sharqi*, ethnography as, 23–29

Facebook, 144, 200
Fahmy, Farida, 69–70, 71–72, 74–75, 96
Farouk (king), 192, 216–17
fath, 58, 69, 86, 190
feminism, 27, 213
    Western, 26–27, 67
firqa komiyya, 54–55, 69–70, 72, 73
fitna, 59, 90, 235n.26
Foster, Susan, 15–16
Fouad, Nagwa, 70, 73–74, 88–89, 90, 114
Foucault, Michel, 161–62
Free Officers, The, 71
Friedman, Vanessa, 75
funun al sha3biyya, 31–32, 69–96, 78*f*, 81*f*, 120–23, 125

galabeya, 55, 80–81
Gamal, Melissa, 158
Garcia, Cindy, 15–16, 50
Gelvin, James, 2
gender, class and, 159, 212–13
    labor, sexuality and, 86, 91, 213
    labor and, 94, 131
    during Mubarak era, 164–65
    nationalism and, 12, 26–27, 34–35, 56, 57–58, 68, 86, 116, 119, 135, 177–78, 191–92, 194

race and, 83–84, 116, 119, 135
reklam and, 186–87
in 2011 revolution, 225
gender, sexuality and, 68, 72–73, 83–85, 90–91, 93–94, 121, 127, 203–4
class, labor and, 86, 91, 213
nationalism and, 12, 24–25, 31, 73, 86, 90–91, 119, 135, 224, 235n.23
in patriarchal system, 207, 220–21
gender constructions, 53–54, 62–64, 84–85, 94, 198
gendered bodies, 50, 106–8, 116, 122, 208
gender embodiment, 58, 62–64, 67–68, 69
gender identities, 56–57, 58–59, 217
gender normativity, 68–69, 72–73, 83–84, 90–91, 94, 153, 156
gender performativity, 53–54, 59, 62–64, 67–68, 69, 72–73, 92–94, 119, 198
Ghannam, Farha, 136
Gulf oil boom, 190
Gulf War of 1991, 112–13
gut instinct and gut knowledge, 8–9, 28, 114–15, 147

Hafez, Sherine, 18–19, 27, 71, 94
heteronormativity, 68–69, 72–73, 90–91, 122, 203–4, 220–21
hip(g)nosis, 54, 83–84
hudur, 26, 86
hyper-femininity, 56–57, 197–98

ihsas, 19, 24, 28–30, 53–54, 86, 91, 124, 216
imperialism, 15, 20, 47, 142–43, 145
Instagram, 4–5, 141–43, 144, 158
InterContinental Semiramis Hotel, 103*f*, 104–5
intersectionality and intersectional analysis, 21, 25–27, 31, 33, 116, 217, 219, 220, 221, 225
Islamists, 152–53, 192–93
Ismail, Khedive, 103–4

Jamarkani, Amira, 18

keet, 187, 190–91, 193, 194–95, 207, 212–13
Kent, Sahra C., 73–74
Kent, Sahra Carolee, 201–2

khaleegy, 52, 57, 79, 104, 106–8, 109, 190, 191
audiences in Cairo five-star hotels, 110–11, 220
audiences in Pyramid Street cabarets, 190, 195–96, 197–98, 201, 203, 207, 209
Khalil, Mohammed, 73, 88–89, 90
Koo Lounge, 164–66, 167–69

Lazreg, Marnia, 26–27
Lorde, Audre, 213

Madison, Soyini, 183
mahraganat, 139, 147, 154–55
in Cairo disco clubs, 146, 147, 157–58, 159, 160–62, 173–74, 180, 221–22
class and, 140
male gaze, 83, 84, 237n.55
Martin, Rosemary, 147–49, 177, 223
masculinity and hyper-masculinity, 72–73, 80, 119, 131, 148, 208–9, 212–13, 225–26
matwua, 157–58
McJihad, 224
meleya luff eskandarani, 127
MENA. *See* Middle East and North Africa
MENAHT. *See* Middle Eastern, North African, Hellenic, and Turkish
mi3allima, 197, 198
Middle East and North Africa (MENA), 1–3, 16, 18, 46–47, 85
Middle Eastern, North African, Hellenic, and Turkish (MENAHT), 5–6, 7–8, 11–12, 13–14, 15, 18–20, 26, 145
Mitchell, Timothy, 223–24
Morsi, Mohammed, 2, 33, 100, 152–54, 216–18, 219–20
Mubarak, Hosni, 2–3, 41, 103, 139, 152, 164–65, 224
Cairo *raqs sharqi* in five-star hotels during era of, 108–9, 112–13
Cairo *raqs sharqi* on boats during era of, 44, 75
economic decline under, 189–90, 192, 194
gender and class during era of, 164–65
neoliberalism and, 41
multiply moving ethnography, 24, 25, 29–35, 183, 226

musannafat, 58, 69, 190, 205–6, 238n.57
Muslim Brotherhood, 2, 17, 33, 152–54, 192–93, 219–20

Napoleon III (emperor), 103
Nasri, Farah, 31–32, 69–96, 78*f*, 81*f*, 121, 139, 151*f*, 152, 217–18
Nasser, Gamal Abdel, 56, 57–58, 80, 103, 110, 189–90, 225
　women's roles during regime of, 71–72, 110
nationalism
　Arab, 71–72
　gender, class and, 12, 26–27, 34–35, 56, 57–58, 68, 86, 116, 119, 135, 177–78, 191–92, 194
　gender, sexuality and, 12, 24–25, 31, 73, 86, 90–91, 119, 135, 224, 235n.23
　global capitalism and, 142
neoliberalism, 3, 20, 41, 56, 100, 189–90
Nile Maxim boats. *See also* Cairo *raqs sharqi,* on *Nile Maxim* boats
　bathroom attendants on, 49–50
　Nile Pharaohs and, 44
　tanoura on, 44, 45*f*
Nile Pharaoh boats, 44
Nile River, boats and boat cruises on, 41–48, 57, 75
nimra, 34–35, 188–89, 190–91, 195–99, 204–11, 224, 225

Oka and Ortega, 136
orientalism, 6–7, 15, 47, 145

paternalism, 2, 76–77, 179–80
patriarchal gender system, 207
patriarchal heterosexual and militarized systems, 220–21
patriarchal masculinity, 131, 212–13
patriarchy, 18, 71, 91, 94, 145, 178, 187–88
　capitalist, 178, 198
　imperialist orientalist, 145
Pyramid Street cabarets, 184–94. *See also* Cairo *raqs sharqi,* in Pyramid Street cabarets

Quran, 37–39

raqs al 3asaaya, 31–32

raqs sharqi, 1, 4–9, 13. *See also* Cairo *raqs sharqi*
　aganib and, 19–20, 22
　awalim and, 67
　embodied, ethnography as, 23–29
　fath and, 58
　foreign dancers of, 47, 56, 112, 240n.14
　funun al sha3biyya and, 69–96
　in Golden Era of Egyptian cinema, 50–51, 55, 56–57, 173, 236n.39
　ihsas in, 19, 24, 28–30, 53–54, 216
　improvisation in performances, 26–27
　male performers, 232n.36
　mejance in, 29–30, 31–32, 51, 52, 54, 59–61, 67, 69–70, 77–78, 81–82, 110–11, 120–21, 122–23, 157, 194
　meleya luff eskandarani and, 127
　in nightclubs and cabarets, 109
　sa3idi in, 31–32, 52, 80–81, 87, 111
　sha3bi in, 31–32, 52, 55, 56, 57
Reda, Mahmoud, 69–70, 71–72, 80
Reda Troupe, 69–70, 71–73, 74–75, 80, 92, 127
reklam, 34–35, 186–87, 190, 199–200, 222, 245n.1
Roushdy, Noha, 14

sa3idi, 31–32, 52, 80–81, 87, 111
Sadat, Anwar, 3, 41, 44, 55, 56, 58, 69, 100, 108, 112–13, 145, 189–90, 191–92
Said, Edward, 6–7, 15, 47
Said, Mona, 54–55, 56–57
Sawerki, Ragab el, 192–93
SCAF. *See* Supreme Council of the Armed Forces
Sellers-Young, Barbara, 160
sexual harassment, 47–48, 118–19, 148, 153, 217–18
sex workers and sex work, 47, 72–73, 106–8, 186–87, 188–89, 239–40nn.7–8
sha3bi, 31–32, 52, 55, 56, 57, 82–83, 235n.18
　in Cairo disco clubs, 154–55, 159, 160–62
　men dancing, 188
　in music videos, 124, 135, 139–40
　wedding parties, 191–92

Shalimar, 189–90
"Shik Shak Shok," 93
El-Sisi, Abdel Fattah, 2, 3, 8, 100, 113, 147, 153–54, 193, 219–21, 224
social mobility, 65–67, 68
Sofinar, 140
Soviet Moiseyev Dance Company, 72
Srinivasan, Priya, 133
Stallybrass, Peter, 161–62
Sunaina, Maira, 18
Supreme Council of the Armed Forces (SCAF), 2, 148, 152
Sweeper, The, 140

tahiyya, 34–35, 191–92, 194–95, 196, 204–5
Tahrir Square, 100, 111–12, 148, 182–83, 217–18, 224, 225
tanoura, 44, 45f, 46–47, 80, 110, 233–34n.5, 234n.7
taqseem baladi, 128–30
tarab, 159
Tet, El, 140–41
tipping
  in five-star hotels, 125–27
  keet, 187, 190–91, 193, 194–95, 207, 212–13
  in Pyramid Street cabarets, 187, 190–92, 193–94, 196–97, 203, 207–8, 212, 213
  tipping wars, 191–92, 193–94, 197, 212–13
toura players, 201–4, 209–10
2011 Egyptian revolution, 1–3, 16, 103–4, 153–54, 192–93, 216, 220–21

Cairo *raqs sharqi* in five-star hotels after, 111–12, 113, 114
gender and class in, 225
Tahrir Square, 111–12, 182–83, 217–18, 224, 225
women's roles and, 224–25

usta, 109, 240n.11

Van Nieuwkerk, Karin, 14, 232–33n.39

Ward, Heather, 147, 160–61
Western gaze, 14–15
Western tourism, in Egypt, 48
White, Allon, 161–62
Widan, Ahmed, 154, 177–78
El-Wikala, 44
women
  bodies of, 18, 71, 192
  citizenship and rights, 94
  roles, 2011 revolution and, 224–25
  roles during Nasser regime, 71–72, 110
  womanhood, corporeality and, 18, 89
working-class cabarets, 19, 30, 35, 96, 127, 161–62
working-class dancers, 96, 114, 123, 127, 133, 144–45, 160–61, 209, 225–26
Wynn, L., 48

Yom Kippur War, 190
Yossry, 20, 202–3, 247n.21
YouTube, 124, 140–41, 154

Made in the USA
Monee, IL
28 April 2026

49136493R00164